Tibet's Relations with the Himalaya

Published by
ACADEMIC FOUNDATION
in association with

FOUNDATION FOR
Non-violent
Alternatives
an institute for developing peace studies

The Foundation for Non-violent
Alternatives (FNVA), New Delhi
Email: office@fnvaworld.org
www.fnvaworld.org

Tibet's Relations with the Himalaya

Edited by

SIDDIQ WAHID

ACADEMIC FOUNDATION
NEW DELHI

www.academicfoundation.org

First published in 2017
by

ACADEMIC FOUNDATION
4772-73 / 23 Bharat Ram Road, (23 Ansari Road),
Darya Ganj, New Delhi - 110 002 (India).
Phones : 23245001 / 02 / 03 / 04.
Fax : +91-11-23245005.
E-mail : books@academicfoundation.com
www.academicfoundation.com

in association with
The Foundation for Non-violent Alternatives (FNVA), New Delhi.

Cataloging in Publication Data--DK
Courtesy: D.K. Agencies (P) Ltd. <docinfo@dkagencies.com>

Tibet's relations with the Himalaya / edited by Siddiq Wahid.
pages cm
Revised version of papers presented at three symposia organized by the Foundation for Non-Violent Alternatives
ISBN 9789332703124

1. Tibet Autonomous Region (China)--Relations--Himalaya Mountains Region--Congresses. 2. Himalaya Mountains Region--Relations--Tibet Autonomous Region--Congresses. I. Wahid, Siddiq, editor. II. . Foundation for Non-Violent Alternatives.organizer.

DDC 327.51505496 23

Typeset, printed and bound by The Book Mint, New Delhi.
www.thebookmint.in

CONTENTS

II
Peoples and Linkages

III

Environment

About the Editor/Contributors

Editor:

Siddiq Wahid has been a Senior Fellow at the Centre for Policy Research, New Delhi. He was formerly Vice Chancellor of Islamic University, Kashmir; Gulab Singh Chair Professor of History, Jammu University and Director, Institute of Kashmir Studies, Kashmir University. He has taught in the United States (US) in his field of study, which are Central Asian and Tibetan History. Professor Wahid has published widely and the latest (2015) is a forthcoming chapter on historical Gilgit, Baltistan, Ladakh and Kashmir for an anthology of the Himalaya.

Contributors:

Claude Arpi, born in 1949 in Angoulême, France, has been living in south India for the past 40 years. He is the author of *The Fate of Tibet* (1999), *Tibet, le pays sacrifié* (2000), *And Dark Shall be the Night: The Karma of Tibet* (2001), *Born in Sin: The Panchsheel Agreement* (2004), and *Tibet: The Lost Frontier and The Negotiations That Never Were: Dharamsala and Beijing*. More recently, he published, *1962: The McMahon Saga and Glimpse of Tibetan History*. He regularly writes on Tibet, China, India and Indo-French relations for *Rediff.com, Indian Defence Review, The Pioneer, The Statesman, The Asian Age* and other Indian publications.

Nani Bath, a recipient of IPSA Young Political Scientist Award, is Professor in the Department of Political Science, Rajiv Gandhi

University, Itanagar. Having done his BA (Hons) in Sociology from University of Delhi, he joined Jawaharlal Nehru University for Masters in International Politics. Dr Bath has written articles for books and journals, and contributes regularly in local newspapers.

Sonam Joldan (PhD), currently works as Assistant Professor in the Rinchen Shah Centre for West Himalayan Cultures, Islamic University of Science and Technology, Awantipora (IUST), Jammu and Kashmir. He has several publications to his credit including a book authored by him and few research papers, besides presenting papers in national and international seminars/conferences.

Sanjay Chaturvedi is Professor of Political Science at Department of Political Science, Centre for the Study of Geopolitics, and Honorary Director, Centre for the Study of Mid-West and Central Asia, Panjab University, Chandigarh. He is the editor of the *Journal of the Indian Ocean Region* and serves on the editorial advisory boards of *Cooperation and Conflict, Geopolitics and Journal of Borderland Studies*. His latest book, co-authored with Timothy Doyle, is *Climate Terror: A Critical Geopolitics of Climate Change* (2015).

Ananta Swarup Bijendra De Gurung is at present a PhD research scholar at the Centre for Indo-Pacific Studies, School of International Studies, Jawaharlal Nehru University, New Delhi. He has published in both national and international journals.

Sunanda K. Datta-Ray (author and columnist) has worked in Britain, India, the US and Singapore. He was Editor of *The Statesman* (Calcutta and Delhi); Editor-in-Residence, East-West Centre, Honolulu; Editorial Consultant, Singapore Press Holdings; and Visiting Fellow, Corpus Christi College, Oxford. His *Smash and Grab: Annexation of Sikkim* (1984), revised and reissued in 2014, is regarded as the only true account of how the protected Himalayan kingdom became an Indian state. His latest book,

Looking East To Look West: Lee Kuan Yew's Mission India, won the Crossword Vodafone prize for non-fiction.

Tashi Phuntsok is at present Secretary for the Information Department of Central Tibetan Administration (CTA). Earlier, he served as a Representative of His Holiness, the Dalai Lama in Pretoria, Paris and Brussels from 1997 to 2005. Since 2005, he was the General Secretary for the Tibetan Homes Foundation, Mussoorie. Later, in 2010, he was appointed as the Chief Representative of the CTA, South Zone, Bangalore. His education includes BA (Hons), BEd, LLB, Counselling and Psychotherapy (Dip).

Sangeeta Thapliyal is a Professor of International Relations at the Centre for Inner Asian Studies, Jawaharlal Nehru University, New Delhi. Earlier, she was Director/Head of the Department for Strategic and Regional Studies, University of Jammu. She is Vice President of the Association of Asia Scholars. Her areas of research include: India's strategic interests in the Himalayas with a special emphasis on Nepal, Bhutan, Tibet and water security in South Asia.

Thubten Samphel is the Director of the Tibet Policy Institute, a research centre of the CTA. He writes extensively on Tibet and is the author of *Falling Through the Roof*, a work of fiction.

Chetan Singh is the Director of the Indian Institute of Advanced Study, Shimla. He is a historian by training and has taught at Panjab University, Chandigarh and Himachal Pradesh University, Shimla. Among the books he has authored is: *Natural Premises: Ecology and Peasant Life in Western Himalaya 1800-1950*. He has also edited, *Recognising Diversity: Society and Culture in the Himalayas*.

Bijay Thapa is presently pursuing his PhD from the Centre for South Asian Studies, Jawaharlal Nehru University, New Delhi. He completed his MA and MPhil from the Department of

International Relations/Politics, Sikkim University, Gangtok, Sikkim.

Tshering Doma Kaleon is presently pursuing her PhD from the Centre for East Asian Studies/Chinese Division, Jawaharlal Nehru University, New Delhi. She completed her MA and MPhil from the Department of International Relations/Politics, Sikkim University, Gangtok, Sikkim.

Man Norbu is at present a PhD research scholar in the Department of Political Science, Rajiv Gandhi University, Itanagar. He has done his post-graduation (2012) and completed MPhil degree (2013-14) from the same University on the topic "People's Perception on Sino-India War of 1962: A Study of Tawang District of Arunachal Pradesh". He did his graduation (2010) in Political Science (Hons) from Government College, Bomdila. Presently, he is working on district administration of Tawang and West Kameng under the supervision of Professor Nani Bath.

Tenzin Norbu was formerly (2008-2013) a civil servant at the CTA, Dharamsala, where he served as the Director of the then Environment and Development Desk under the Department of Information and International Relations. He has represented the CTA at various regional and international environmental forums. Before joining CTA, he was a senior researcher at the Environmental Engineering Programme of the Asian Institute of Technology in Bangkok, and conducted research on many environmental projects. At present, he is working on a Tibetan nomad project and co-authoring a book on the same subject with a former UC Berkeley Professor in California.

Foreword

The Foundation for Non-Violent Alternatives (FNVA) has been engaged in very useful and innovative, people and environment-oriented non-political work relating to Tibet. This book is the end product of a particularly commendable initiative taken by the Foundation. It contains texts of papers presented at conferences held at Leh, Gangtok and Itanagar in 2012-13 on the broad theme of "Tibet's Relations with the Himalaya".

The people who have lived in the Himalayas have interacted with each other for aeons, fundamentally unfettered by whoever may have been their temporal ruler at any particular point of time. The ethnology and ethos of the Himalayan peoples has been profoundly shaped by their continually evolving interactions with the peoples of the equally remote cold desert plateau of Tibet. Socio-cultural and economic interaction amongst these peoples was a natural phenomenon with little or no consciousness that notional frontiers divided the territorial domains they lived in and were familiar with. In the process, a virtual knowledge bank of traditional beliefs, concepts, philosophy and practices came into being, which is an integral and invaluable part of the intellectual, socio-cultural and spiritual heritage of mankind. It is imperative that this heritage is documented and preserved.

One of the paradoxical by-products of the end of the imperial and colonial eras was the rise of indigenous regimes of states in and around the Himalaya. Imbued with strongly nationalist sentiment, and suspicion regarding the intentions of the neighbour inevitably resulted in the imposition of restrictions on what had heretofore been free movements and interactions. Frontiers were transformed into borders and with each passing year this 'cross-border' interaction was increasingly monitored and regulated, forcing the people to be segregated from one another by and into artificially created 'political' compartments. This runs counter to the reality of fluid movement of peoples across mountain landscapes that had no preordained, rigid national boundaries. Even if one has to accept that this ground reality is here to stay, enlightened statesmanship should be able to allow state-centric relationships to be complemented by freer people-oriented exchanges and encouragement "to document, preserve, improvise and improve on the knowledge, methods and materials of the Himalaya....and an unfettered continuation of the civilisational dialogue that has formed the warp and weft of their lives", as Professor Siddiq Wahid has so eloquently pleaded in his excellent Introduction to this book. This exercise, hugely useful in itself, could also be a small but desirable step in the potential lessening of 'cross-border' tensions.

An unfortunate reality is that border management policies followed by China and India in particular, are formulated in the capitals which are not only geographically distant from the Himalayan 'borders' but psychologically much more so, seemingly completely oblivious to the inherited legacies, needs and feelings of the people who live in and around the Himalayas. It is imperative that some methodology be found to ensure that the voices of the people who live in the borderlands are adequately taken into account in the formulation of policies for the management of borderlands. This will not only be useful in itself, but will also serve as a potential corrective to the overweening security overhang in the formulation of borderland management policies. This book should be viewed as a valuable contribution to this process.

FNVA needs to organise further seminars to cover fields not addressed and other Himalayan regions not included in this book. This can contribute to a deeper realisation that border regions have in the past and continue to be inhabited by real people that have enjoyed their own traditions of movement and exchange, and who we need to visualise them as legitimate inheritors of these new 'borderlands', intrinsic stakeholders in our plural societies. Their voices should command attention in the capitals.

India's new Prime Minister, Shri Narendra Modi, has been particularly proactive on the foreign policy front. Amongst his many innovative approaches is highlighting the importance of people, of culture, of people-to-people interaction, of greater inter-cultural discourse. It is my fervent hope that the aspects that have been mentioned will draw the attention of the government to include, facilitate and indeed enlarge discourses amongst and between the peoples of the Himalayas and Tibet. This is an eminently desirable and implementable people-oriented confidence building measure. Indeed the government would do well to proactively support the kind of work that institutions like FNVA have been engaged in.

— Ranjit Gupta
Former Indian Ambassador

Acknowledgements

This book would not be in your hands but for the help, encouragement, advice and whole-hearted support of the Foundation for Non-violent Alternatives (FNVA) team, trustees and advisors; our sincere thanks to each one of them. It would be impossible to list everyone who helped shape this work, but we owe special gratitude to some.

First and foremost, we are truly grateful to Professor Siddiq Wahid whose erudition is reflected throughout this volume. In addition to his untiring pursuit to interaction with the authors to revise their papers in the light of discussions held and editing of the content, wherever necessary, he also helped FNVA to choose a publisher.

Thirteen remarkable and diverse individuals from different regions, age-groups, professions and dispositions who have contributed to this volume have made this book what it is. The complete list of contributors appears elsewhere in the book. We are grateful to each one of them.

FNVA also places on record its gratitude the logistical support it received at Leh, Gangtok and Itanagar. We would like to record our grateful thanks to Ven. Lama Lobzang, Secretary General of IBC and Tashi Motup of Larisa Hotel in Leh; and Professor Manish Srivastava, Head of Department (HOD) of International Relations and Political Science, University of Sikkim for his untiring zeal in organising the programme and motivating his students and staff members to participate academically in it.

We are especially grateful to Dr B.P. Singh, the then Governor of Sikkim and a friend and well-wisher of FNVA from its very inception, for inviting all the participants over to tea at the Raj Bhavan.

Professor Nani Bath, HOD Political Science, Rajiv Gandhi Central University, also deserves our thanks for graciously hosting us and for organising the seminar in his department. We are grateful to Professor Tamo Mibang, Vice Chancellor, Rajiv Gandhi Central University, for his participation in the opening session and appreciating the importance of the theme of the seminar.

A special mention is made for the presence of Mr Kiren Rijiju, currently Minister of State, Home Affairs, Government of India, on the last day of the programme and for hosting the entire delegation at his residence.

Grateful thanks are due to Ambassador Ranjit Gupta for writing the Foreword to this volume. His presence at Itanagar helped ensure a safe passage for the entire group through a violent state-wide *bandh* in Assam.

Our trustee Tempa Tsering is especially thanked for his encouragement and advice during the entire series. Our special thanks also go to Shri Krishan Varma, who joined FNVA as a trustee in 2014, for his encouragement and active involvement in the preparation of this book.

Last but not the least, we record our deep appreciation for Chok Tsering, Research Associate at FNVA. He showed exemplary patience in dealing with all the authors and never tired of following up with all concerned. There is hardly any aspect of this publication which escaped his watchful eyes.

Our thanks are due to Ms Punam Thakur for copy-editing all the papers.

Academic Foundation, the publishers, have done a commendable job in bringing out this volume. They deserve our appreciation.

Needless to say, amidst all the great things that others have contributed, any shortcomings in the book are solely ours and in no way reflect on others who were connected with this publication.

New Delhi

— REBON BANERJEE DHAR
and O.P. TANDON
Founding Trustees
The Foundation for Non-violent Alternatives

SIDDIQ WAHID

Introduction

I

The essays in this anthology are a result of a series of seminars entitled: "Tibet's Relations with the Himalaya", from which is derived the title of the volume. Three seminars were held over a two-year period with the aim of exploring exchanges between the peoples of the Tibetan Plateau, the Himalayan belt and the South Asian peninsula. A key assumption of the meetings—held in Leh, Gangtok, and Itanagar—was that the Himalaya represented an assimilative space for the seepage of ideas, material exchanges and institution building northwards from the Indic civilisation and southwards from Tibetan civilisation; furthermore, these ideas and customs also mingled with the autochthonous equivalents that existed in the folds of the Himalaya. The topics addressed by the seminar's participants ranged from international relations to trade, religion to politics, and climate change to ecology.

Some of the thematic questions of the seminars were: how did the enclaves of the many small 'encysted' cultures respond economically through trade, socially through shared experiences and politically through institutions? Intellectually, how did these cultures respond to the two large oceans of civilisation represented by Buddhism in Tibet and Hinduism in India? Then, as they were confronted by modernisation, how did they respond to the ideas of modernity? Were the responses mere reactions to occidental colonial expansion or was there more to it? And what of the responses following the withdrawal of western colonialism in the mid-20th century when revised encroachments asserted themselves on the peoples who live in spaces—such as mountains, valleys and high altitude deserts—

that are difficult to define sociologically and to control politically? Were there localised visions of modernity? And what does the future hold for the cornucopia of cultural expressions that is the Himalaya?

The format for the series of meetings which resulted in the essays presented in this volume was to have the authors present their papers, followed by panel discussions between all the participants. With each meeting, the participants revised their papers to consider contributions that were made by colleagues until the chapters took final shape. We did not, of course, envision that the meetings would yield defining or even comprehensive answers to these questions. That task calls for a much larger enterprise. Our exercise is best described as an exploration towards formulating some of the critical questions. A prime objective was to make sure that the questions are asked so that they do not fade away. This is important for two reasons.

First, there is a need to document and acknowledge Tibetan civilisation's contribution to Himalayan culture. This is important because this contribution is in danger of being lost to our memory due to Tibet's presently diminished status as an independent political entity or a fully autonomous cultural source. Diminished political status and restrained cultural impetus weaken a nation's ability to make such contributions or a culture's ability to fully flower. More importantly, they endanger the inspiration source and the wellspring of this knowledge.

It is often forgotten that the geographic position of the many cultural enclaves of the Himalaya—sandwiched between two civilisational oceans and political giants of present-day India and China—is also home to indigenous knowledge, culture and life-ways of its autochthonous peoples. The second objective of our exercise was to ensure that what is left of the indigenous knowledge and its perspective in the various fields of study addressed in this volume—economic, social, political and intellectual—are incorporated into the world's knowledge bank so that lived experiences of and from the Himalaya, from the cultural outposts of Gilgit-Baltistan in the west to that of Arunachal Pradesh in the east, are preserved and expanded on.

To be sure a volume as slim as the present one cannot pretend to answer such questions comprehensively or formulate all the questions that need to be asked. For example, indigenous Himalayan contributions to the methods and wisdom in the fields of agriculture, art and literature, among other knowledge fields are not touched upon in this volume. In this context, the symposia organised by the Foundation for Non-Violent Alternatives (FNVA) was intended more as an exploration and an inventory of what some of the questions might be. It is hoped that the questions will serve as a beginning for scholars who participate in knowledge banking and practitioners who participate in policymaking. The questions raised in this volume need to be horizontally expanded on and vertically deepened so that our understanding of the precious mosaic of the Himalayan cornucopia is not lost amidst aggressive state-building exercises by the many independent nation-states—specifically Bangladesh, Bhutan, China, India, Myanmar, Nepal and Pakistan—that form the borderlands of the Himalayan expanse and the juggernaut of homogeneity facilitated by the introduction of 'rapid' (and all too often uncritical) modernisation through the devices of technology, instant communications and ease of transport.

The first two chapters set the stage for the theoretical questions that emerged from our deliberations. In the last decade and a half, Willem van Schendel and James Scott have generated a creative dialogue between anthropologists, historians and geographers. The basic premise, first mooted by Schendel, of this thesis is that the societies that inhabit the Tibetan Plateau and the Himalaya were protected from expanding and powerful states because of their location and the difficulty of the terrain in which they lived. Scott expanded this theory to other regions and contended that societies also sought refuge in the hills so as to avoid being ruled by aggressive 'state-making' processes, more often than not violent and oppressive.

Chetan Singh, in the opening essay, nuances this thesis with the observation that the Schendel-Scott arguments do not explain "the emergence of well-structured states in the region" in the late modern period. This is a valid question, because it was between the late 18th and the mid-19th centuries that the Himalaya (one could also say western and eastern Turkestan or Central Asia) witnessed many states—Bhutan, Nepal, Jammu & Kashmir, Sikkim and several other smaller ones—crystallising as modern entities and negotiating their futures with the larger states that either wedged them in or directly dominated them. The complexity of the process of state-building, Singh argues, allows the smaller entities to become 'transitory' and 'threshold' units as they adapt themselves to new realities socially, culturally and politically. He illustrates his argument with a discussion on how Kinnaur and the Kinnauras have adapted themselves to both modernisation and the idea of modernity.

In Chapter 2, Sanjay Chaturvedi addresses the question of Tibet's position in the comity of nations. He argues that modern Tibet, along with the Central Asian states and Afghanistan (one could add other similar states as well) has been a victim of "colonial cartographies" and "neo-liberal geopolitics" in the recent past. This tends, he points out, to gloss over the fact that it has been subjected to "excessive geopolitics". This phenomenon, combined with a forced exoticism of its location and civilisation, has caused us to forget that geopolitics cannot ignore "human-cultural geographies" which need to transcend state-centric negotiation along borders. With this in mind, Chaturvedi urges, "China and India to acknowledge collectively that the histories of mobility throughout the Himalaya are much longer than the histories of borders" setting the stage for a perspective on Tibet's relations with the Himalaya in light of the 'peoples' of both, rather than merely as 'trade route', geo-political 'buffer zone' or territorial possession.

The discussions during the seminar series, which give this volume its content, were Tibet-centric in that it they sought to record and expand on Tibetan contributions to the life of the Himalaya's ethnicities, languages, political histories and even, in its role as the 'Third Pole', a custodian of the environment of its sprawling neighbourhood of South Asia and Southeast Asia. Chapters 3 and 4 are devoted to establishing this perspective. Thubten Samphel's contribution returns the focus of our discussions to the "Geopolitical Importance of Tibet" for the diverse citizens of the Himalaya and South Asia in history and for the future. His discussion focuses on the criticality of fairness towards the Tibetan Plateau in the use of its minerals (over 130 varieties of them) and as the "Water Tower of Asia", arguing that neglect by the international community on fairness of use in these activities will be to the detriment of the world as a whole. In Chapter 4, Tashi Phuntsok gives us an overview of the Himalayan peoples' current relationship with Tibet, including a historical overview of perspectives and an update on the status of Tibetans in exile.

The next cluster of three chapters is devoted to Tibet's relationship with the Himalayan kingdom-states of Tehri, Sikkim and Ladakh over the centuries.

Claude Arpi, in Chapter 5, examines the case of a dispute between the Tehri state and Tibet, which has spilled over not just between British India and pre-1950 Tibetan interests but also to the current Sino-Indian border position. It represents an interesting study on how some lingering legacies of border problems are addressed. Sunanda K. Datta-Ray's essay, "Sikkim Can Be Put in India But Tibet Can't Be Taken Out of Sikkim" (Chapter 6) is a classic rendition of the debt that is owed to Tibet culturally, historically and politically by an erstwhile Himalayan kingdom. He narrates how a non-Buddhist-non-Tibetan Nepali majority, "find it more than ever necessary to cling to the Tibetan legacy for its own survival as a distinct entity in India." This case of calling for the opposite of majoritarian cultural domination and highlighting a now-minority civilisational identity for a state is surely a subject that deserves a few doctoral theses in the context of identity politics that is so pronounced in political discourse today.

Sikkim lost its independent status in 1975 when it was annexed to India. The kingdom of Ladakh was annexed to the emergent Dogra state of Raja Gulab Singh in 1842. With the birth of the Dogra state of Jammu & Kashmir in 1846, its territory became the largest portion of the by-now 'Territories of Maharaja Gulab Singh'. But the ethnic, linguistic and cultural definition of Ladakh as 'Tibetan' had begun in the 9th century. This phenomenon is summarised by Sonam Joldan in his review (Chapter 7) of the historical, cultural and trade relationship between Ladakh and Tibet over 2,000 years. It is interesting to note how the relationship between these two 'trans-Himalayan' regions (depending on which side of the Himalaya one is looking at!) were sustained even though they were separated by three months of travel on yak and horse-back. Joldan concludes Chapter 7 by asserting the importance for Ladakhis of "the restoration of normal border trading and cultural relations" with Tibet. He also underlines the criticality of consulting borderland dwellers about their future, rather than having policy directed exclusively from the capitals of the large and powerful status quo states.

The original intent of the seminar series was to also include the sovereign states of Bhutan, Nepal and Pakistan—all of whom have a Tibeto-Himalayan connection along their northern borders—with *in situ* symposia and interpretations from the citizens of these sovereign nation-states. However, the scarcity of time and funds prevented the organisers from continuing the series. But we are happy to be able to include Sangeeta Thapliyal's contribution. Chapter 8 explores the implications of an independent country with a non-Tibetan and non-Buddhist majority, interacting with a significant ethnic and religious minority. Thapliyal's take is to examine, among other things, "Buddhism as a link between India, Nepal and China." She points out that these were forged when the political elites of China, Nepal and India were open to exploring cultural linkages between them, suggesting a return to emphasis on them. "States cannot ignore...cultural realties." The implication of this appears to be that cultural dialogue is just as important, if not more so, than political negotiations which often tend to be exclusively territorial in nature.

Chapter 9 directly addresses the complexity of the contentious claim and counter-claim between India and China from the point of view of Tibet's relations with Tawang in Arunachal Pradesh. The essay by Man Norbu and Nani Bath illustrates this complication. The essay cites evidence showing that Tawang was clearly a Tibetan territory from medieval times. Tibet lost its political independence in 1950. It is now India's official position to regard Tibet as a part of China. If such be the case, then what are we to make of China's claim to it? Between the Indian and the Chinese positions, the chapter tells us, is the aspiration of the people of Tawang, namely, that it is not a part of China. As in the case of most intractable international disputes, Tawang also represents a conundrum in the context of the larger question of Tibet. A conundrum that will undoubtedly have to find a solution that accommodates not only the status quo states but also, most importantly, the people directly influenced by state-based territorial acquisitiveness.

Bijay Thapa's essay (Chapter 10) focuses on how Tibetans in Darjeeling and Sikkim are addressing the question of identity. His argument is not dissimilar to the one proffered by Datta-Ray earlier in this volume: "Tibetans and Tibetanness prevail, represent and define the historicity and landscape of Sikkim-Darjeeling hills." In this context, it dwells on how the ethnic and linguistic Tibetans in these regions tend to ensure that they rigorously preserve their distinctiveness whether it is in the realm of their vocation, social relations, politics or religion.

In Chapter 11, Tshering Doma Kaleon focuses on trade links between Sikkim and Tibet which helped to shape the earlier majority Sikkimese Tibetan identity. She argues passionately for the restoration of border trade, not as part of some nostalgic romanticism but as a meaningful material linkage that can help bolster the identity of the Tibetan, and now-minority, ethnics of Sikkim.

Chapter 12 by Tenzin Norbu augments the argument for the importance of Tibet from the point of view of the environment. His is a passionate argument for an understanding of the 'Third Pole' not just as a source of water for a considerably portion of humanity but also as a source of knowledge on how to preserve the ecology of the region. His aim is "to understand and bring forward the ground realities of what is actually happening, how our forefathers have protected the ecology, and how we must act together to protect the environmental degradation and loss of ancestral cultures in the process of development".

A lacuna in the series of dialogues that we held around the topic of Tibet and the Himalaya was the absence of Chinese perspectives because of the shortage of time for networking and the scarcity of financial resources. However, we are thankful to Ananta S.B. de Gurung (Chapter 13) for not letting the volume be blank on this important perspective. His chapter examines the reasons why Tibet is materially important to China: water, minerals and the territorial expanse to allow for the migration of the majority population. He concludes: "Chinese presence in Tibet has transmogrified into a need-based issue because of the cushioning it can guarantee against non-conventional security concerns, for example, [the] destabilising effect that may arise from energy and food security in the country".

II

Over much of the known history of its mountainous belt, the diverse peoples and cultures of the Himalaya have been alternately ignored, appeased or pacified by the empires and states that have bordered them. In the last couple of centuries, with the rise of modern state-building and greater efficiency in territorial acquisitiveness, many territories and their inhabitants have been incorporated into the established nation-states. In late modernity and after the British withdrawal from southern Asia, while the incorporation of the Himalaya into the larger states (some very new) has been formalised, the process of equitable integration of these regions and peoples has yet to be completed. In part this is because the process of state-building in the mainstream land of the countries that border the Himalaya is still a work in progress.

Two major premises inform the seminar series. First, that it is precisely in the present that the half-dozen modern nation-states bordering the Himalayan belt must recognise the importance of not only being sensitive to the needs of the peoples of the region but engaging with them to document, preserve, improvise and improve on the knowledge, methods and materials of the Himalaya. Given the relative fluidity of interaction along the Himalayan regions' borders with the six odd states that surround it, the multiplicity and diversity of the 'Indic' and sub-cultural influences from their southern neighbours will continue as a dialogue. However, the second premise is that from the north, given the current political status of Tibet, the trend of a hard nationalism in China threatens homogenisation of and Han hegemony over Tibet. This in turn threatens that the wellspring of Tibetan cultural influences for the Tibeto-Himalaya will dry up. So the seminars and the contents of this volume are intended to launch a dialogue that will forestall this possibility.

As has already been said, this is a rather large project. Nor is this the first attempt at such a discourse. However, the laudable FNVA seminar series and its outcome can still lay claim to some 'firsts'. Tibet's contribution through its vernacular interpretation of Buddhism is well known, whereas its contribution to other aspects of life less so. Therefore, we have made a conscious effort to concentrate on Tibetan contributions to the Himalaya historically, culturally, commercially and socially. Also, we have 'unpacked' the Himalaya by attempting to represent as much of its internal diversity and modest but invaluable autonomies in our discourse. Once again, it has not been possible to do full justice to this ambition. It would have enriched this volume, for example, to have a chapter on how the people of Baltistan, which is today in Pakistan, are reintroducing the Tibetan script in order to preserve the language as also an important Tibetan Buddhist site not far from Skardu its capital. Similarly, a chapter on Mustang (ethnically, linguistically and culturally Tibetan, but territorially in Nepal) or another on the plight of Bhutanese citizens of Nepali descent would not have been out of place. But then we have to draw a line somewhere. By far the most important first in the seminars and the contributions to this volume is that the participants have been overwhelmingly 'Himalayans'. Out of the 14 authors of this volume, 11 are from the Himalaya and many of them are young scholars. And what is more, a majority of them still live there.

Some authors in this volume have pointed out, either directly or indirectly, that the Himalayan region suffers from a discourse that originates and ends in the capitals of the status quo states. That is, between New Delhi, Beijing, Islamabad, Dhaka, Kathmandu and Thimpu. This book is a fervent advocacy for this to change so that the everyday citizenry of the Himalaya—the Himalayans who live on the borders—are consulted without prejudice to the centuries of influences that have seeped into the fabric of their lives from the south and, more particularly, the north. They deserve to be allowed the civilisational dialogue that forms the warp and weft of their lives no matter from which direction. And most of all, they deserve to be allowed to have a say about the future of their lives that is substantive, transparent and organic.

I

Histories and Backdrop

1

CHETAN SINGH

Thresholds in the Wilderness

Identities, Interests and Modernity in Western Himalayan Borderlands

The Search for Highland Essentialities

Willem van Schendel's (2002) audacious postulation that the enormous expanse of Asian highlands—including the Himalaya, the Tibetan Plateau and the uplands of the Southeast Asian peninsula—was a distinct identifiable region has evoked much academic interest. He contended that societies in these highlands had persistently, and successfully, resisted the domination of large and powerful states at the peripheries of which they were located. Furthermore, the sparse and scattered highland population of this region exhibited greater cultural diversity than the more homogenised lowlands. To this extensive and impressive land mass, van Schendel gave the interesting name 'Zomia' (originating from north-eastern India).

James Scott (2009), subsequently, developed the idea of Zomia in his study of the Southeast Asian Massif. This extensive region includes the upland territories of several countries. Scott's (2009: x) principal argument was that the most significant social intent in the peripheral uplands was to escape domination by any state. It is not simply environmental conditions and cultural considerations that determined the nature of family, community institutions and economic strategies of these communities. In fact, the options available were rather restricted after people in the highlands had made the initial political choice of escaping the stranglehold of powerful agrarian states and seeking shelter in the mountains (Scott, 2009: xi). These marginalised 'shatter zones' adjoined states and provided refuge to people who were periodically buffeted by the oppressive and violent processes of "state-making and state-unmaking" (Scott, 2009: 7). A history of long-term resistance to state domination gave the highland societies the ability to change and adjust very rapidly, "turn on a dime" as Scott puts it (Scott, 2009: 24). Resistance was sustained by a social structure which was easily "disaggregated and reassembled". For this purpose a "mixed portfolio of subsistence techniques was adopted as it provided greater economic advantage" (Scott, 2009: 211). Three critical ideas determined how hill people perceived themselves and structured their society: "equality, autonomy, and mobility" (Scott, 2009: 217). Adoption of an oral tradition was yet another method of escaping state control. The virtual absence of writing and texts offered "freedom of manoeuvre in history, genealogy, and legibility that frustrates state routines" (Scott, 2009: 226). According to Scott, the ambiguity accompanying oral methods of remembering created "multiple histories" that mountain people used "singly or in combination depending on the circumstances" (Scott, 2009: 329). It was "in their interest to keep as many of their options open as possible, and what kind of history to have is one of those options. They have as much history as they require" (Scott, 2009: 330).

Geographers, anthropologists and historians explored the idea of Zomia in a special issue of the *Journal of Global History* in 2010. Despite its theoretical appeal the concept is based on generalisations that are rather difficult to substantiate empirically. Fairly developed state formations occurred quite early within the extensive highland region defined as Zomia by van Schendel and Scott. If Zomia is conceived primarily as a region of refuge for societies that had escaped state control, the emergence of well-structured states within the region is a contradiction. One can, however, argue that state control over societies in the mountains was often quite weak, and in some places even non-existent. Lack of state intervention enabled mountain people to assert their identities and interests in opposition to the stricter 'mainstreaming' efforts of the more powerful, agrarian states.

The Idea of Modern Development

The perceived isolation of mountain people from larger socio-political trends of the lowlands seemed to allow greater freedom to hill societies from state control. Not surprisingly, this also gave rise to the notion that hill societies remained non-conformist or even 'backward' till they were radically transformed by state-sponsored developmental activities. Change in western Himalayan societies is, therefore, usually seen as a result of modern development. Two sets of theoretical and methodological assumptions underlie the present thinking on the impact of modernisation on different regions of the world. This is especially true of geographical spaces (like mountains) whose isolation caused them to be mistakenly seen as unchanged and unaffected by major trends that radically transformed the world in modern times.

Development, Modernisation and Modernity

The first set of assumptions consists of three overlapping concepts: development, modernisation and modernity. There is a logical, and perhaps even sequential, connection between the ideas of development and modernisation. With the decline and collapse of colonial empires by the mid-20th century, the impoverishment of the peoples of the former colonies became apparent to the world. The compelling necessity for bringing about 'development' in these newly liberated countries was justified by the anticipated material benefit that 'modernisation' ensuing from development would bring to them. Considerable academic work focused upon the linkages between development and modernisation. Quantifiable material change was integral to development and modernisation. The visibility of the 'things' that modernisation brought to a society that it touched was an important measure of its success.

In the 1950s, the embedded objective of developmental planning at the global level was to modernise previously colonised societies. This was particularly so where the burden of social tradition was regarded as a hindrance to progress. As a result "modernity" came to be regarded as "a value in and of itself" (Ortiz, 2000: 255). It was here, too, that the relationship between development and modernity acquired greater complexity. Unlike the materially recognisable aspects of economic 'modernisation', the concept of 'modernity' often comes loaded with qualitative issues and asks questions dealing with values, norms, beliefs, rationality, subjectivity, individuality and a host of intangible ideas. In short, modernity engages more directly with the world view of a society and its methods of analysis and explanation. Modernisation might successfully alter the material condition of societies. But it may not always engender in them the emergence of 'modernity' as a different and systematic way of seeing, explaining and changing the world.

The Presumed Marginality of the Western Himalaya

The second set of assumptions is directly relevant to our present purpose. In part at least, the attraction of exploring changes in social identities and interests of communities of the region was derived from their presumed historical marginalisation. The premise here was that because the peripheral nature of the region had inhibited change, contemporary transformations caused by 'development' would, for that reason, become more apparent. This would also, therefore, make the disjuncture between tradition and modernity in such societies measureable.

These suppositions, however, require an empirical understanding of the nature of society as it might have existed before 'development', and also of the changes introduced thereafter. Societies of the western Himalayan borderlands were earlier drawn into the competing interests of colonial empires and were subsequently required to follow nationally determined 'developmental' activities. To discover the world view that steered these borderland societies before the age of 'development' and 'modernisation' is a difficult task. Little has been written about popular mentalities in the western Himalaya prior to the colonial encounter—though some of the better recorded religious beliefs do reveal something about secular wisdom. More interestingly, trading and commercial activity (with its complexity of negotiations) provides some useful insights into the minds of societies that engage in it.

Early European Perspectives on the Western Himalaya

Early observations of European travellers and colonial administrators—albeit impressionistic—are quite easily available to historians today. Western Himalayan societies' introduction to modernization and modernity began earlier than scholars have cared to notice. Prior to the concept of 'modernisation', it was the colonial rulers' idea of introducing 'civilisation' and its accompanying material accessories to the mountain people that influenced altruistic thinking in British India. J.G. Gerard (1824: 314), a British doctor stationed in Sabathu (in present-day Himachal Pradesh) in 1824, was convinced that:

> The example of European character and intelligence has not been lost upon the hill population. The Chiefs have beheld with pleasure many of the arts and sciences and the comforts of civilized life and have adopted several useful and laudable customs. I allude here to articles of dress, household furniture, implements of husbandry, glass windows, grates and chimneys, the cultivation and cookery of the potato, medicine and chemistry, and it is quite delightful to observe the daily disuse and abandonment of hereditary prejudices and the development of energy and civilization all over the country.

Gerard evidently believed that the introduction of modern science and technology would result in the dilution of traditional practices and customary beliefs that came to be classified as 'hereditary prejudices'. To early colonial officials, this represented a change in thinking that could facilitate the transition to modernity. It appears that western Himalayan borderland societies shared certain socio-cultural characteristics that influenced how they responded to external developments. To a considerable extent, these characteristics were probably influenced by their geographical and socio-political locations.

Transitory Zones and Transformation

These societies were quite clearly situated in what can be called transitory zones. The physical space and that they occupied compelled them to interact with, and even accommodate, the beliefs and practices of at least two major religions, cultures and peoples.

Their location at the peripheries of two dominant civilisations enabled some distinct territories of the western Himalaya (such a Kinnaur, Lahaul, Spiti and Ladakh) to remain discrete cultural areas. Throughout the region as well as in adjoining western Tibet, were to be found numerous locations that functioned as socio-cultural (even political) thresholds. These thresholds, as would be expected, had a dual character. They marked the point at which two grand civilisations separated. But these were also locations where the essential elements of two major cultural traditions met, transacted exchanges and sustained a diversity of beliefs and practices.

Fisher's (1987: 96, 189) study of Tarangpur traders of Nepal in the Nepal-China border area, inhabited by Magars and situated between the Buddhist and Hindu traditions, is a case in point. He argued that:

> The problem is not only the integration of an encysted ethnic minority into a complex society, but also the mode of accommodation reached between two major systems. The symbol systems of two different great traditions compete for commitment, so that executing the transactional chain requires a double-edged Janus-faced form of impression management—hence the present cultural heterogeneity of Tarangpur—of a society which is nominally Buddhist, strongly Hinduized and still partly tribal.

The intermediate position of certain western Himalayan societies between two large cultures offered them enormous opportunities. Their location in a transition zone encouraged them to acquire multiple identities for different purposes. They needed to accommodate in their society what were apparently contradictory social and cultural arrangements. The ability to do so probably lent them a flexibility and willingness to deal with ideas and institutions that were new and unfamiliar. This was so even as their commitment to community, village and local religious beliefs persisted.

The larger geographical context within which major long-term historical trends occur is not always easy to identify, even though they might offer interesting explanations. Braudel's (1978) seminal study of the early modern Mediterranean world is one such outstanding example. Using this study, Wong (2003: 13) argues that even for Central Asia one could adopt a similar model, and "consider the cultural dynamics of regions by tracking the institutions among people crossing cultures and carrying ideas." He argues that: "regions there offer a scale of observation that encourages recognition of difference and connection." He emphasises that "the northwestern frontier of China was a region in which four civilizations—the Han Chinese, Tibetan, Mongolian and Islamic—have met since the sixteenth century" (Wong, 2003: 14). However, this meeting place had very extended linkages that went deep into the economies and societies of the neighbouring civilisations. In this extensive part of Central Asia, "the connections among peoples of the region were often less important than those formed with other sedentary systems that bordered them" (Wong, 2003: 35).

Ladakh Borderland: Trade and Society

Several adjoining parts of Tibet and Central Asia, further north, witnessed this remarkable interaction among different people of diverse backgrounds. Leh, for instance, was a place where traders—Kashmiris, Punjabis, Yarkandis and others—from distant regions gathered to exchange goods that they had in turn brought from even more far-off markets (Nakshahbandi, 1850: 377; Vigne, 1981: II: 343). The long and difficult journeys they undertook required an equally long period of preparation. Their extended residence in Ladakh for this purpose enabled greater social interaction and understanding.

Yarkand, in Central Asia, had a system of administration that was quite conducive for trade. Administrative control over the town was shared between a Muslim *Hakim* and two Chinese *Ambans*. While the *Ambans* supervised customs, police and criminal justice, a chief judge appointed by the *Hakim* settled civil disputes. Yarkand lay a difficult 40-day journey from Leh, and yet Yarkandi, Kashmiri and Ladakhi traders were to be found in both places. The Kashmiris were taxed at a lower rate than the others at the custom-house. The close association of Yarkand with trade, and the transitory character of a large part of its trading population is reflected in the use of the term *musafir* (traveller). The term was used for every foreign trader resident in the town, even though some of them had settled there long enough to have local wives and children living with them (Izzatullah, 1843: 305; Nakshahbandi, 1850: 372-85). The mixed milieu of the town is illustrated by the fact that though the governor of the city was a Chinese *Amban*, the Muslim *Qazi* of the town was regarded with great respect, as were the *Ulema*. It was further noted that, "whenever a dispute arises between a Mahomedan and a Chinese, it is settled according to the Mahomedan law. The Chinese are also sent to the *Hakim*, and he, with common consent, settles their disputes by Mahomedan law" (Nakshahbandi, 1850: 383).

In fact, trade was an extremely important economic aspect of the trans-Himalayan highlands, and treaties between states refer to its regulation quite meticulously, as, for example, does the 1684 treaty between Tibet and Ladakh (Ahmed, 1968: 353-54). In adjoining Tibet, and further north in Central Asia, there were towns where trade acted as a binding factor. This was accompanied by attempts by different states to regulate routes, impose taxes and ensure some kind of administrative presence. In western Tibet, the administrators (*Jongpen*) had a personal interest in trade from which they profited and this may have resulted in its close regulation. Such regulation did sometimes restrict the free movement of goods through western Tibet. An important trading town of the Changthang region of western Tibet was Gartok, and it was sometimes described as not much more than a temporary trading camp. When Moorcroft visited it in July 1817, he described it as a collection of black tents and little else (McKay, 1992: 410, 412, 414-15). The smallness of the scale does not, however, detract from the fact that the trade was of great importance for the societies that engaged in this exchange. In many respects, it was crucial for their existence.

Not surprisingly, therefore, the Tibetan Plateau and the mountain region bordering it in the south and west was not a 'no-man's land' despite its desolate appearance. Even in this apparent wilderness there existed imagined and real thresholds where traders and travellers were carefully watched. Nain Singh and his brother, who were tasked by the British with the assignment to secretly survey Tibet, soon discovered how carefully the movement of people across the border was monitored. In March 1856, they first attempted to cross into Tibet through the Nepal border in the guise of Bashahris, but were turned back by an official who knew only too well that Bashahri traders did not use the Nepal route to enter Tibet (Singh, 2008: 477-48). The high passes, too, were therefore thresholds in the wilderness that were points of political and economic regulation. Even in this bleak and sparsely populated landscape, it did not take long for people to identify each other. While, once again, pretending to be a Bashahri travelling for business in Tibet, Nain Singh was closely questioned by suspicious Kashmiri traders who soon penetrated his disguise, though they did not reveal his true identity to the Tibetan authorities (Montgomerie, 2008: 431).

Kinnaur and Modernity

It must, nevertheless, be remembered that these thresholds were equally a passage for crossing from one side to the other. The societies that lived and prospered by such crossing seem to have exhibited an impressive ability to negotiate and understand diverse cultural and political nuances. Gerard's (1824: 315) early account suggests that such adaptability was to be found amongst Kinnauras. He made an interesting distinction between formal education on the one hand and 'civilisation, morality and knowledge' on the other. The latter, according to him, had "made the greatest progress in the remote and secluded regions of Koonawur." Gerard believed that, "Koonawur, in spite of the defects of the Bussahir government and its remoteness from the capital, ranks above every other State in point of intelligence, active industry and good feeling..." He pointed out that:

> There are no Brahmins in that country and there is much less of blind devotion in religion, but more of superstition. Education is there less cultivated than the actual acquirement of knowledge, which their intercourse with the Chinese, their commercial pursuits and habits of hardihood encourage and establish (Gerard, 1824: 315-16).

The lack of Brahmanical control over society in the Himalaya was seen as a window of opportunity for introducing crucial transformational changes. Through modern education and the "introduction of the morality of Christianity and the arts and comforts of civilization," in particular, "the moral and political improvement" of the people could be carried out (Murray, 1824: 274). Interestingly, the freedom enjoyed by women in mountain regions was seen as a something that promised "hope of future improvement" (Murray, 1824: 274).

What reinforced British conviction that the Himalayan society was more amenable to change was the prevalence not only of equality "to a greater degree than is to be found in any other portion of India" but also the existence of "a parity of ignorance" (Gerard, 1824: 314). This seemed to present a kind of clean slate opportunity to the colonial rulers to insert a greater measure of European influence. For the British, it was probably easier to prevail over 'irrational' belief in magic and superstition than to confront carefully formulated religious doctrines spelt out by orthodox Brahmins. Gerard's confidence in being able to effect a change in Kinnaur might have been derived from his success in making small-pox inoculation acceptable in the mountainous area as early as the 1820s, while resistance to it persisted in various parts of India through the 19th century (Swinton, 1824: 305). Many Tibetan lamas, who probably travelled through Kinnaur, were convinced of its efficacy. They had offered themselves for vaccination and had even requested Gerard to carry out vaccinations at the border (foreigners were not permitted into Tibet) so that others in Tibet could benefit too (Murray, 1824: 276-77). Gutzlaff (1850: 226), in fact, mentions that every year large numbers of nomadic people in the Tibet Plateau areas died of smallpox.

The absence of Brahmins in certain South Asian societies did not, however, invariably mean that such societies remained 'simple' or 'primitive' and therefore likely to succumb more easily to external intellectual and religious influences. In fact, the so-called 'Hindu' belief system presented itself in diverse ways in different parts of South Asia, and the Brahmin characterised only the more formal facet of orthodox Brahmanic religion. The absence of Brahmins, therefore, did not necessarily indicate the absence of beliefs derived from Brahmanical prescriptions. Kinnaur, even today, retains a very eclectic approach towards religion.

Markets, Money and Exchange

The ideas of commerce and exchange permeated the structure of Kinnaur social organisation. Despite the difficult topography of the area, money and commodities were essential elements of life in Kinnaur. Travel over long distances for trade was an integral part of the annual cycle of activities and the Kinnaura capacity to negotiate in culturally diverse situations is not to be underestimated. Their ability to understand different identities and interests, too, had been remarkably sharpened over centuries. Trade routes connecting Tibet and India had existed for centuries prior to the widening of the Hindustan-Tibet road by the British. The economic and cultural baggage that passed along these routes and the opportunities for gain that this offered had always been factored into the Kinnaura world view.

European travellers invariably referred to the trading and manufacturing activities of the Kinnauras. Among the early references, Moorcroft, on the basis of information obtained in Ladakh, writes about two kinds of local plants that were exported as 'tea' in considerable quantities from Kinnaur to Ladakh (Moorcroft and Trebeck, 1970: 209-10). Fraser mentions the production of wine, iron, lead, copper in limited quantities—but most importantly the "fabrication of woollen cloths of several sorts, and in this they excel the inhabitants of all the countries between Sutlej and the Alaknunda" (Fraser, 1982: 272-74). Rampur is described by him as a town that "was once a flourishing place" where commodities from Kashmir, Ladakh, 'Bootan' (Tibet), Kashgar, Yarkand, etc., could be bought (Fraser, 1982: 256-57). The implication seems to be that the highly exploitative period of Gorkha rule had taken a toll on its prosperity. Soon after, in 1824, however, Murray, the Deputy Superintendent of the Shimla Hill States, referred to the availability of "tea from China" and "bars of silver" from Yarkund and toys from Russia at the Rampur fair, while in Kinnaur were to be found "Mandarin chopstick, cups and saucers" (Murray, 1824: 292).

Rampur became once again a prosperous place where trade fairs were held thrice a year in May, October and December and where "people of many countries, characters and customs" came (Murray, 1824: 286-87; Lloyd, 1840: 183).

Not surprisingly, then the Kinnauras were more prosperous than the peasantry in other parts of Bashahr. This prosperity was noted also by Gerard (1993: 76-77) who travelled through Kinnaur in 1822. He mentions two different occasions on which he ran short of money and had no difficulty in borrowing it from local Kinnauras who were very happy to loan him whatever amount he required. Kinnauras obtained a good income from trade and pastoralism, and this enabled them to earn "more than enough to pay their contribution" of the revenue demanded by the Bashahr state (Gerard, 1993: 282, 289). The state was, moreover, "fully aware of the singular situation and the importance of this commerce, upon which it is so dependent" (Murray, 1824: 289). The Bashahr Gazetteer of 1910 [part of the Shimla Hill States Gazetteer (SHSG)] while referring to the revenue settlement of Bashahr of 1894 observed that the inhabitants of Kinnaur were on "the whole better off than those of Rampur and Rohru. Good profits are made in trading, they have plenty of cattle, and they make a considerable income from fruit and forest products, as well as from wool and homespun cloth" (SHSG, 1911—Bashahr: 76). The *bandobast* report of Chini tehsil carried out in 1928 reiterated that the people of the tehsil were by and large traders and sold goods at the Lavi trade fair in Rampur after "increasing the prices by a large margin of profit" (Bhuj, 1928: 21).

There is also an interesting reference to the existence of a committee that oversaw the transaction of trade between Kinnaura and Tibet traders. Each group of Kinnaura traders had its counterpart in Tibet with which they had to transact business and the infringement of rules was punishable (SHSG, 1911—Bashahr: 62). Nevertheless, people from Kinnaur had considerable freedom of movement in Tibet. This is proved by the fact that when the British sent an expedition to explore the eastern watershed of the upper Indus river, they had to send in a person disguised as a Bashahri trader along with a group of genuine Bashahris (Montgomerie, 1870: 208).

The remarkable familiarity of the people of Kinnaur with fairly complex commercial transactions and their dependence on conducting business with traders from distant places situated them in a place rather different from ordinary agro-pastoral peasants of the region. Even forest produce of the area, such as *zeera* and *neoza* were successfully marketed by Kinnauras on a regular basis (Llyod, 1840: II: 272). It would be important to keep this factor in mind while attempting to understand the possible impact that developmental activity might have had on their thought processes. The 'simplicity' of a pre-modern society or the theoretical 'clean slate' often assumed by colonial officials because of the geographical inaccessibility of Kinnaur certainly did not exist. On the contrary, the region portrays far more intricate socio-economic characteristics than those found in some simpler peasant societies situated in close proximity to the political centre of India.

Society and Social Organisation

While taking a closer look at Kinnaur society in the context of modernisation and its trajectory towards modernity, there are at least two features that seem to merit closer examination. These were not exclusive to Kinnaura society, but they did occupy an important place in it. The first was the religious practice of Buddhism in some areas along with the institutions associated with it, and the second was the fairly common social practice of polyandry with all its economic and political implications.

The existence of Buddhism as a formal, institutionalised religion has a long history in upper Kinnaur, going back more than a thousand years. For the colonial period, Alexander Gerard makes one of the earliest references to it. When he visited the village of Sangnam in 1817, he was received by about 80 Buddhist lamas and 50 or 60 nuns belonging, according to him, to "six populous villages". He further writes that the convent at Sunam had 32 nuns and several lamas (Gerard, 1993: 21, 120). Rose (1970: III: 453) noted later that while the largest nunneries of Kinnaur were located in the villages of

Kanam and Sangnam, a few *jomos* or nuns were to be found in almost every village. Andrew Wilson who travelled through the region in the 1880s mentions that his baggage was sometimes carried by "lama nuns" when pressure of work kept the lay people too occupied to render this service. Apart from cultivating the land attached to the monastery, these nuns also hired out their labour during the harvest season (Wilson, 1979: 189-90).

But the most interesting aspect of the monastic nature of Buddhism in Kinnaur—in so far as our present project is concerned—is that as a result, a fair number of people in certain parts of the region were engaged in reading and writing the scriptures. Alexander Gerard writes, "all lamas can read and write, and I never saw one who did not instantly recognize the few sentences in Captain Turner's Thibet" (Wilson, 1979: 118). The ability to at least read and write was not restricted to monks. The nuns, too, were encouraged to read the religious texts and would often be engaged in writing. Rose mentions that Kanet girls, who did not marry, were expected to live in nunneries and "devote their time to the study of the Tibetan scriptures" (Rose, 1970: III: 453). Wilson saw a connection between polyandry and the existence of a large number of nuns when he argued that, "of course, there is a large number of surplus women under this polyandric system, and they are provided for in the Lama nunneries where they learn to read and copy the Tibetan scriptures, and to engage in religious services" (Wilson, 1979: 189).

The population of Kinnaur appears to have remained small, and an estimate of six members per household was arrived at by Alexander. Quite possibly, each (Kanet) household in upper Kinnaur would have one or more family member entering the religious order. They might, by that connection, also have become familiar with the merit of reading and writing—even though they did not engage directly in activities that were dependent upon these skills. Did these linkages, albeit tenuous, of the Kinnaura families—not merely with religion but with the world of formal learning—affect their understanding of their world and its functioning? Were smaller peasant-oriented territories within a large part of Kinnaur bound together by the larger vision of Buddhism and the secular functioning of its institutions despite the fact that they sometimes spoke different languages and dialects? Alexander Gerard explicitly mentioned the differences in the languages spoken in Kinnaur. He wrote: "the inhabitants of Soognum speak a language totally different from Koonawuree and Tartar dialects.... There are to the best of my knowledge, no fewer than five distinct tongues spoken in Koonawur..." (Llyod, 1840: II: 230). Did the economic activities of the monasteries—which often included trade—introduce greater social and commercial complexity in what might otherwise have remained a simple, subsistence-oriented barter of products between peasant communities? Polyandrous families, I have argued elsewhere, were among the more prosperous ones in the areas where the practice existed (Singh, 2011: 98-120).

To complicate the situation further, there also existed a parallel hierarchy of local deities associated with each village. The Chini Tashil Settlement Report (Bhuj, 1928: 3) observed that:

> Most of the inhabitants of this tehsil follow the Buddhist religion, yet they also have a different *deota* in every *chak* who is called a family *deota* (*kul deota*) and who is not like the *deota* of the entire *ghori* as is the case in Rohru and Rampur.

In southern Kinnaur, this hierarchy existed not within the ambit of Buddhism, but was attached to the Brahmanical order. All village temples here had a number of functionaries attached to them. They managed the affairs not only of the *deota* and the temple, but also of the village itself (Rose, 1970: III: 447). The deity could only be approached through one or the other of these temple officials. A list of temples was made out by Rose and he pointed out that the deities were not all equal—they were in fact arranged in a hierarchy that reflected their importance. The absence of Brahmins in Kinnaur has already been mentioned earlier, and not surprisingly, the *pujaris* of these temples were all Kanets (Rose, 1970: III: 450, 470).

This hierarchy of *deotas* seems to be of immense significance for the administration of Bashahr state. Their connection with the monarch, who ruled on account of his claim to some amount of divinity, was quite intimate. The link between the two appears to have been renewed every year at the Fag *mela* held in Rampur—at which a large number of deities marked their presence before the ruler. This was a religio-political link that bound the ruler with his subjects through their deities. It represented the conduit through which passed subtle impulses not only of authority and consent, but also of autonomy and dissent. It was the channel through which the subjects expressed their anguish and a form of disagreement that sometimes bordered on rebellion. This was, perhaps, the tried and tested means through which mountain kingdoms accommodated dissent. Are the popular agitations against large hydro-electric projects that recur in the area similar to the remnants of older forms of protest that still struggle to survive? Is the modern democratic state, with its emphasis on the individual, attempting to alter the language and idiom of autonomous decision-making of traditional village-level communities?

Some Questions about Altered Western Himalayan Identities

Modernisation (riding on the presence and overwhelming demands of the Indian state) through the scheduled tribe (ST) status and corresponding need of social mobilisation within a democratic polity has made Kinnaura ethnicity more pronounced. Perhaps Kinnaura ethnic consciousness has developed a unity today that could not have emerged in pre-modern times. But does this mobilisation involve a shift away from earlier methods of invoking the village *deota*, and towards a more secular discourse within constitutional institutions? Or was the earlier intervention of the *deota* actually political in essence and religious only in form, and therefore its continuance even today is quite logical? Does this consciousness once again reassert and consolidate traditional norms in new forms? If so, has not 'development' based modernisation stalled the emergence of modernity at least in the European sense of the 'individual' and the nuclear family being the fulcrum of social organisation and instead reinforced the traditional notion of communal, or rather community, identity?

References

Ahmed, Z. (1968). "New Light on the Tibet-Ladakh-Mughal War of 1679-84", *East and West* 18 (3-4): 340-61. *http://www.jstor.org/stable/ 29755343*

Bhuj, C. (1928). *Report Tarmeem Bandobast: Tahsil Chini.* Typescript in Devanagari. 24 pages.

Braudel, F. (1978). *The Mediterranean and the Mediterranean World in the Age of Philip II.* Sian Reynolds (tr.). London: *Fontana/Collins.* 2 vols. First published in France in 1949.

Fisher, J. (1987). *Trans-Himalayan Traders: Economy, Society and Culture in Northwest Nepal.* Delhi: Motilal Banarsidass.

Fraser, J.B. (1982). *The Himala Mountains.* Delhi: Neeraj Publishing House. First published 1820.

Gerard, A. (1993). *Account of Koonawur in the Himalaya etc. etc. etc.* George Llyod (ed.). New Delhi: Indus Publishing House. First published in 1841

Gerard, J.G. (1824). "Letter of Dr J.G. Gerard, Assistant Surgeon, 1st Nusseeree Battalion, to Captain C.P. Kennedy, Assistant Deputy Superintendent, Soobathoo, dated 20 Nov. 1824", in *Punjab Government Records.* Lahore: Punjab Government Press, 1911, 8 vols. 10 parts. Vol. I: Delhi Residency and Agency Records, 1807-1857. pp.312-19.

Gutzlaff, Ch. (1850). "Tibet and Sefan", *Journal of the Royal Geographical Society of London* 20: 191-227. See p.226. *http://www.jstor.org/stable/179803*

Izzatullah, M. (1843). "Travels Beyond the Himalaya", *Journal of the Royal Asiatic Society of Great Britain and Ireland* 7 (2): 283-342. *http:// www: jstor.org/stable/ 25207596*

Journal of Global History (2010). *Journal of Global History* 5. London School of Economics.

Llyod, George (1840) (ed.). *Narrative of a Journey from Caunpoor to Boorendo Pass in the Himalaya Mountains by Major William Lloyd and Captian Alexander Gerard's Account of an Attempt to Penetrate by Bekhur to Garoo and the Lake Mansarowara, with a Letter from the Late J.G. Gerard Detailing a Visit to the Shatool and Boorendo Passes.* London: J. Madden & Co. 2 vols.

McKay, A.C. (1992). "The Establishment of the British Trade Agencies in Tibet: A Survey", *Journal of the Royal Asiatic Society* (Third Series) 2(3): 399-421, November. *http://www.jstor.org/stable/25182574*

Montgomerie, T.G. (1870). "Report of the Trans-Himalayan Explorations Made During 1868", *Proceedings of the Royal Geographical Society of London* 14 (3): 207-14. Stable URL: *http://www.jstor.org/stable/1799050*

————. (2008). "Report of a Route Survey made by Pundit ___, from Nepal to Lhasa and thence through the Upper Valley of the Brahmaputra to its Source", in U. Bhatt and S. Pathak (eds.), *Asia ki Peeth Par: Pandit Nain Singh Rawat: Jeewan, Anweshan Tatha Lekhan.* Nainital: Pahar. pp.447-509. First published in *Journal of the Royal Geographical Society.* London, 1877.

Moorcroft, W. and G. Trebeck (1970). *Travels in the Himalayan Provinces of Hindustan and the Punjab; in Ladakh and Kashmir and Bokhara, by Mr William Moorcroft and Mr George Trebeck from 1819 to 1825.* Prepared for press by H. H. Wilson. Patiala: Languages Department. First published Calcutta: Asiatic Society, 1837.

Murray, W. (1824). "From Lieutenant W. Murray, Deputy Superintendent, Shimla Hill States to C. Elliott, Agent to the Governor-General, Western Provinces, dated Camp Subathoo, 6 July 1824", in *Punjab Government Records.* Lahore: Punjab Government Press, 1911, 8 vols. 10 parts. Vol. I: Delhi Residency and Agency Records, 1807-1857. pp.251-99.

Nakshahbandi, A.S. (1850). "Route from Kashmir via Ladakh to Yarkhand", *Journal of the Royal Asiatic Society of Great Britain and Ireland,* 12: 372-385. Based on M.S. Persian dated 1846. Tr. by J. Dowson. *http://www.jstor.org/stable/25228626.*

Ortiz, R. (2000). "From Incomplete Modernity to World Modernity", *Daedalus* 129 (Winter 1: Multiple Modernities): 249-60. *http://www.jstor.org/stable/20027922*

Rose, H.A. (1970). *Glossary of Tribes and Castes of the Punjab and the North West Frontier Province.* Patiala: Punjab Languages Department. 3 volumes.

Scott, J.C. (2009). *The Art of Not Being Governed: An Anarchist History of Upland Southeast Asia.* New Haven/London: Yale University Press.

SHSG (1911). "Simla Hill States 1910", Vol. III in Punjab States Gazetteer. Bashahr. Lahore: The Civil and Military Press.

Singh, N. (2008). "Extracts from a Diary kept by Pundit ___ during his Journey from Nepal to Lhasa, and from Lhasa through the Upper Valley of the Brahmaputra to the Source of that River Near Mansarowar Lake.", in U. Bhatt and S. Pathak (eds.), *Asia ki Peeth Par: Pandit Nain Singh Rawat: Jeewan, Anweshan Tatha Lekhan.* Nainital: Pahar. pp.447-509. First published in *Journal of the Royal Geographical Society.* London, 1877.

Singh, C. (2011). "Polyandry and Customary Rights in the Western Himalaya", in Chetan Singh (ed.). *Recognizing Diversity: Society and Culture in the Himalaya.* New Delhi: Oxford University Press. pp.98-120.

Swinton, G. (1824). "Secretary to Government in the Political Department, Fort William to C. Elliot, Agent to Governor General, Delhi, dated 27th August 1824", in *Punjab Government Records.* Lahore: Punjab Government Press, 1911, 8 vols. 10 parts. Vol. I: Delhi Residency and Agency Records, 1807-1857. pp.300-06.

van Schendel, W. (2002). "Geographies of Knowing, Geographies of Ignorance: Jumping Scale in Southeast Asia", *Environment and Planning D: Society and Space* 20(6).

Vigne, G.T. (1981). *Travels in Kashmir, Ladakh and Iskardo.* New Delhi: Sagar Publications. 2 vols.

Wilson, A. (1979). *The Abode of Snow: Observations on a Tour from Chinese Tibet to the Indian Caucasus, through the Upper Valleys of the Himalaya.* Kathmandu: Ratna Pustak Bhandar. First published in 1886, London: G. P. Putnam's Sons.

Wong, R.B. (2003). "Between Nation and World: Braudelian Region in Asia", *Review* (26)1: 1-45. *http://www.jstor.org/stable/40241564*

2

SANJAY CHATURVEDI

Remapping Tibet

Colonial Cartographies, Neoliberal Geopolitics and Return to Himalayan Human-Cultural Geographies

Introduction

The key puzzle before this chapter, prompted by intellectual-academic concerns that are more exploratory in nature than normative is why is it that despite diverse geographical locations on the world map certain 'places'—for example Afghanistan, 'Central Asia' and Tibet—are approached, remembered and even speculated upon in overwhelmingly geopolitical terms? Is something inherently wrong with their respective geographic locations? Or could it be that they continue to be the objects of 'excessive' geopolitics—excess accumulated over centuries by the ways in which various centres of power have treated these places as 'buffers', 'frontiers' or 'routes' on highly territorialised imperial-colonial and even national maps of pride and prejudice. This is not to belittle the importance of the given geographies of Tibet's location *per se* (a long-standing concern and focus of classical geopolitics) but to highlight the serious and wide-ranging implications of the written geographies (focus of a critical geopolitics) that are forced, at times quite violently, by the powers that be on diverse and dynamic social-cultural landscapes of the peripheral regions. My key argument in this chapter is that for most of the colonial epoch in Asia, Tibet was subjected to an excessive geopolitics produced by the imposition of various imperial as well as nation-state centric geopolitical and military-strategic mappings that territorialised as well as trivialised the dynamic human-cultural geographies of Tibet as a place. Tibet was implicated in the Great

Game (Hopkirk, 1994; Scott, 2008; Upshur, 2011) and continues to be so imagined in its new avatars (North, 2011).

I begin my exploration with a brief theoretical engagement with the power and politics of mappings/maps with special reference to the role played by imaginative geographies. I distinguish 'imaginative geographies' from 'imagined geographies' which continue to contest reductionism inherent in and induced by the former. This is followed by a brief geo-historical account of how 'Tibet' was framed in western imaginations and the legacies that the colonial mapping has left behind on various Tibetan landscapes, including cognitive-mental. The manner in which Tibet is currently implicated in the geo-economics qua geopolitics of neoliberal globalisation is the theme to which I turn next. I conclude with a plea to a return to dynamic human and cultural geographies of Tibet as a place with a rather complex spatiality that is connected to the Himalayas on the one hand, and marked by diasporic identities, on the other.

Power and Politics of Mappings and Maps: Imaginative *versus* Imagined Geographies

Critically approached, mapping implies "the intellectual process of creating, communicating and accepting geographical conceptions whether at individual or socio-cultural level" (Edney, 1997). As pointed out by Dennis S. Cosgrove (1999), mapping presents both epistemological and interpretative challenges. The politics and power of 'cartography' need critical attention. In his view, the "measure of mapping" should not be confined only to the mathematical. Mapping can equally be spiritual, political or moral.

> By the same token, the mapping's record is not confined to the archival; it includes the remembered, the imagined, the contemplated. The world figured through mapping may thus be material or immaterial, actual or desired, whole or part, in various ways experienced, remembered or projected (Cosgrove, 1999: 2).

My contention, drawing upon the point made above, is that both the process and the outcome of the mapping of Tibet are influenced by the classical and critical versions of geopolitics. This needs some explanation. I agree with the point made by Kelly (2006) that whereas the two major versions of geopolitics, namely 'classical' and 'critical', will continue to compete with one another in some respects, it is worthwhile to look for mutually enriching connections between the two. Doing so, he argues, will facilitate not only the scholarly advancement of both a classical version that treats geography as an 'aid to statecraft' while offering advice to statecraft and foreign policy establishments and the critical version that aims at exposing the power-knowledge nexus and remains highly skeptical of grand narratives. In its classical version, Kelly (2002: 1) defined geopolitics as:

> A foreign policy approach and an international relations theory that stresses an awareness of relative position among countries and a corresponding response of statesmen to advantages and vulnerabilities that territorial and maritime space may bring to foreign affairs and national security.

'Critical geopolitics', according to its leading proponents (see Tuathail, 1989; 1996; 1999; Agnew and Corbridge, 1996; Agnew, 1998; 2010; 2013; Dalby, 2010) is a relentless interrogation of how various spatial perceptions of 'we' and 'them' are invoked in various architectures and technologies of domination. In the words of one of the leading proponents of critical geopolitics:

> The focus of critical geopolitics is on exposing the plays of power involved in grand geopolitical schemes.... Fundamental to this process is the power of certain national security elites to represent the nature and dilemmas of international politics in particular ways... These representational practices of national security intellectuals generate particular 'scripts' on international politics concerning places, peoples and issues. Such scripts then become part of the means by which hegemony [by the great powers] is exercised in the international system (Tuathail, 1989: 439).

A critical geopolitics remains highly suspicious of the manner in which both the grand deterritorialising regional and global geoeconomic narratives of globalisation and reterritorialising state-centric geopolitical discourses of borders and national security displace and dismiss the impulses and imperatives of human-cultural geographies of minorities on the margins.

According to John Agnew (2010: 569):

> The hegemonic calculus of the past 200 years has involved the imposition of a set of normative rules and practical constraints on states and other actors, reflecting the uneven distribution of global power and a common "script" of world politics thereby written more in some places than in others. Though this script has had powerful continuities to its core themes, it has also involved important shifts over time with the rise and fall of dominant actors who have brought different conceptions and practices to bear within it.

Agnew (2010) also rightly points out that:

> To date, the overwhelming body of work in critical geopolitics has focused on the contemporary United States and the European colonial powers, often as if they were the sole active forces in world politics toying with the docile masses in the rest of the world.

The point made by Agnew is relevant for the purposes of this chapter.

Imaginative geographies play a central role in the production of excessive geopolitics. According to Derek Gregory (2004: 17), "Imaginative geographies imply, representations of other places—of peoples and landscapes, cultures and 'natures'—that articulate the desires, fantasies and fears of their authors and the grids of power between them and their 'Others'." The imaginative geographies deployed by the centres of power are partly factual and partly fictional and tend to downplay and downgrade the histories and geographies of those perceived on the margins. Gregory (2004: 262) in his seminal study entitled "The Colonial Present" reflects on the possibility of the decolonisation of mind and imaginations. In his view:

> [F]or this possibility to be realized—for us to cease turning on the treadmill of the colonial present—it will be necessary to explore other spatializations and other topologies, and to turn our imaginative geographies into geographical imaginations that can enlarge and enhance our sense of the world and enable us to situate ourselves within it with care, concern and humility.

Gregory (2004: 262) further emphasises that in the broadening and deepening of a collective, inclusive global socio-spatial consciousness need not be construed as a call for an empty relativism:

> [T]here will still be disagreements, conflicts, and even enemies. But in order to conduct ourselves properly, decently, we need to set ourselves against the unbridled arrogance that assumes that 'We' have the monopoly of Truth and that the world is necessarily ordered by—and around—Us.

I will return to some of the issues raised in my concluding reflections.

Liberating 'Tibet' from Colonial-Western Cartographies: Impositions and Resistance

What do we mean by 'Tibet' and 'Tibetans' today? How do we approach and map out the given human-cultural geographies of contemporary Tibet in the light of the fact that there are multiple voices, perspectives and narratives coming from "Tibetan refugees in McLeod Ganj, India, Kathmandu, Nepal, and Boston, USA—key places where diaspora is in process, where individuals are making and remaking their lives" (Houston and Wright, 2003: 218). I will return to the complex and compelling issue of Tibetan diaspora shortly. At this point, it will be useful in my view to note in passing some of the given geographies of Tibet as the homeland of Tibetans. As Fischer (2010: 235) puts it succinctly:

> Tibetans are those people who call themselves Bodpa (Tibetans) or some recognized sub-group of Tibetans (e.g. Amdowa, Khampa), speak various dialects derived from the written language, referred to as bod-yig (Tibetan), and/or refer to their indigenous territory as Bod (Tibet), or some recognized subdivision thereof (as for example, Amdo, Kham etc.). This understanding is actually not contentious given that all Tibetan subgroups, with few exceptions, were recognized by the RRC as one group called zang-zu (the Chinese term for Tibetans) when the Chinese Communist Party (CCP) conducted its official enumeration of nationalities in 1950s.

Whereas 'Tibet', comprising highland areas (nearly 25% of China's landmass) at average altitudes exceeding 3000 meters, generally refers to "all of the Tibetan areas in China, including the Tibetan Autonomous Region (TAR) and the Tibetan areas that have been incorporated into the provinces of Qinghai, Gansu, Sichuan and Yunan" (Fischer, 2010). Barring a few disagreements over the borderlands of Eastern Tibet, "the administrative definitions of the PRC are almost identical to the definition of Tibet used by the Tibetan Government in Exile" (Fischer, 2010).

Having noted in passing the given physical-human geographies of 'Tibet' and 'Tibetans', I turn next to the politics behind the written/imposed geographies of these two categories. My key argument here is that the present and futures of both Tibet and Tibetans cannot be divorced from the imperial and colonial ethnographic mappings. Dibyesh Anand's seminal study on Tibet as a 'geopolitical exotica' is a powerful reminder that what is of paramount importance in the pursuit of a genuinely 'postcolonial IR theoretical approach', is an imagined geography that "challenges the commonplace ignorance of the history of imperialism and colonialism in the analysis of supposedly 'intractable' political problems in the postcolonial world." He, therefore, underlines:

> ...the centrality of the concept of representation to the Western enterprise of knowledge production about its Others. It bares the "real" impact of rhetorical utterances and practices. Geopolitical Exotica explores asymmetrical power relations in the discursive production of "Tibet" as a specific site of West-non-West encounter in and beyond the twentieth century. It emphasizes the (re)productive relation between representation and identity and performs a deconstructive cultural analysis of Western images of Tibet by looking at the poetics of representation, which entails recognition of the contingency of identity without giving up the notion of agency. It theorizes Tibetan identity discourses as constitutively and performatively produced in relation to Western imaginaries and imageries, the politics of representation (Anand, 2007: kindle locations 1717-1723).

Dibyesh Anand's passing reference to knowledge production about Tibet in China deserves serious attention. In his view, "Knowledge production about Tibet, especially since the mid-twentieth century when the Chinese Communists consolidated their political control, is no longer the preserve of Europeans. Very much in the tradition of Orientalist scholarship and British imperialist writings, the manufacturing of scholarly truths about Tibet within the Chinese academies is implicated in the service of the political regime" (Anand, 2007). In his view, "Chinese representations of Tibetans as essentially backward, primitive, and barbaric" can be seen both in some of the popular and official discourses. At the same time, "the notion of Tibet's lack of development due to 'cultural backwardness' has been very strong in Chinese state policies since the 1951 Seventeen Point Agreement." According to Anand (2007), "Unfortunately this has resonance with the self-justificatory tone of the civilizing mission within Western imperialism."

One of the most seductive grand narratives of all times, driven by geographical determinism and politics of fear is the 'Great Game'. The manner in which Tibet has been implicated in both the 'old' and the 'new' great games deserves a close scrutiny. Three names on the British imperial-colonial canvas that deserve special mention in this regard are: Lord Nathaniel Palmer Curzon, Halford J. Mackinder and Sir Olaf Caroe. The first two have received much greater scholarly attention and citation than Olaf Caroe.

Thomas Neuhaus has shown at length how towards the end of the 19th and early part of the 20th century the key drivers behind western interest in Tibet changed from "a desire to live adventures and explore the religion and natural environment of the area" to "a more organised and political form of assertiveness, culminating in a military expedition to Lhasa under the guidance of Colonel (later Sir) Francis Younghusband" (Neuhaus, 2012: 25). Tibet came under the gaze of wider imperial geopolitical vision and its 'civilizing mission', which was ably supported by "European technology, a flowering 'forward' school in military strategy, as well as a sense of cultural superiority" (Neuhaus, 2012). As Neuhaus (2012: 29) puts it:

> While schemes to sell tea from British India to Tibetans, or even to scout for gold in Tibet, may have played a part in awakening interest in the region, what was really behind the wish to assert British power in Inner Asia was a desire to assert British strength

ideologically, culturally and geopolitically. The immediate conditions for the Younghusband mission arose from what has been called the 'Great Game', an extension of earlier competition between Russia and Britain in Asia.

The imaginative geographies of the Great Game carried both 'the White Man's Burden' and the 1903-04 expedition of the Younghusband was projected as a benign move to 'open up' Tibet to the benevolent influences of the British empire. The expedition was essentially the brainchild of Lord George Nathaniel Curzon, who was appointed Viceroy of India in 1899. As pointed out by Parshotam Mehra (2012: 219), "Curzon's obsession with Russia and the Great Game is also important in his dealings with Afghanistan and Tibet." Tibet in his imperial world view was a highly strategic space where the British geopolitical interests were likely to be challenged by the growing Russian influence. In his book entitled *Frontiers*, Curzon (2011, kindle edition: locations 64, 101, 246) would implicate Tibet in broader terms of British colonial mentality and geopolitical vision:

> Time was when England had no Frontier but the ocean. We have now by far the greatest extent of territorial Frontier of any dominion in the globe. In North America we have a Land Frontier of more than 3,000 miles with the United States. In India we have Frontiers nearly 6,000 miles long with Persia, Russia, Afghanistan, Tibet, China, Siam, and France.... The most arduous struggle in which we have been engaged in India in modern times was waged with Frontier tribes.... Backed as they are by the huge and lofty plateau of Tibet...the Himalayas are beyond doubt the most formidable natural Frontier in the World.... *Had the Tibetans respected our Frontiers, we should never have marched three years ago to Lhasa.* Think, indeed, of what the Indian Frontier Problem, as it is commonly called, has meant and means; the controversies it has provoked, the passions it has aroused; the reputations that have flashed or faded within its sinister shadow (emphasis added).

Present in the audience and listening with rapt attention to some of the lectures by Curzon on 'frontiers' was the British geographer Halford J. Mackinder, widely known as the leading proponent of classical geopolitics, although he avoided using the term 'geopolitics' and perhaps even disliked it. In a lecture delivered to the Royal Geographical Society, London, in January 1904, Mackinder announced before his audience that the Columbian epoch (1500-1900), characterised by the dominance of sea power, was now coming to a close due to a tectonic shift in the 'natural seats of power', in favour of land power. Consequently, "the oversetting of the balance of power in favour of the pivot state, resulting in its expansion over the marginal lands of Euro-Asia, would permit the use of vast continental resources for fleet-building, and the empire of the world would then be in sight. This might happen if Germany were to ally herself with Russia" (Mackinder, 1904: 432). It was the latter scenario that alarmed Mackinder the most. While mapping out what he saw as opportunities and threats before the declining British empire at the dawn of the 20th century, Mackinder pinpointed three regions with varying power potential on the face of the globe: the geographical pivot or the gigantic natural fortress (re-designated as 'the heartland' in later work); the inner crescent; and the outer or insular crescent. In a book written soon after World War I, entitled *Democratic Ideals and Reality* (Mackinder, 1919), largely with the intention of influencing the Versailles Peace negotiations, Mackinder (1919: 150) (renaming what he called Euro-Asia as the "World-Island" and the "pivot area" as the "Heartland") offered his well-known geopolitical dictum: "Who rules East Europe commands the Heartland, Who rules the Heartland commands the World-Island; Who rules the World-Island commands the world".

A number of scholars have criticised Mackinder's Pivot-Heartland thesis as being overly simplistic and deterministic. According to Tuathail (1996: 27):

> Underpinning this [Mackinder's] argument is an unquestioned ethnocentrism, an ethnocentrism that initially sustained the belief that certain regions of the world political map were blank, undiscovered, and unoccupied and is now proclaiming the world political map a close system of space, settled, occupied, and named. The barbaric chaos of unknown space has been replaced by the civilizational certainties of the scientifically unveiled, one and only true geography of the planet. What Mackinder does not anticipate...is

that the British, European, and more generally, Western domination of global geopolitical space would be challenged profoundly in the new century. The struggle over geography had only begun.

Mackinder's heartland thesis has its supporters and admirers too (see Blouet, 2005). Colin S. Gray (2005: 30), writing *In Defense of the Heartland*, argues that Mackinder's grand theory dealing for the first time with a truly 'global context' was the result of his concern with the security and prosperity of the British empire. For Gray:

> The Pivot-Heartland theory rested upon geographical realities. Such is the arrangement of the continents that potentially lethal menaces to the security of the West plausibly could come only from the Eurasian landmass. Some critical theorists may disagree, but Mackinder's concepts were hewn out of bedrock. The concept of the Pivot-Heartland is of course a constructed one, but it reflected material facts and truth about location.

Mackinder wrote in 1999, Tibet "has no parallel on earth for combined height and area, or in a single word, for massiveness" and went on to argue that "when the Sahara will be crossed and recrossed daily by the traffic of civilization, it is probable that Tibet, the 'roof of the world', will still deflect around its flanks and widely separate overland routes into China and India" (cited in Brobst, 2005: 69).

No doubt both Curzon and Mackinder emphatically located Tibet on the military-strategic chessboard of British imperial interests. But their self-proclaimed geopolitical supervisions proved no match to the Great Game centric mappings of Tibet by Sir Olaf Kirkpatrick Caroe, who served as foreign secretary to British India's government throughout the duration of the Second World War. A keen observer of developments in regional and global geo-politics, Caroe was deeply interested in discerning underlying continuities in the geographical patterns of regional and global power politics. For those interested in meticulously researched details of Caroe's geopolitical-strategic thinking on wideranging issues refer to a pioneering study by Peter John Brobst (2005). All that I would venture in the next few paragraphs is to pinpoint Caroe's take on Tibet in the context of what he saw as the "permanence of the Great Game and its imperatives"

(Brobst, 2005: 1), drawing rather liberally on the insights offered by Brobst.

One of the key reasons why Olaf Caroe decided to form a 'Viceroy's Study Group' in 1942 and reflect over the future of the Great Game was his "longstanding concern that in the official planning for India's independence the imperatives of strategy and geopolitics received too little attention" (Brobst, 2005: 1). Caroe argued in favour of an appreciation "in the highest places that India cannot build a constitution unless the frontiers are held the ring fence in some manner kept standing" (cited in Brobst, 2005: 35). The so-called "ring fence"—approximately 3000 miles stretch from west to east, from the Persian Gulf round India's north to Burma—comprised what Caroe describes as "a double line of inner and outer entrenchments." The inner ring or crescent consisted of princely states or tribal areas that were internal to the Indian empire, such as Baluchistan and the Naga Hills. However, the outer ring or crescent was composed of countries that the British recognised as 'independent', or at least 'autonomous', including Persia, Afghanistan and Tibet.

In the imaginative geographies of Caroe's version of the evolving 'new great game', Tibet (along with Burma/Myanmar) received highest consideration, if for no other reason than Caroe's fear that China's ambitions, if unchecked, "would be likely to lead to constant attempts at Chinese encroachment on the North-Eastern frontier [of India]" (cited in Brobst, 2005: 68). He therefore stated with all emphasis at his command that despite advances made in modern military and scientific-technological domains, Tibet's autonomous position with its high latitudes, large deserts and 'strategic depth' held one of the major keys to India's defence. Tibet, in other words, must not lose its strategic value as a major 'political buffer'.

Howsoever sound and seductive the strategic narratives of Caroe might have sounded (and still might sound) to strategic-defence communities, they significantly contributed to the production of excessive geopolitics as far as Tibet was concerned. The struggle over Tibet's strategic location did not end with the withdrawal of the British from the Indian subcontinent. It would continue and soon acquire new meanings and symbols against the erosion of human-cultural-intellectual geographies. As Parshotam Mehra (2012: 46) reminds us: "All through the ages Lhasa's monasteries had often been centres of teaching, home to its artists, writers and men of learning, who were nurtured and trained there." Blatantly oblivious of this reality, what the British were aiming at was to keep a "permanent political vacuum" (Mehra, 2012: 142).

We need to pause for a while and reflect briefly over the various ways in which 'Tibet' and 'Tibetans' were located and re-located on the geostrategic maps of the ideological geopolitics of the Cold War. Writing at the height of the Cold War, Dawa Norbu (1988: 375) argued that among other things what the Cold War, and various events that unfolded in its shadow, revealed beyond doubt was that the Chinese Communists, "who were strategists par excellence through their lifelong guerrilla warfare, realized early the strategic importance of Tibet and decided to shut China's backdoor in 1950." Especially in the wake of events such as the Tibetan rebellion of 1959 and the Sino-Indian border war of 1962, Chinese sensitivities to the geopolitical and strategic location of Tibet deepened. "No sooner had the PLA troops entered eastern Tibet than they began building roads" (Norbu, 1988: 375). In other words, the project of connectivity was initiated, which, as the decades of capitalist development would unfold, will result in far-reaching implications for Tibetans at 'home' or in 'diaspora'.

Neoliberal Globalisation and Tibet: Towards New Reterritorialisation, Relocations and Displacements?

According to Cosgrove, the Cold War cartography is becoming increasingly obsolete, even though it has not entirely disappeared. Various facets of globalisation (political, economic, technical and cultural) force us to revisualise and rethink maps and mappings. In his view, in a world of radically unstable spaces and structures, it is unsurprising that the idea of mapping (and for the purposes of this chapter especially with regard to Tibet) should require rethinking. There is little evidence to support American strategist Edward Luttwak's (1990; 1993) much-touted thesis that geo-economics underpinned by a space-opening logic is replacing geopolitics with its space-closing logic. For him, this shift implied national leaders and security experts using a different set of 'grammar': conducting foreign policy and international relations with a view to protecting "vital economic interests by geo-economic defences, geo-economic offensives, geo-economic diplomacy, and geo-economic intelligence" (Luttwak, 1993: 19).

Tibet with its rich mineral-resource and hydrological endowments is no exception to the trend where 'connectivity', especially physical-infrastructural, is perceived as a prerequisite for 'economic growth' and 'human development' within the overarching, rather overwhelming context of crony capitalism, commodification and consumerism. Matthew Sparke (2013) draws attention to urban spaces where these forces become quite pronounced. He is quite right in pointing out that:

> The tension between territorial fixity and geographical expansion at the heart of uneven development also operates at sub-national spatial scales to create other unstable entanglements of growth and decline. Geoeconomic plans for global integration here take the form of more localized efforts by the government of cities, regions, and local economic development zones to reach beyond national territory and fix global financial flows in local space (Sparke, 2013: 297).

In the case of Tibet, Tashi Nyima (2008) has shown how, in less than two decades, as a result of government sponsored "scientific development" projects and demographic change induced by the migration from China's inland provinces, Lhasa is no more a "Tibetan town" and stands transformed into a "Chinese city", "in which local Tibetans have to struggle for economic as well as cultural survival" in a climate of fear. Conspicuous by their absence in the current development discourse are "concepts such as rights-based development, local empowerment and participation" and "if this situation persists, it will contribute to further tension in Tibet" (Nyima, 2008: 257). Nyima (2008) puts it so succinctly:

> Indeed, since the deepening of economic reforms in the early 1990s, Han migrants have come to dominate virtually all new economic activities in Lhasa, whether tailoring, taxi driving, restaurant ownership, or vegetable sales. The intensified marketization and state

> investment into development projects brought by the Open Up the West campaign in 2000 further accelerated the arrival of migrants, as did the completion of the Qinghai-Tibet Railway in 2006...Many Tibetans in Lhasa now live on an economy of Han rents. In the Lhalu neighborhood, Tibetans whose farmland has been expropriated for urbanization make a living renting out their courtyard space and houses to Chinese migrants, who run shops and businesses... Though a religious, cultural, and political center for centuries, Lhasa has been deterritorialized and reterritorialized as a backward periphery of the PRC that urgently needs to be developed. (Yeh, 2013: Kindle Locations 271-77, 280-83).

As noted by Yeh, the manner in which the state-led development projects continue to deterritorialise and reterritorialise Lhasa, substantiates the point made by Matthew Sparke with regard to the complex interplay between geopolitics and geo-economics. According to Yeh, the territorialisation, "a deeply material and embodied process that involves the transformation of both subjectivities and landscapes" (Yeh 2013: kindle Locations 301-08) has been steadily unfolding in Tibet since early 1950s, "with a particular focus on development in the making of hegemonic social-spatial relations." In her view:

> From the 1950s through the 1980s, this embodied process was framed as both cause and effect of Tibetan gratitude for socialist liberation, whereas since the 1980s, the framing has shifted toward one of Tibetan gratitude for the gift of development. Throughout, the transformation of the material landscape of Tibet has often been enacted through the labor of Tibetans themselves, transforming their subjectivities in ways that help naturalize Tibetans' association with the PRC even as they may simultaneously resist this association. The exploration of state territorialization in Tibet brings into view the contradictory and complex nature of development and belonging in ways that are not immediately apparent from a surface reading of the landscape.

As the 21st century unfolds, are we then talking of erosion, even demise, of Tibet as a 'place' in all its human-cultural diversity in the shadow of neoliberal globalisation? Is Tibet not being reduced to yet another 'extraction zone' in the national and global quests for economic-energy-resource security; while being 'connected' to the highly nebulous but seductive cartographies of flows and networks? As Tibet gets relocated on the map of neoliberal geopolitics (see Roberts *et al.*, 2003), a map based on the geopolitical assumption that 'disconnection defines danger', one wonders what could be the implications of 'new' connections/connectivity for the local political economy of life anchored in the indigenous systems of knowledge. Questions such as these are not easy to answer but remain compelling in the case of Tibet for several reasons.

Return to Human and Cultural Geographies: Opportunities and Challenges

According to Cronon (1991), the identity of a place needs to be understood by its connections to the 'outside world': "through the paths that lead in and out" (Cresswell, 2004: 43). In a classical geopolitical sense then, 'location' on constantly evolving maps—political, social, cultural, economic, environmental etc.—remains decisive in the geographical politics of identity. At the same time, locations are better approached and understood as relative rather than as absolute. A geo-historical perspective on the changing locations and representations of Tibet reveals a rather complex politics of the making and the unmaking of Tibet as a place through various ethnographic-geopolitical mapping projects undertaken by the colonial powers. We have also seen how both Tibet and Tibetans were lodged and dislodged, located and re-located, on various maps of meaning from time to time. The process continues. Does this imply that 'erosion of place' is now a reality for the Tibetans to reckon with on a daily basis?

Edward Relph was one of the first humanistic geographers who systematically engaged with the themes of place and placelessness. Some of the key findings of this chapter force us to critically reflect on Relph's incisive insistence on acknowledging the "distinction between the experience of insideness and outsideness in the human experience of place" (Cresswell, 2004: 44). Relph argued that, "to be inside a place is to belong to it and identify with it, and the more profoundly inside you are the stronger is the identity with the place" (Relph cited in Cresswell, 2004: 44). The existential outsideness, on the other hand, caused largely by mobility, would lead to a sense of alienation from the place. Relph even argued that in the modern world a large humanity is faced with some kind of "creeping placelessness marked by an authentic relationship to a place because new placelessness does not allow people to become existential insiders" (Creswell, 2004: 44). For many Tibetans in exile, a diasporic identity might represent a sense of being 'in-between' which does not perhaps mean the same thing as being 'place-less'. I have argued elsewhere with Joe Painter (Chaturvedi and Painter, 2013: 388) that places continue to matter as homeland and motherland to their inhabitants, even when truncated and trivialised by the quest of profit seeking neoliberal capital for a friction free space, in search of strategic resources, markets and consumers. In our view: "it is useful to draw a distinction between the 'objects' and the 'subjects' of the emerging world order. Geo-politically speaking, the world order is not as 'global' in nature, scope and functioning, as many of us believe it to be or would like it to be. In other words, emerging world order is not as placeless as those who are fascinated by the time–space compression of globalization would like to imagine."

It is important to acknowledge in my view that there are worlds beyond the territorial-geopolitical realms of the 'nation-state'. Agnew (2013: 1) reminds us:

> The past 20 years or so has seen a reframing of political thought away from the totally state-centered narratives that tended to prevail previously. Much of this has had to do with the rise of thinking about globalization that puts in question the modern territorial state as the sole unit of contemporary political account...But some has also arisen from questioning the extent to which the world has ever been organized completely in terms of the territorial 'nation-states' upon which so much political debate has long been focused...The term 'territory' provides a plausible basis for extending political analysis beyond the state. Only in one relatively modern meaning does it relate exclusively to the state... This is when it is used to signify the areal extent and limits of state sovereignty.

It is to these somewhat eroded non-territorial realms of human-cultural geographies that we need to return in order to find new routes to and from Tibet that cannot and should not be divorced from indigenous socio-cultural roots. This is certainly not to suggest that societies and cultures are frozen in time and space but to propose that they promise to act as an antidote to excessive geopolitics and its partitioning effects. One such critically important realm, resting on a complex but compelling route/root interface, is that of Buddhism.

While making a plea in favour of a return to human-cultural geographies of the Himalayas, in which Tibet is situated, I remain aware of the argument made by McConnell (2013: 163) with regard to the geopolitics of religion. According to her, "Buddhism is often perceived as geopolitically unthreatening and thus insignificant" whereas in her view "a focus on Buddhism more generally has the potential to" open up productive new lines of inquiry in religious geopolitics. She is quite persuasive in her argument that such a critical focus is likely to reveal complex questions around political and religious succession and leadership, contestations over sources of political legitimacy and problematise in the process the conceptual boundaries that are often drawn between "the secular and the religious, the traditional and the modern".

While I agree with her that "a sustained critical geopolitical engagement with Buddhist communities, leaders and politics" (McConnell, 2013: 162) is important, I do believe at the same time that scholars of geopolitics should also engage with the issue of 'every day religion' as understood and practiced in various parts of the Himalayas.

Once Tibet is seen and understood from the human-cultural lens of a dialogue among civilisations, the following insights offered by Tony Huber (in reference to his attendance at the Dükhor Wangchen held at Amaravati in January 2006 in the Indian state of Karnataka; a place where Tibetan Buddhists believe the Buddha himself gave the very first teaching of the 'wheel of time' acquire enormous significance and salience:

> As events which employ the modern Buddhist holy land as a ritual setting like no other, the Dükhor Wangchen can draw together almost

> an entire society, along with its closest supporters and coreligionists, and set in motion a remarkably rich interplay of persons, symbols, and discourses with greater social significance.

My appeal to a return to human-cultural geographies of the Himalayas does include a plea to rejuvenate and revitalise Buddhist studies in Asia in general and the Himalayan Asia in particular but is not exhausted by it. In apparently mundane but quite significant terms the return could simply imply more focus on 'Tibetans', including those in diaspora and their struggles for human and livelihood security. However, the issue of the Tibetan diaspora demands and deserves much greater attention. Houston and Wright (2003: 229-30), while grappling with the complexity of Tibetan diaspora, point out insightfully that:

> Although such sentiment has considerable utility and power, we know that the Tibetan diaspora is also a process involving the making and remaking of Tibetan identities. By wrestling with the questions of what it means to be a Tibetan refugee in different exile communities we find that context influences the production of identities, which are, in turn, heterogeneous. Indeed, life stories in each community not only always make reference to His Holiness and the Tibetan homeland, but they also depart from nationalist rhetoric to tell their own complicated tales of Tibetan diasporic identities. They invoke a repertoire of tactics of resistance to cultural extermination and assimilation as well. For instance, either choosing citizenship or choosing officially to remain a Tibetan refugee presents individuals with different means of access to political power. Specifically, refugee identity affords long-term international recognition whereas citizenship (of Nepal, the USA or India) facilitates an easier everyday life. Each title grants types of identity benefits and restrictions associated with different axes of power. Analysing how exiles weigh these and other options provides insights into how diasporic Tibetans negotiate their lives.

Houston and Wright (2003) are quite right in pointing out that:

> Approaching "as condition and process" could be helpful in understanding the diversity of experiences that the category of Tibetan diaspora encompasses. In their view this is just one among

several perspectives that demand further research. For example, what does it mean when we talk of "return within a diaspora"? A serious and systematic research is needed to 'consider the metaphorical interpretation of return within a diaspora. In this view, re-turn does not invoke a physical return to a homeland, but rather a repeated revisiting to the concept of homeland via texts, imagery and social and religious rituals. How this plays out over time and space may provide vital insight into diasporic identities and lived refugee experiences.

Equally important is research on how the younger generations of Tibetans in various locations perceive the phenomena of dispersion and diaspora.

Concluding Reflections

Globalisation induced interconnections/interdependencies offer dangers (as pointed out earlier in this chapter) as well as opportunities. In order to make good some such opportunities it is necessary to recall and revive the geographies of mobility, especially human-religious-cultural, in Asia. As pointed out by Sen (2010: 34), "India and China have had over 2000 years of exchanges and interactions, either directly or through intermediaries. These exchanges were multifaceted, complex and had their ebbs and flows." He reminds us that:

> While the initial route of the transmission of Buddhist ideas from India to China is still debated by scholars...overwhelming evidence suggest that the first transmitters were Parthian and Indo-Scythian traders. Some of the earliest Buddhist missionaries in China were also natives of Central Asia and present day Iran...Monks from India started arriving more frequently only after the third century. *Three other multicultural features of the transmission of Buddhist ideas from Southern to Eastern Asia need to be highlighted here: one, the extensive translation activity in China (and later continued by the Khitans, Tanguts, and the Tibetans) and the composition of indigenized texts; two, the process through which some of the 'peripheral regions' became important Buddhist centres and pilgrimage sites; and three, the contribution of intermediary states in Southeast and Central Asia in sustaining the Buddhist networks between Southern and Eastern Asia...*

> *By the end of the first millennium, India-China interactions had entered a new phase. The Buddhist-centred exchanges were gradually replaced by connections established through commercial interactions.* This created new links between Southern Asia and China and embedded India-China interactions more deeply into the wider network of intra-Asian exchanges...A noteworthy aspect of India-China interactions during this period is participation of Muslim traders belonging to different ethnic groups (Sen, 2010: 36-37) (emphasis given).

Sen also reminds his readers that the nature and scope of Buddhist interactions between India and China during the first millennium included but were not exhausted by "the study of the transmission of religious doctrines from India to China" (Sen, 2010: 45). In reality these interactions "must be understood as a multicultural phenomena that had significant impact on almost every religion of Asia" (Sen, 2010).

Once China and India come to acknowledge collectively that the histories of mobility throughout the Himalayas are much longer than the histories of borders—which can and should be made more porous, negotiable and crossable, especially for the border communities—endless possibilities for what Kurian (2014) has described as "conversations beyond state" could emerge. I fully endorse Raja Mohan's (2012) contention that the opportunities that are emerging before us to broaden and deepen trans-border commercial exchanges must not be lost.

> The current border trade mechanism at Nathu-la between Sikkim and Tibet is under-utilised and the two sides could consider facilitating deepening trade exchanges. Delhi and Beijing should also consider re-opening the old trade route between Kalimpong (West Bengal) and Lhasa (Tibet) through the Jelep-la pass and the Chumbi valley. Linking China's improved transport infrastructure in Tibet with the rail and road networks on the Indian side could be a bold move. A move in that direction could act as a much-needed political spur for the rapid modernisation of infrastructure on the Indian side. India and China could also consider a coordinated effort to develop the many pilgrimage sites on either side of the Tibetan frontier and provide a big boost to religious tourism (Raja Mohan, 2012).

The 21st century has been variously described as the century of climate affairs, the 'new American century', 'Asian century' etc. Painter and Chaturvedi (2007: 392) have argued that, "what is also unfolding before us is a century of resistance marked by a number of silent, often invisible, revolutions, demanding justice and dignity." What appears to be unfolding beyond a rather elitist human rights framework of international law is various social movements, such as women's movements, indigenous movements, labour movements, and gay and lesbian movements, as alternative sites of resistance and models of social justice. Be it the demonstrations by hundreds of thousands of people in the United States against changes in immigration laws (Rajagopal, 2003), or the ongoing demonstrations demanding democracy in Hong Kong or the ever rising number of social protest movements in rural China (Tilt, 2010), the writing on the wall is clear: 'ordinary' people are on the march, demanding 'extraordinary', emancipatory socio-economic transformations in favour of a more decentralised and humane political governance. The futures of Tibet (irrespective of the location of Tibetans) cannot be divorced from such movements both in China and elsewhere. In China:

> Even during the Cultural Revolution (1966-1976), the height of the socialist experiment and the point at which the power of the Chinese state was nearly absolute, this tradition of public engagement in civic affairs remained visible. Citizens were encouraged to purge intellectuals and other "bad elements" from their midst and also to "struggle" against corrupt leaders who abused their political power. For all its brutality, the Cultural Revolution kept alive the tradition of justified public protest. Civil-society mobilization today—whether they seek to address political, religious, economic or environmental issues—bear the stamp of this legacy (Tilt, 2010: 122).

Tilt draws attention to the positive role that economic liberalisation has played in facilitating decoupling of industry from state. This in turn has acted as a fillip to the growth of environmental civil society. In his view:

> The subtle bourgeoning of environmental civil society in China today reminds us that no matter how solid a grip the central government

appears to have on its citizens and on local officials, its control is never hegemonic; those at the margins possess creating strategies for attracting the political system' (Tilt, 2010: 157).

May be in the years to come the Tibetan demand for autonomy may find some of its most vocal supporters and allies inside China.

Imaginative 'strategic' geographies, anchored in classical geopolitics, irrespective of where they come from, will continue to implicate Tibet in various rings, crescents and circles but not without inviting resistance. Demands for decentralisation of power and a genuine autonomy—one that is integral to the process of democratisation—are likely to multiply as the 21st century unfolds. Once conceived primarily in non-territorial, socio-cultural terms, such demands need not pose a threat to the 'territorial integrity' of any nation-state. Mahatma Gandhi had once talked about majestic oceanic circles, that is about the independence of the grassroots. According to Gandhi, a centralised government is inherently prone to violence. By contrast, he advocated the decentralisation of political power. Explaining his metaphorical vision of the structure of a future non-violent society, Gandhi wrote:

> Life will not be a pyramid with the apex sustained by the bottom. But it will be an oceanic circle whose centre will be the individual always ready to perish for the village, the latter ready to perish for the circle of villages, till at last the whole becomes one life composed of individuals, never aggressive in their arrogance, but ever humble, sharing the majesty of the oceanic circle of which they are integral units (cited in Murthy, 1987: 189).

Imagined geographies of this nature are both desirable and feasible, and create much-needed space to question, tame and trim excess of geopolitics and its imaginative geographies.

References

Agnew, J.A. (2013). "Territory, Politics, Governance", editorial in *Territory, Politics, Governance* 1(1): 1-4.

Agnew, J. and S. Corbridge (1996). *Mastering Space: Hegemony, Territory and International Political Economy*. London: Routledge.

Agnew, J. (1998). *Geopolitics: Re-visioning World Politics*. Routledge: Psychology Press.

———. (2010). "Emerging China and Critical Geopolitics: Between World Politics and Chinese Particularity", *Eurasian Geography and Economics* 51(5): 569-82.

Anand, D. (2007). *Geopolitical Exotica: Tibet in Western Geopolitical Imagination*. Minneapolis, London: University of Minnesota Press.

Brobst, P.J. (2005). *The Future of the Great Game: Sir Olaf Caroe, India's Independence and the Defense of Asia*. Akron, Ohio: the University of Akron Press.

Chaturvedi, S. and J. Painter (2007). "Whose World? Whose Order? Spatiality, Geopolitics and the Limits of the New World Order", *Cooperation and Conflict* 42(4): 375-95.

Cosgrove, D. (ed.). (1999). *Mappings*. London: Reaktion Books.

Cresswell, T. (2004). *Place: A Short Introduction*. Oxford: Blackwell.

Curzon, George Nathaniel (2011-08-11). *Frontiers* (Kindle Locations 99-101). E. Kindle Edition.

Dalby, S. (2010). "Reconceptualizing Violence, Power and Nature: The Next Twenty Years of Critical Geopolitics", *Political Geography* 29(5): 280-88.

Edney, M.H. (1997). *Mapping an Empire: The Geographical Construction of British India, 1765-1843*. University of Chicago Press.

Fischer, A.M. (2010). "A Land Called Tibet", in Ira Pande (ed.). *IndiaChina: Neighboring Stranger*. Noida: Harper Collins. pp.234-50.

Gregory, D. (2004). *The Colonial Present: Afghanistan, Palestine, Iraq*. Oxford: Wiley-Blackwell.

Hopkirk, P. (1994). *The Great Game: The Struggle for Empire in Central Asia*. New York: Kodansha.

Houston, S. and R. Wright (2003). "Making and Remaking Tibetan Diasporic Identities", *Social & Cultural Geography* 4(2): 217-32.

Kelly, P. (2002). "Geopolitics of Paraguay: Pivotal Position within a Model of Geopolitics", *Historical Text Archives*.

———. (2006). "A Critique of Critical Geopolitics", *Geopolitics* 11(1): 24-53.

Kurian, N. (2014). *India-China Borderlands: Conversations Beyond Centre*. New Delhi: Sage.

Luttwak, E. (1993). "The Coming Global War for Economic Power: There Are No Nice Guys on the Battlefield of Geo-Economics", *The International Economy* 75: 18-67.

Luttwak, E. (1990). "From Geopolitics to Geoeconomics: Logic of Conflict, Grammar of Commerce", *The National Interest* 20: 17-23.

Mackinder, H.J. (1919). *Democratic Ideals and Reality: A Study in the Politics of Reconstruction*. New York: Holt.

McConnell, F. (2013). The Geopolitics of Buddhist Reincarnation: Contested Futures of Tibetan Leadership', Area (45). 2: 162–169.

Mehra, P. (2012). *Tibet: Writings on History and Politics*. Oxford: Oxford University Press.

Murthy, S. (1987). *Mahatma Gandhi and Leo Tolstoy Letters*. Long Beach Publications: Long Beach.

Neuhaus, T. (2012). *Tibet in the Western Imagination.* Palgrave Macmillan Monographs. Kindle Edition.

Norbu, D. (1988). "Chinese Strategic Thinking on Tibet and the Himalayan Region", *Strategic Analysis* 32(4): 371-94.

North, A. (2011). "India and China, the New Great Game", *BBC News Asia*, 13 December, *http://www.bbc.com/news/world-asia-16149397.*

Nyima, T. (2008). "The Chinese Development of Tibet: Lhasa in Transformation", *Forum for Development Studies* 35(2): 257-77.

Ó Tuathail, G. (1989). "The Bush Administration and the 'End of the Cold War: A Critical Geopolitics of US Foreign Policy in 1989", *Geoforum* 23: 437-52.

————. (1996). *Critical Geopolitics: The Politics of Writing Global Space*. Minneapolis: University of Minnesota Press.

————. (1999). "Understanding Critical Geopolitics: Geopolitics and Risk Security", in C.S. Gray and G. Sloan (eds.). *Geopolitics: Geography and Strategy,* London: Frank Cass. pp.107-24.

Raja Mohan, C. (2012). "India China Talks Today, Tibet Holds Key", *Indian Express.* 16 January.

Rajagopal, B. (2003). *International Law from Below: Development, Social Movements and Third World Resistance.* Cambridge: Cambridge University Press.

Roberts, S., A. Secor and M. Sparke (2003). "Neoliberal Geopolitics", *Antipode: A Radical Journal of Geography* 35: 886–97.

Scott, D. (2008). "The Great Power 'Great Game' between India and China: 'The Logic of Geography'", *Geopolitics* 13:1–26.

Sen, T. (2010). "Changes and Exchanges", in Ira Pande (ed.). *IndiaChina: Neighboring Stranger.* Noida: Harper Collins. pp.234-50.

Sparke, M. (2013). *Introducing Globalization: Ties, Tensions and Uneven Integration*. Oxford: Wiley-Blackwell.

Tilt, B. (2010). *The Struggle for Sustainability in Rural China: Environmental Values and Civil Society.* New York: Columbia University Press.

Upshur, Jiu-Hwa L. (2011). "The Great Game and Tibet", *Michigan War Studies Review. http://www.miwsr.com/2011-020.aspx.*

Yeh, E.T. (2013). *Taming Tibet: Landscape Transformation and the Gift of Chinese Development.* Studies of the Weatherhead East Asian Institute, Columbia University. Cornell University Press. Kindle Edition.

3

THUBTEN SAMPHEL

Geopolitical Importance of Tibet

Among scholars and strategic thinkers in Asia and elsewhere, there is a new recognition of the enormous geopolitical and environmental importance of Tibet to the continent, which is home to nearly half of the earth's population.[1] This recognition is driven home by China's stunning economic growth for the last more than 30 years. It is no accident that China's dynamic economic growth coincided with Beijing's discovery of Tibet as a vast and hitherto untapped source of minerals, water and energy. The new appreciation of the importance of the Tibetan Plateau also grew out of Chinese scientists' discovery that the plateau is the world's Third Pole and the 'Water Tower of Asia'. In addition, Chinese geologists have identified more than 130 minerals in Tibet "with significant reserves of the world's deposits of uranium, chromite, boron, lithium, borax, and iron."[2]

What China does with Tibet's natural resources is its business, as long as this is done responsibly and sustainably, although there is little evidence of this. Already, there are street protests in Tibet where Tibetans complain bitterly of rampant mining activities that pollute river waters that in turn harm the health of humans and animals. However, what China does with the waters of the 10 major river systems that originate from Tibet and sustain the life of about 47 per cent of the world's total human population is another matter. From a problem confined to the Tibetan people alone, it becomes a pan-Asian problem.

---

1. An example of the growing recognition of the importance of Tibet is the seminal new book by Chellaney (2011).

2. Environment and Development Desk (2000).

What are China's real intentions of damming and diverting rivers from the south to the north and the likely consequences of such actions on downstream nations?

> Anxieties about China's intentions were inflamed in 2005 by the publication of the provocatively titled Tibet's Water Will Save China. Though it was not an official statement of policy, it was written by a former officer of the Chinese People's Liberation Army, Li Ling, and its wide circulation gave it sufficient stature in Indian eyes to merit careful scrutiny. Ling's enthusiasm for diverting Tibet's rivers, including the Brahmaputra, to northern China to alleviate the acute water crisis there fitted enough of the facts to set alarm bells ringing.[3]

Damming of rivers and the proposed river diversion schemes in Tibet come in the wake of the looming water crisis in Asia. Experts say water is poised to overtake oil as the world's scarcest vital resource. China's plans for the various uses of water of rivers originating from Tibet are intensifying the heated debate about their likely consequences for downstream nations. Already there is the talk of water wars.

> The protection of the sources of water demands that no party withdraw or divert water in such a way as to affect the ecosystems. ...Although intrastate water-sharing disputes have become rife in several Asian countries—from India and Pakistan to Southeast Asia and China—the potential intercountry conflict over shared water resources should be of greater concern (Chellaney, 2011: 10).

Central to all these discussions is Tibet. The environmental importance of Tibet as the maker of the Asian monsoon and as the retainer of the largest concentration of glaciers, outside of the two poles, that feed the life-giving waters of the 10 major river systems that sustain millions downstream, are recent discoveries. However, Tibet's geopolitical importance was highlighted during the days of the British Raj. Its geopolitical importance is based on its mass and bulk, and the reason why China is in Tibet in the first place. Tibet is the world's highest and largest plateau, covering an area of 2.5 million square kilometres, with an average elevation of more than

3. *http://www.newstatesman.com/asia/2010/01/india-china-tibet-chinese*

4000 metres thrusting up above the sea level. The plateau snakes, snarls and stretches across 2400 kilometres from east to west and 1448 kilometres from north to south. Its entire southern rim is flanked by the Himalaya, the word's highest mountain chain.

In any age, even in our nuclear age, such a landmass constitutes a formidable buffer or barrier for any power operating beyond Tibet. Although Tibet itself posed no existential threat to China, there were periods in history when the Tibetans burst out of the plateau and wrested the prosperous oasis towns of Khotan, Kucha, Karashar and Kashgar in Turkestan from Tang China around 666 (Tucci, 1967: 27). "The Tibetan empire ruled the Southern Route of the Silk Road and most of Gansu Corridor, including Khotan, Lob-nor, and Dunhuang, for over fifty years from the late 8th to the mid 9th centuries" (Takeuchi, 2000). In 763 Tibetan troops captured the Chinese imperial capital, Ch'ang-an (Xian of present-day China) and put a new emperor on the throne" (Tucci, 1967: 27-28).

This period of Tibetan military activities outside the plateau, sustained by a line of energetic kings, lasted at the most for 300 years. The last great king of Tibet's imperial age was Tri Relpachen, who, while concluding a peace treaty with China (821-822), made sure that Buddhism made its greatest penetration into his domain during his reign (Tucci, 1967: 27-28). After Tri Relpachen, the Tibetan empire collapsed and Tibet disintegrated into smaller and constantly feuding kingdoms. Meanwhile, Tibet's successful incorporation of Buddhism as one of the core values of the Tibetan people tempered the martial instincts of the Tibetan people with Buddhist quietism and the contemplative way of life. Since then, Tibet by itself posed no threat to China.

All this changed with the steady takeover of the Indian subcontinent by the British. This fact brought home to China the geopolitical importance of Tibet. Western dominance of the world then threw up two empires competing for spheres of influence. The Great Game, or the Tournament of Shadows, was a strategic rivalry between the British and Russian empires for the mastery of Central Asia.

> From the British perspective, the Russian empire's expansion into Central Asia threatened to destroy the 'jewel in the crown' of the British empire, India. The British feared that Afghanistan would become a staging post for a Russian invasion of India.[4]

By the 1890s, Central Asian states were made into Russian vassals one after the other "with Central Asia in the Tsar's grip, the Great Game now shifted eastward to China, Mongolia and Tibet. In 1904, the British invaded Lhasa, a pre-emptive strike against Russian intrigues and secret meetings between the 13th Dalai Lama's envoy and Tsar Nichoals II."[5] The 13th Dalai Lama fled to Mongolia and China.

The invading British army found no evidence of any Russian influence in Tibet. However, the greatest impact of the British invasion of Tibet was felt in Manchu China. Throughout its history, China faced threats from the marauding nomads of the vast, open grasslands of Mongolia and Manchuria who usurped the Chinese imperial throne and established their own dynasties. In the 19th century, China faced a new threat from beyond the oceans in the form of western colonial powers, which, joined by fast-rising Japan, exacted humiliating trade and territorial concessions from a crippled Manchu empire. In view of the constant threats to China from the grasslands of Mongolia and now this new threat from beyond the oceans, China continued to look at Tibet as an effective buffer and its 'secure backyard'. The British breach of the buffer disabused Manchu China of this notion.

With the breach of the buffer, an enfeebled Manchu China was convinced that the British might mount an invasion on China through Tibet. The only way to prevent this from happening was to take control of Tibet. As one Manchu official put it, "Tibet is the buttress on our national frontiers—the hand, as it were, which protects the face."[6]

---

4. *http://en.wikipedia.org/wiki/The_Great_Game*
5. Ibid.
6. Ibid.

The man selected to invade Tibet was General Zhao Erfeng who occupied eastern Tibet in 1906 and marched to Lhasa in 1910, "only to find that the Dalai Lama had fled, this time to India, together with his leading ministers" (Snellgrove and Richardson, 1968: 234).

Manchu China's invasion of Tibet brought about the collapse of the key operating principle of Central Asian diplomacy. The priest-patron relationship, which Tibet had developed with the Mongols and the Manchus, both of whom embraced Buddhism, was based on the priests of Tibet providing spiritual ministry to the emperor of the day, who in turn provided protection and security to the realm of his priest. This form of diplomacy, or what this writer calls 'Tiblomacy', never anticipated the possibility that the protector would one day turn on his protected.

When this happened, Tibet turned to British India for protection:

> Although the British had precipitated the trouble, they continued to look the other way, until the Chinese Revolution of 1911 enabled the Tibetans to shake off once and for all their unwanted connection with the Manchus (Snellgrove and Richardson, 1968: 234).

When the news of the October 1911 revolution, led by Sun Yat-sen reached Lhasa, the Manchu garrison in the Tibetan capital mutinied. The Tibetan government expelled the troops to China through India. The 13th Dalai Lama returned to Lhasa in January 1913. He issued a decree to all Tibet, which came to be considered by Tibetan people as a formal declaration of Tibetan independence (Shakabpa, 1984: 146).

Meanwhile, the 1911 Chinese revolution which started with much promise, descended into warlordism and a dilapidating civil war that invited Japanese invasion and occupation. The Chinese civil war ended in 1949 when Mao Zedong and his Communist comrades in arms expelled the nationalist Chinese to the island of Taiwan. Mao Zedong promised to 'liberate' Tibet and the island of Hainan soon.

Before invading Tibet, Mao Zedong wanted an insurance. He consulted Stalin. Here is the gist of the conversation between the two dictators, as recounted in *Mao: The Unknown Story*.

When Mao Zedong saw Stalin on 23 January 1950, he asked if the Soviet Air Force could transport supplies to Chinese troops "currently preparing for an attack on Tibet." Stalin's reply was: "It's good that you are preparing to attack. The Tibetans need to be subdued ..." Stalin also advised flooding Tibet and other border regions with Han Chinese: "Since ethnic Chinese make up no more than 5 per cent of Xinjiang's population, the percentage of ethnic Chinese should be brought to 30 .... In fact, all the border territories should be populated by Chinese..." This is exactly what the Chinese Communist regime then proceeded to do (Chang and Halliday, 2006: 552).

The acquisition of the entire Tibetan Plateau by the new Chinese Communist empire gave China extraordinary strategic depth in luring potential intruders and repulsing them as well as enormous military reach in operating offensives on multiple fronts and sustaining them: "Tibet was vital to Chinese strategic calculations for the simple reason that the Himalaya presented by far the best vantage point for China's defensive or offensive needs" (Shakya, 1999: 424). Complementing this advantage was another factor. Despite its spatial vastness, because of its sparse population stuck in material 'backwardness', Tibet was not a significant market. However, Tibet was spiritually and culturally potent, the centre of a distinct culture, a magnet for the best minds of the Tibetan Buddhist civilisation, "stretching from Ladakh in the west to the borders of the Chinese provinces of Szechuan and Yunnan in the east, from the Himalaya in the south to the Mongolian steppes and the vast waste of northern Tibet..." (Snellgrove and Richardson, 1968: 271).

With China's invasion and occupation of Tibet, the world lost an immense landmass of enormous strategic and environmental importance and an ancient and rich culture of vital relevance to how human beings should lead their lives. The wonder was not how Tibet was lost but how the world let it happen: "Civilization of the Tibetan people is disappearing before our very eyes, and apart from a few gentle protests here and there the rest of the world lets it go without protest and without regret" (Snellgrove and Richardson, 1968: 15).

The World's Apathy is Best Explained by Tsering Shakya

There was a general consensus that there was nothing that the United Nations (UN) could do to help Tibet. The Americans hoped that a debate would serve as anti-Communist propaganda, but they were not prepared to take any action to place it on the agenda. Both Britain and India shared the view that any UN resolution should be limited to a statement calling on both sides to settle their differences by peaceful means because "stronger resolution (e.g. calling on China to withdraw its forces from Tibet and to restore the status quo) would merely be ignored by China" and therefore "the UN would lose prestige." (Shakya, 1999: 59).

The world's indifference then to the plight of the Tibetan people sealed Tibet's fate. The loss of Tibet is obviously a loss for the Tibetan people. But with a new understanding of the role played by Tibet, either as a primary shaper of Asian monsoon patterns or the source of water for much of Asia or as home to significant mineral reserves, the Tibetan people's loss is also Asia's loss. With the possibility that China might turn the tap off in Tibet leaving most of Asia high and dry, the people of Asia cannot continue to adopt the attitude that Tibet is the Tibetan people's problem and not a challenge for the whole of Asia. Damming of rivers to regulate their flow, serious plans to divert river waters from the south to the north, increasing mining of minerals precariously close to river banks and the potential for massive pollution of river waters that flow to the rest of Asia make Tibet a pressing issue for all of Asia to take up with China. To convince China to see the wisdom of allowing the Tibetans to exercise real autonomy is also to ensure that Asia as a whole continues to prosper. Brahma Chellaney, a leading Indian strategic thinker and analyst, succinctly advances this argument. He writes:

> The Tibet issue has been presented more often than not in the international literature in political or cultural terms, with the Chinese government and ethnic Tibetans supposed to be the principal players. But the Tibet issue is much larger and more fundamental: It is about Asia's water and climate security and its ecological interests. It is also about vital resources. Fundamentally, it is about securing Asia's future (Chellaney, 2011: 113).

However, there is a way for Asia to solve its water problems with China. In 2008, in Beijing, the two envoys of His Holiness the Dalai Lama, Lodi Gyari and Kelsang Gyaltsen, handed to the Chinese government a copy of a Memorandum on Genuine Autonomy for the Tibetan People (Department of Information and International Relations, 2010: 31-38). This memorandum contains the core demand of the Tibetan people, which is real autonomy under a single administration for all the Tibetan people. This demand, which is within the scope of the constitution of the People's Republic of China, was rejected by the Chinese government.

The rejection of the latest Tibetan proposal for autonomy should come as no surprise. No power which thinks it holds all the cards at the negotiating table would ever make even the slightest concession. China's economy is the world's second largest economy with military might to match. Some scholars predict that soon China might displace the United States (US) as a global power. Although shaken by the Bo Xilai scandal and embarrassed by the great escape of a blind dissident lawyer, Chen Guangcheng to the American embassy in Beijing, China's political system seems stable. With these advantages, there is no compelling incentive for China to make any concessions to a disgruntled group of people inhabiting its vast imperial periphery.

However, what should come as a surprise is that these talks were held at all. Tibetan exiles' contacts with Beijing from 1979 to 1993 and from 2002 to 2010 make for fascinating reading. Never in China's long and distinguished history have the representatives of a group of 'barbarians' been allowed to sit in the imperial capital to demand their just dues. That the talks took place at all means that China wants something from the Tibetans which it does not have: legitimacy. It is for the Tibetan people to give or withhold from Beijing 'the mandate of heaven' to rule Tibet. As long as their reasonable demands are not satisfactorily addressed by China, the Tibetan people will refuse to give Beijing legitimacy for its presence in Tibet, the latest evidence of this is the more than 51 fiery deaths, engulfing eastern Tibet that echoed and re-echoed calls for freedom for Tibet. As long as China does not have this legitimacy, it would want to talk with the Tibetans.

Another factor that strengthens the case for Asia to collectively press China to address the grievances of the Tibetan people is a spiritual one. Tibet and much of Asia have Buddhism in common as one of the cores of their value system. Restoring the Tibetan people to their traditional role of a responsible steward of the ecologically fragile plateau, which they have managed to do so sustainably for thousands of years, is in the best interest of Asia. When they are restored to their traditional role of being the guardian of the Tibetan Plateau, the Tibetan people will base the management of the plateau on Buddhist principles. They will regard the Tibetan Plateau as:

> A zone of peace, based on the principles of non-violence, compassion and protection of the natural environment, deriving inspiration from the Buddhist principles of compassion, justice and equality ... Future Tibet will strive for balance and harmony—both a balance between human and human and between human and the environment—realising the fact that everything is interconnected....This vision incorporates an attitude of sharing, harmony and co-operation between the people.[7]

All of Asia speaking to China on behalf of Tibet accords well with the best thinking prevailing in China today. Some of the leading lights of China, including Liu Xiaobo, the imprisoned Chinese Nobel Laureate, Fang Lizhi, the late physicist, considered one of the Three Voices of Freedom in China and many other public intellectuals have come in support for the Middle-Way Policy as articulated by the Dalai Lama. Given its current fluid political situation in which the premier of the nation is calling for the absolute necessity for political reform, these voices of moderation and tolerance of China's nascent civil society will shape China's attitude towards Tibet. For Asia to demand that China put in place a better treatment of the Tibetan people and let them manage the Tibetan Plateau sustainably and efficiently is in line with the forward-looking thinking in China. This act also amounts to Asia demanding that its tap in Tibet not be turned off.

7. Environment and Development Desk (2004).

References

Chang, Jung and Jon Halliday (2006). *Mao: The Unknown Story.* London: Vintage Books.

Chellaney, Brahma (2011). *Water: Asia's New Battleground.* New Delhi: Harper Collins, India. A joint venture with India Today.

Department of Information and International Relations (2010). *The Middle-Way Policy and All Related Documents*. Dharamsala: Central Tibetan Administration.

Environment and Development Desk (2004). *Guidelines for International Development Projects and Sustainable Development in Tibet*. Dharamsala: Department of Information and International Relations, Central Tibetan Administration. p.9.

————. (2000). *Tibet 2000: Environment and Development Issues*. Dharamsala: Department of Information and International Relations of the Central Tibetan Administration. p.86.

Shakabpa, Tsepon W.D. (1984). *A Political History of Tibet*. New York: Potala Publications. p.146.

Shakya, Tsering (1999). *The Dragon in the Land of Snows: A History of Tibet Since 1947*. London: Pimlico. p.424.

Snellgrove, David and Hugh Richardson (1968). *A Cultural History of Tibet*. Delhi: UBS Publishers Distributors. p.234.

Takeuchi, Tsuguhito (2003). "Military Administration and Military Duties in Tibetan-ruled Central Asia (8th-9th century)", in Alex McKay (ed.), Tibet and Her Neighbours: A History. London: Edition Hansjorg Mayer. p.43.

Tucci, Giuseppe (1967). *Tibet: Land of Snows*. Calcutta, Bombay, New Delhi: Oxford and IBH Publishing Co.

4

TASHI PHUNTSOK

Current Relationship between the Himalayan Region and the Tibetan People

Introduction

This is a short and preliminary commentary on the current relations between the Himalayan region and Tibetans in exile. It concentrates mainly on the cultural and religious aspects of the relationship with special reference to the north-eastern region of India.

Although the commentary reflects on both the past and current situations, it provides more details for the period after 1959.

General Reflection on the Past Relationships

The Himalayas, despite their inhospitable nature and terrain, have nurtured a unique trans-Himalayan Buddhist culture from the 7th century. The sacred mountains have been the abode of snow, great *yogis* and saints. The isolated caves in the rugged mountains and the monasteries on the craggy ridges nurtured the hardy monks and nuns in their meditational retreats. Political boundaries did not exist. Like the free migrant birds that graced the Himalayan sky, intrepid travellers and seekers of the Buddha Dharma trudged across the blistering wind and barren landscape of the Tibetan Plateau.

To the south of Tibet are the Himalayan communities of Ladakh, Lahual, Spiti, Kinnaur, Sikkim and Arunachal Pradesh in India, upland Nepal and Bhutan. Taken together, they constitute a Buddhist world, a coherent cultural, religious and linguistic bloc with deep ties and connections over many centuries. This whole belt predates interventions of the great powers: the British Raj, China and modern India. It was a porous life that for long had brought water, wool, salt, pilgrims, lamas and religion down from the Tibetan Plateau, while carrying up from the lowlands and through the mountains cotton, pilgrims and great Indian masters. This rich history of two-way traffic, of goods and ideas, commodities and mind training, brought the Himalayan peoples closer together, overcoming all hardship of a steep terrain.

The spiritual renaissance, also called the Latter Diffusion of Buddhism in Upper West Tibet, originated from the Himalayan region of Spiti, Kinnaur and Ladakh in India and Ngari and Guge in Tibet. Lochen Richen Sangpo (958-1055), Lochung Legpai Sherab, Atisha, Marpa and Milarepa exemplified the crisscrossing of Buddhism across the Himalaya (Arpi, 2013; Mckay, 2003a).

Royal patronage from Guge, especially by King Yeshi Yod, was responsible for the invitation of Indian Master Atisha. Lotsawas Phagpa Sherab from Zhangskar is associated with restoration of Jokhang Temple and Samye (Bray, 2011).

Thangston Gyalpo (1385-1462), popular saint-engineer and patron of Tibetan opera, built a suspension bridge (*chaksam*) over Tawang river near Kraling village, seven miles south-east of Tawang. The bridge, which still survives, connects Mukto and Kitpi areas of Tawang (Sarkar, 1978).

Tana Mendelkhang, where the palace of King Gyalpo Kala Wangpo of Tawang once stood, became the site where the famous Tawang Gonpa (monastery) was founded by Merak Lama Lodre Gyatso in 1680-81, in accordance with the wishes of the 5th Dalai Lama (Sarkar, 1978). The monastery belongs to the Gelugpa School and had a religious association with the Drepung Monastery in Lhasa before 1959.

The peoples of the Himalayan region looked north to Lhasa and Tibet, to trade, to go on pilgrimage, to seek a teacher for the village, to rebuild a monastery, to find an artist to repaint murals and to seek authentic connections to a lineage of mediators.

Indeed monks from the Indian Himalaya could gain admission to and avail of all facilities in major Tibetan monasteries just like any Tibetan. Ngari Khangtsen, Spiti Khangtsen, Tsawa Khangtsen and other hostels were reserved for them. This tradition continues till date.

Buddhism in the Himalayan Belt

Historically, Indian Buddhist institutions such as Nalanda and Vikramasila were the centres of excellence for propagation of Buddhist ideas. Indian influence and role were pivotal in the establishment of Mahayana Buddhism in Tibet. The knowledge and literature of Buddhism, rather than being available in India, was preserved, got ingrained and further developed in Tibet before it declined in India. In mid-20th century, when the People's Republic of China (PRC) took over Tibet, that very knowledge pool came back to India with Tibetan exiles (Institute for Defence Studies and Analyses [IDSA], 2012).

Despite the prevailing situation inside Tibet, a cultural and spiritual relationship still exists amongst the exiled Tibetans and the Himalayan peoples who follow Buddhist traditions. It is the revival and establishment of various Buddhist monasteries and centres that has kept this relationship intact throughout the Himalayan belt.

In Ladakh, there are 37 monasteries of different sects and more than 90 elderly monks who had been to various monasteries in Tibet before 1959. The Hemis Monastery, for instance is the largest monastery of the Drukpa Kargyu School of the Great Mahayana culture. It was founded in 1630 by Tagtsang Repa Ngawang Gyatso (1574-1651) under the patronage of King Sengye Namgyal (Mckay, 2003b). The monastery now has about 350 monks with its various branch monasteries in over 50 villages all over Ladakh (IDSA, 2012).

Phyang and Shachukul monasteries in Ladakh follow the Drikung Kagyu lineage. Matho Monastery, about 26 km from Leh, is the only monastery that follows the Sakya sect. It was established in the early 15th century by the Tibetan Sakya scholar, Dorje Palsang for the benefit of the local community. Thak Thog Monastery that follows the Nyimgma sect in Sakti village, about 45 km from Leh was founded in the late 16th century. Alchi Monastery that follows the Gelukpa sect was built by the great translator Guru Rinchen Zangpo between 958 and 1055. Other Gelukpa sect monasteries in Ladakh include Thikse and Likir monasteries (IDSA, 2012).

Tabo Monastery, in Tabo village, Himachal Pradesh (HP), was founded by Lotsawa Rinchen Sanpo in 996. It is located on the left bank of Spiti river. It was built by King Yeshi Yod. It is noted for being the oldest continuously operating Buddhist enclave in the Himalaya. It is protected by the Archaeological Survey of India (ASI) and is a listed United Nations Educational, Scientific and Cultural Organization (UNESCO) heritage site.

Key Monastery is said to be founded by Dromton (1008-1064), a well-known pupil of Atisha. It is close to Spiti river and is the largest monastery in the Spiti Valley.

The Himalayan kingdom of Sikkim became the 22nd state of India in 1975 and though the majority of its population follows traditional Hindu cultures and rituals (about 70%), in the northern part of the state the Bhutias and Lepchas are Buddhists.

The Monpas and Khampa peoples of Arunachal Pradesh have also been Buddhists. Looking back in time, the 6th Dalai Lama, Tseyang Gyatso was born at Urgelling Monastery, 5 km from Tawang. He was a Monpa by ethnicity.

It may not be out of place to mention here that with the exception of the Khamptis in Lohit District, the Monpas are the only people in the North-East Frontier Agency who can claim to have a script (Chakravarty, 1973).

Besides various Buddhist monasteries, Buddhist institutes like the Central Institute of Buddhist Studies in Ladakh, the Namgyal Institute of Tibetology (NIT) in Gangtok and the Central Institute of Himalayan Culture Studies in Arunachal Pradesh, serve as centres of learning and preservation of Buddhist culture.

In 1957, the foundation stone for NIT was laid by His Holiness the 14th Dalai Lama. Over the years NIT has sponsored and promoted research on the religion, history, language, art and culture of the people of the Tibetan cultural area, which includes Sikkim. The NIT library holds one of the largest collections of Tibetan works in the world outside Tibet and has a museum of Tibetan iconography and religious art (NIT, 2013).

In 2010 the Union Cabinet approved the establishment of the Central Institute of Himalayan Culture Studies (CIHCS) at Dahung in West Kameng district of Arunachal Pradesh, as an autonomous institute under the Ministry of Culture. The current director of CIHCS, Lama Tashi, was born in Kameng district and received his Buddhist education from the Drepung Loseling Monastery at Mundgod, Karnataka. He was also the principal chant master of this monastery and travelled extensively around the world (Central Institute of Himalayan Culture Studies, 2013).

Tibetan Exile (1959)

China's occupation of Tibet forced His Holiness the 14th Dalai Lama and some 80,000 Tibetans to leave Tibet. They moved to India, Nepal and Bhutan. His Holiness, escaping the Chinese army, crossed into India on 30 March 1959 and spent some days resting at the Tawang Monastery before reaching Tezpur in Assam on 18 April. Early Tibetan refugee settlements, monastic communities and schools were established here.

While China systematically destroyed ancestral cultural and religious centres in Tibet, these Tibetan establishments, set up all across India, became the central hope for safeguarding the unique cultural and religious traditions of Tibet.

His Holiness the Dalai Lama has been the esteemed guest of the Government of India (GoI) since 1959. The Central Tibetan Administration (CTA) has been based in Dharamsala as well. All these would not have been possible without the generous help and kind consideration of the people and the GoI.

Current Relationships

The exiled Tibetan community, with generous support from the Indian government, has successfully thrived in many Indian states. According to the latest demographic census released by the Planning Commission (CTA) in 2010, the Himalayan states of Himachal Pradesh, Uttarakhand, Jammu & Kashmir (J&K), Sikkim and Arunachal Pradesh have a total of 25 Tibetan settlements with a total population of about 50,500 people (Figure 4.1).

Figure 4.1

Tibetan Population in Indian Himalayan States

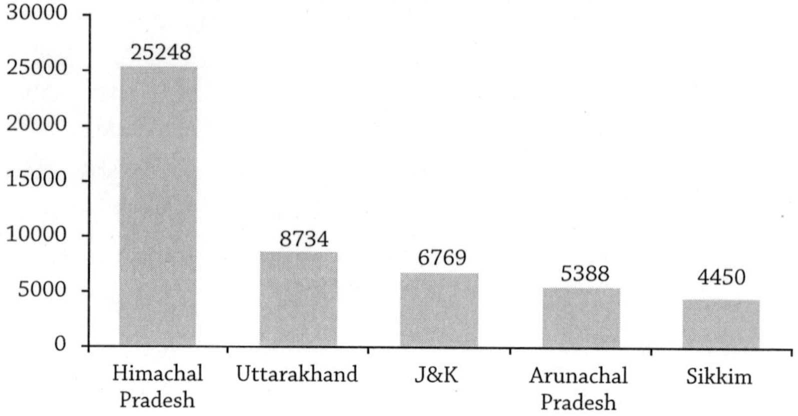

Source: The Office of the Planning Commission, CTA (2010).

Figure 4.2

Students Enrolled in Tibetan Schools in Himalayan States (2013)

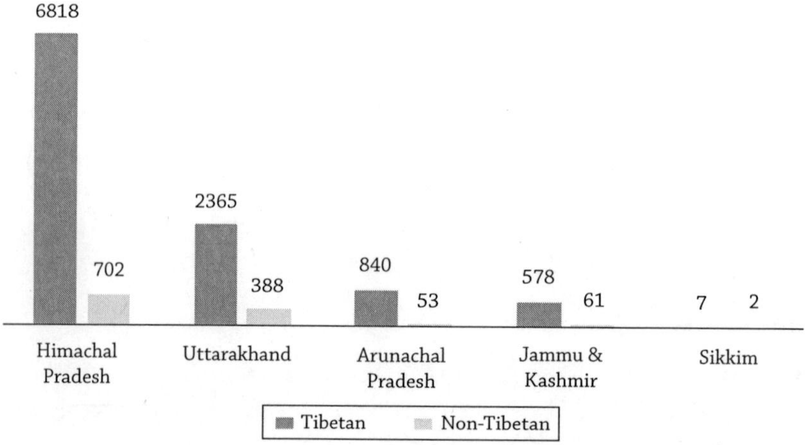

Source: Department of Education, CTA (March 2013).

These Himalayan states are also home to various Tibetan boarding and private schools. Most of them are administered by the

Department of Education (CTA, Dharamsala), Tibetan Children's Village (TCV), Dharamsala and Tibetan Homes Foundation (THF), Mussoorie. As of March 2013, 32 schools imparted modern education to more than 11,800 students, of whom 1,206 students were non-Tibetans (Figure 4.2). For more information, please refer to Appendix A-4.1.

In addition, TCV had 1,214 students of whom 1,050 were boarders and 164 day scholars. TCV in Choglamsar, Leh and Ladakh, had seven homes for the local children and THF had 71 students from the north-east Himalayan region alone.

The current rate of young Himalayan scholars enrolling in the various monasteries, religious and cultural centres and Tibetan schools is encouraging. It is a positive indication of the ability of the Himalayan peoples to retain, practice and preach this unique Buddhist philosophy and its teachings in a free country. For instance, according to the 2011 records maintained by the Department of Religion and Culture of the CTA, in north-east India alone, there were about 53 Tibetan-run Buddhist monasteries and religious centres that educated more than 4,400 monks from various ethnic backgrounds. According to the available data, more than 80 per cent of these monks were non-Tibetan or monks from the other Himalayan region (refer to Figure 4.3 and for more details, see Appendix A-4.2).

As reflected in Figure 4.4, peoples from the Himalayan regions (Kinnuar, Spiti, Ladakh, Mon, Nepal, Bhutan and Sikkim) make up roughly 25 per cent of the total monks and nuns in the major monasteries in south India.

In and around Dharamsala, several Buddhist monasteries, nunneries and religious institutes also educate many students (comprising monks, nuns and lay people from the Himalayan region). According to a report published in 2011 by the Department of Religion and Culture, there were over 400 monks and nuns enrolled in various Tibetan monasteries and nunneries in Dharamsala (Refer to Figure 4.5 and for more details, see Appendix A-4.3).

Figure 4.3

Number of Monks Enrolled in North-east Buddhist Monasteries Managed by Tibetans

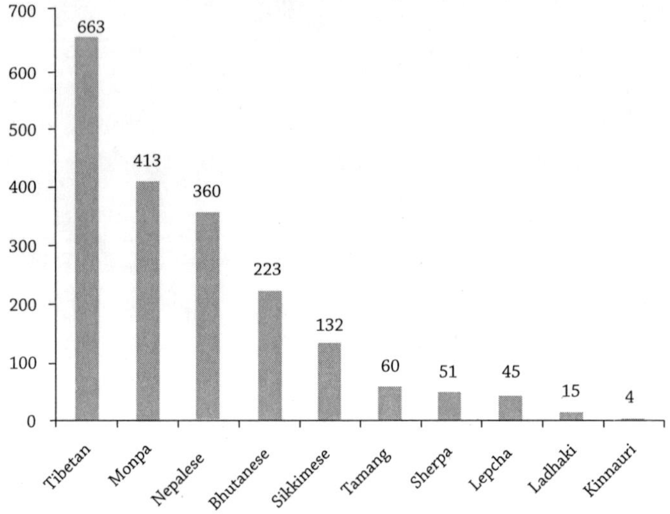

Source: Department of Religion and Culture, CTA (2011).

Figure 4.4

Number of Monks and Nuns in Tibetan Buddhist Monasteries in South India

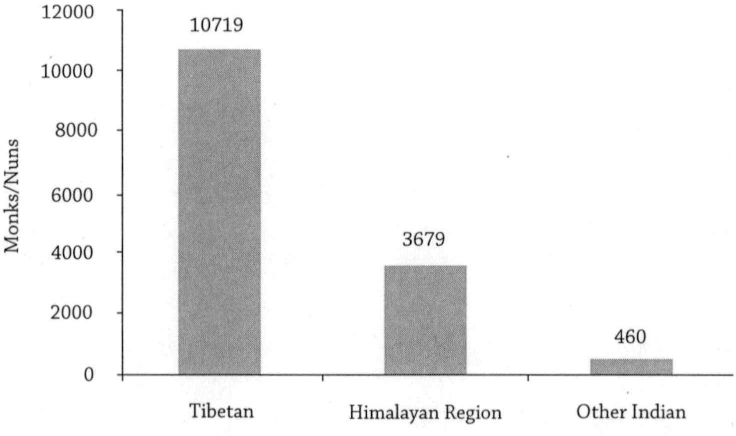

Source: Department of Religion and Culture, CTA (2011).

Tibetan monasteries in the Himalayan regions are now becoming the main learning centres for local people. In due course, a majority of the spiritual scholars will likely be from the Himalayan region. Their linguistic know-how and cultural and spiritual affinity give them an edge to excel and become renowned Buddhist scholars and high priests. This should be comforting for those researchers who have shown great concern regarding the "Tibetanization of the Himalayan Regions" (IDSA, 2012). It is clear that these monastic institutions and religious centres will become the main centres for future Buddhist studies and practitioners.

Figure 4.5

Number of Monks and Nuns Enrolled in Various Tibetan Monasteries in Dharamsala

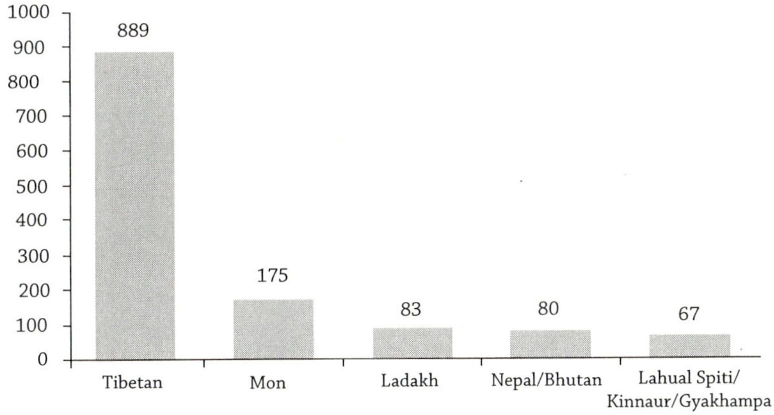

Source: Department of Religion and Culture, CTA (2011).

Already many eminent spiritual scholars from the Himalayan region have adorned the leadership in Tibetan Buddhist hierarchy. The current Gaden Tripa (the throne holder of the Gelugpa school), His Eminence Rizong Rinpoche, is from Ladakh; Khenrinpoche Jangchup Choeden, Abbot of the Gadhen Shartse, is from Spiti; and Khen Rinpoche Lobsang Tseten, Abbot of the Tashi Lhunpo Monastery is also from Ladakh. Geshi Lharampa Guru Rinpoche, Abbot of Tawang Monastery, is a Monpa from Arunachal Pradesh. This list is random and not comprehensive. There are several other eminent religious teachers, abbots, directors of religious and cultural institutions, high authorities in managerial posts of the monasteries of all Buddhists schools and nunneries who are from the Himalayan region.

His Holiness the Dalai Lama's Role

His Holiness the 14th Dalai Lama has made special efforts for the improvement of the quality of learning, re-strengthening the confidence of the people and in the revival and promotion of Buddhist culture in the Himalayan region. His tireless commitment has taken him 52 times to the region since his arrival in India. Excluding areas around Dharamsala, His Holiness has visited places in the Himalayan regions of HP 17 times; J&K 18 times; Sikkim 5 times; West Bengal 7 times; and Arunachal Pradesh 5 times. Please refer to Appendix A-4.4(a) for details of the visit of His Holiness in the region.

His Holiness has also conferred the Kalachakra Initiation, the highest form of Buddhist empowerment, seven times in the region. The first was granted in Leh, Ladakh, J&K in 1976 followed by Tabo in Himachal Pradesh in 1983; Zanskar in J&K in 1988; Gangtok in Sikkim in 1993; Jispa in HP in 1994; Tabo in HP in 1996 again; and Kyi in HP in 2000. His Holiness gave the 33rd Kalachakra at Shewai Tsel by the Indus river-side in Leh in July 2014.

For the people of Tawang, in Arunachal Pradesh, it was a great blessing when the GoI supported His Holiness the 14th Dalai Lama's 'socio-religious' visit to Tawang in 2009. During that trip, His Holiness inaugurated a museum at the historic Tawang Monastery and told the reporters that he was getting emotional as he had crossed this town in 1959 while fleeing from Tibet following the armed repression by the government of the People's Republic of China (CTA, 2009).

On 25 March 2013, His Holiness the 14th Dalai Lama was invited to Sikkim to consecrate the colossal 128 foot hammered copper statue of the Buddha, which he had earlier named Tathagata Tsal at Ravangla, south Sikkim district. The site was chosen within the larger religious complex of the Rabong Gompa (monastery), itself a centuries-old place of pilgrimage. Also nearby is the Ralang Monastery, a key monastery in Tibetan Buddhism. This statue was built and installed through the joint efforts of the Sikkim government and its people and has now become a key stop on the 'Himalayan Buddhist Circuit' (CTA, 2013).

Conclusion

The shift caused in the relationship because of the Chinese occupation of Tibet has proven beneficial and enriching for the Himalayan region. Far more importantly, and for posterity, the revival and robust growth of cultural and spiritual institutions in the region will have far-reaching consequences for Tibetan Buddhism. It is apparent that both the people of the Himalayan region and the Tibetans have mutually benefited from each other. They have in fact collaborated, under most tragic time for the Tibetans, to usher in a new era—the revival and the easy access of the higher standards of Buddhism in the Himalayan region of India.

Having said so, this preliminary commentary—as admitted in the beginning—needs further consolidation of facts and a deeper analysis of the data thus generated. This work is incomplete in many ways. The vast scope of the study will need more serious attention.

I would like to thank Mr Tenzin Norbu, Ms Tashi Yangzom, Mr Jigme Norbu and Mr Tempa Gyalsten for their assistance in preparing the paper.

References

Arpi, Claude (2013). *Glimpses on the History of Tibet*. Dharamsala: The Tibet Museum, DIIR, Central Tibetan Administration-Dharamsala.

Bray, John (2011). *Ladakhi Histories*. Dharamsala: Library of Tibetan Works & Archives.

Central Tibetan Administration-Dharamsala (2009). *His Holiness the Dalai Lama says Tawang Visit to Promote Universal Human Values. http://tibet.net/2009/11/10/his-holiness-the-dalai-lama-says-tawang-visit-to-promote-universal-human-values/*

———. (2010). *Combined Report of Tibetan Demographic Surveys, 1998-2009 and Socio-Economic Issues Survey 1998-2001*. The Office of the Planning Commission.

———. (2013). *His Holiness the Dalai Lama Consecrates Tathagata Tsal and Begins Teaching in Sikkim. http://tibet.net/2013/03/26/his-holiness-the-dalai-lama-consecrates-tathagata-tsal-and-begins-teaching-in-sikkim.*

Chakravarty, L.N. (1973). *Glimpses of the Early History of Arunachal*. Shillong: Research Department, Arunachal Pradesh Administration.

Department of Religion and Culture (2011). *Background History and Accounts of the Tibetan Monasteries in Exile* (Tibetan version, volumes 1-3). Dharamsala: Central Tibetan Administration.

Institute for Defence Studies and Analyses (IDSA) (2012). *Tibet and India's Security: Himalayan Region, Refugees and Sino Sino-Indian Relations*. Task Force Report. May. *http://www.idsa.in/system/files/book_Tibet-India.pdf*

Mckay, Alex (2003a). *Tibet and Her Neighbours, A History*. London: Edition Hansjörg Mayer.

———. (2003b). *The History of Tibet, The Modern Period: 1895-1959*. London: RoutledgeCurzon.

Sarkar, N. (1978). *A Historical Account of Tawang Monastery*. Shillong: RESARUN, Directorate of Research, Government of Arunachal Pradesh.

Websites and Others:

Central Institute of Himalayan Culture Studies (2013). *http://indiaculture.nic.in/indiaculture/pdf/CIHCS.pdf*

Namgyal Institute of Tibetology (2013). *http://www.tibetology.net/*

Appendix A-4.1

Students Enrolled in Tibetan Schools in the Himalayan States

States/Schools	*Tibetan*	*Non-Tibetan*
Arunachal Pradesh		
CST Tezu	99	2
CST Tenzingang	241	42
CST Rawangla	105	4
CST Miao	395	5
Sikkim		
TSTS Gangtok	7	2
J&K		
TCV, Hanley	146	39
TCV, Sumdho	35	0
TCV, Menlha	101	11
TCV, Agling	189	7
TCV, Nyima	60	0
TCV, Choglam	47	4
Uttarakhand		
TNMF, Clement Town	236	70
Ling Tsang School	14	65
CST Herbertpur	142	251
THF, Mussoorie	1,341	0
THF, Rajpur	490	0
STS Dekyiling	142	2
Himachal Pradesh		
TCV, Mcleod	124	26
TCV, Suja	898	2
TCV, Selakui	384	5
TCV-SOS, Suja	424	55
TCV Upper Dharamsala	1,704	169
TCV, Lower Dharamsala	594	75
TCV, Gopalpur	1,187	34
STS Manali	59	13
STS Chauntra	362	38
STS Puruwala	67	0
CST Shimla	288	265
STS Bir	72	0
STS Gangkyi	205	0
Mewoen Tsuglag Petoen	87	0
STS Paonta	363	20
Total	10,608	1,206

Source: Department of Religion and Culture of the Central Tibetan Administration-Dharamsala (2011).

Appendix A-4.2

List of Tibetan Monasteries and Nunneries in North-east India and Bhutan

S. No.	Name	Place		Founder	Year		No. of Students
		Shegon	*Jaygon*		*Shegon*	*Jaygon*	
NYINGMA							
1	Sangdog Palri Pemaod-ki Phodrang	Kabug		Duljom Jigdral Yeshi Dorjee			Tibetan 10, Bhutanese 25, Nepalese 37
2	Guru Kubum Taglung Sangchoe	Gangtok		His Holiness the Dalai Lama & Zongna Tulku			Tibetan 10, Ladakhi 1, Monpa 1, Tamang 6, Sharpa 9
3	Tashi Choeling	Mao	Tezu	Jeydrung Dakpa Gyaltsen	16 Century	1962	Nil
4	Ogyan Choeling	Tezu		Lama Tenzin Sherab		1967	
5	Gonjang Ogyan Donag Choekhorling	Tingkey Utsang	Gangtok	Rigzing Pema Chophel	19 Century	1980	Tibetan 5, Sikkimese 30, Monpa 14, Bhutanese 17, Nepalese 27
6	Gonjang Samten Choephug	Tingkey Utsang	Darjeeling	Rigzing Pema Chophel	18 Century	1972	Tibetan 8, Bhutanese 2, Nepalese 6
7	Palyul Choekhorling	Nanital, India		Kyapjay Pema Norbu		1960	Tibetan 2, Sikkimese 3, Khunu 4, Nepalese 6
8	Phuntsok Pema Choekhor Ling	Darjeeling		Golog Tulku		1961	
9	Vari Rigzin Gatseling	Gampa Zong, Utsang	Shari, Gangtok	Vari Lama	12 Century	1983	Tibetan 6, Monpa 1, Sikkimese 1, Sharpa 2, Tamang 1

contd...

contd...

10	Phuntsok Nayab Choekhorling		Darjeeling	Jadrel Sangay Dorjee Rinpoche		1959	15
11	Ogyan Kunsang Choekhorling		Darjeeling	Kagyur Rinpoche		1960	67
12	Lhagon Jangchup Choeling	Derge, Kham	Tezu	Rigzing Jatson Nyingpo	1950	1962	
13	Drejong Thupten Dhargyeling	Rawangla		Lobsang Tenpa		1984	16
14	Pema Choeling	Mao, Chophelling		Mao, Tibetan Settlement Office		1978	14
15	Drejong Thupten Choekhorling	Lachen Thanko, Sikkim		Tsewang Lama		1984	14
16	Pemakod Nyesang Donag Jangchup Dhargeyling	Tuting, Arunachal Pradesh				2001	95
17	Pakong Katok	Drejong					
18	Kachoe Pema Woeling Nunnery	Gangtok, Sikkim		Dakyap Khamtrul Rinpoche		2006	Bhutanese 2, Sikkimese, Sharpa and Tamang 22
19	Khachoe Dechenling Nunnery	Darjeeling		Jadrel Sangay Dorjee Rinpoche		1980	
20	Ogyan Choekhorling Nunnery	Gangtok, Sik-kim		Sikkimese Ani Bhumo			Sikkimese, Sharpa and Bhutanese 30
21	Drupdhe Neysang Tagtenling	Bhutan					

contd...

contd...

22	Lhalung Thekchok Rabgay Choeling	Bhumtangshing, Bhutan					
23	Drupdhe Neysang Tagtenling	Bhutan					
24	Ogyan Dongag Choeling	Thimpu, Bhutan					Tibetan 2, Bhutanese 3
25	Padro Sechen Drupde Thekchok Choekyi Gyatsel	Pado, Bhutan		Sheychen Rabjam Rinpoche			
26	Lhodrak Khachududjomling	Lhodak, Utsang	Bhumthang Chamkhar, Bhutan	Jangpa Yapsay	1679	1994	155
27	Yidmon Dechenling		Lhongtso, Bhutan				
28	Sechen Ogyan Choezong Nunnery	Derge, Kham	Thimpu, Bhutan	1st Shalam Rabjampa	1698	1971	Tibetan 6, Bhutanese 80
KARMA KAGYUE							
29	Rumtek Shedrup Choekhorling	Toelung Tsurphu	Rumtek, Gangtok	Ist Karmapa	1189	1961	340
30	Borkhar Nyedon Choekhorling	Dongjang, Toe Ngari	Darjeeling	Karma Sherap Woeser Rinpoche	1920	1984	Tibetan 173, Sikkimese 105, Lowa 25, Yolmo 85, Ladakhi 3, Monpa 74, Bhutanese 45, Nepalese 69, Indian 7
31	Drug Sanag Choeling	Lhokha	Darjeeling	Druk Khukhen Pema Karpo			Tibetan 87, Indian 3, Khunu 48, Spiti 2, Ladhaki 64, Monpa 5, Bhutanese 25, Nepalese 18

contd...

contd...

32	Palchen Choeling	Toelung Tsurbhu	Rawangla, Sikkim	1st Karmapa	1189	1981	570
33	Pal Karmai Zhurmang Shadrup Choekhor-ling		Gangtok	Drung Masey Loedoe Rinchen	1423	1992	Tibetan 36, Sikkimese 9, Ladakhi 2 Monpa 88, Bhutanese 51, Nepalese 66, Lepchapa 45
34	Kagyud Thekchenling		Lawa, Kabug	Kongtrul Karma Lodoe		1988	Tibetan 20, Khunu 18, Ladakhi 15, Bhutanese 12, Nepalese 60
35	Samdrup Dhargye-Choeling	Sonata, Darjeeling		Kullu Rinpoche		1966	
36	Kagyud Tsechokling	Domo, Utsang	Gangtok, Sik-kim	Tenzin Nyinda Rinpoche	1770	1987	40
37	Nyingde Rabtenling	Lhodak	Bhutan	5th Karmapa		1959	20
38	Ralung-gon Dechen Choekhorling		Thimbu, Bhutan	Karsa Kunphen-ling Settlement		1970	50
39	Lhodrag Shekhar Dratsang	Bhutan	Bhumtang, Bhutan	Marpa Choeke Lodoe		1963	
SAKYA							
40	Sakya Choepheling Thorim Tshuglag Lobnyerkhang		Darjeeling	Khenchen Jampa Tenzin		1979	Tibetan 47, Indian 3, Bhutanese 3 , Nepalese 2
41	Nyagton Gyudpai gdansa lelung Choede		Toe, Utsang	Nyag Lama Shangtro		2008	15

contd...

contd...

42	Sakya Gurugon		Darjeeling	Amdo Lama		1909	Tibetan 30, Bhutanese 4, Nepalese 40, Indian 2
43	Pal Sanyor Choetsok		Gangtok	Dolma Phodrang		1909	Tibetan 20, Sharpa 35, Monpa 1, Tamang 20, Lowa 4, Nepalese 4
44	Sakya Kunga Shedrup ling		Darjeeling			1999	Tibetan 11, Sharpa 14, Tamang 12, Bhutanese 3, Lowa 10, Nepalese 4
GELUG							
45	Bodgyon Gaden Tashi Choeling Phegyalling		Shillong	Tsampa Lama		1957	12
46	Gontse Gaden Rab-gayling	Tsona	Bumla, Tezu		1111	1963	Tibetan 10, Monpa 199, Bhutanese 3
47	Palden Sradgyud Dratsang	Shigatse	Kabug	Dulnakpa Palden Sangpo	1450	1970	Tibetan 30, Indian 3, Monpa 2, Bhutanese 2, Nepalese 18
48	Sangchen Magon Palden Sradgyud Dratsang	Shigatse	Salugara	Dulnakpa Palden Sangpo	1450	2001	Tibetan 111, Monpa 4, Bhutanese 1
49	Ganden Tharpa Choeling		Kabug	1st Domo Geshe		1922	Tibetan 20, other 25
50	Zerkhar Choede Kyitsel-ling	Toe Shalkar	Kabug	Jetsun Jampa Tenphel	1400	1987	Tibetan 11, other 11
51	Gum Yidam Choezin		Drajeeling			1850	Tibetan 3, Indian 10, Mongolian 1
52	Kirti-gon Ganden Tashi Choeling		Darjeeling	Ladhak Lama Ngawang Samten		1950	

contd...

contd...

53	Gyepheling	Kabug	Ngagrampa Tenpa Choeden	1979	
YUNGDRUNG BON					
54	Zhurizhing Yung-drung Kundragling	Rawangla	Shuyae Namgyal Tenpa	1984	Tibetan 3, Monpa 13, Nepalese 2

Source: *The History of Exile Tibetan Monasteries, 2011*. Three Volume. Published by Department of Culture and Religion, Central Tibetan Administration.

Appendix A-4.3

Monks/Nuns from Himalayan Regions in the Monasteries and Nunneries in Dharamsala

S. No.	*Name of Monastery/Nunnery*	*No. of Students*
1	Gadong Seljey Ling	Tibetan 5, Monpa 12, Ladakhi 1
2	Kirti Monastery	Tibetan 154, Nepalese 18
3	Cheme Gatsel Ling	Tibetan 14, Spiti 1, Nepalese 47
4	Nechung Monastery	Tibetan 50, Khunu 4, Spiti 1, Monpa 33
5	Tsechok Ling	Tibetan 27, Nepalese 23
6	Gyutoth Monastery	Tibetan 267, Spiti 15, Ladakhi 52, Monpa 89, Bhutanese 5, Nepalese 5,
7	Gaden Choeling	Tibetan 109, Khunu 2, Spiti 5, Ladakhi 17, Monpa 3, Garsha 1, Gyagar Khampa 6
8	Riglam Lobnyer Khang (IBD)	Tibetan 105, Spiti 3, Ladakhi 4, Monpa 2, Khunu 7
9	Dolma Ling	Tibetan 158, Spiti 22, Ladakhi 17, Bhutanese 5, Nepalese 5
10	Namgyal Monastery	Tibetan 180, Ladakhi 13, Monpa 8

Source: *The History of Exile Tibetan Monasteries, 2011. Three Volume*, Published by Department of Culture and Religion, Central Tibetan Administration.

Appendix A-4.4(a)

Visits of His Holiness the Dalai Lama in the Himalayan Region

Himalayan States	*No. of Visit*	*Date*
Arunachal Pradesh		
Tenzingang	3	March 29-April 10, 1983; October 10-13, 1997; April 29-May 1, 2003
Dahung	1	April 29-May 1, 2003
Bomdila	4	May 1-3, 2003: October 10-13, 1997; March 10-11, 1983; April 29-May 4, 1983
Dirang	3	May 3, 2003; October 14-15, 1997; May 17-29, 1983
Tawang	3	April 3-9, 2003; October 15-21, 1997; April 11-17, 1983
Tezu	3	December 13-15, 2003; December 11-14, 1996; March 24-27, 1983
Miao	3	December 11-13, 2003; December 8-11, 1996; March 27-29, 1983
Itanagar	1	May 4-6, 1983
Himachal Pradesh		
Spiti	1	July 9-15, 2009
Tabo	4	June 12-16, 2004; May 21-26, 2003; June 18-July 5, 1996; July 12-27, 1983
Kullu	4	August 16-17, 2010; May 11-15, 2005; October 13-24, 1966; October 22, 1962
Manali	7	August 1-2, 2000; June 4-10, 1985; August 3-5, 1983; September 15-25, 1977; April 8-14, 1975; September 7-13, 1964; October 22-23, 1962
Jispa	2	August 18-20, 2010; July 12-24, 1994
Dakar	1	June 16-17, 2004
Kyi	4	June 17-18, 2004; August 3-17, 2000; June 10-12, 1985; July 3-August 2, 1983
Rekong Peo	2	June 23-24, 1978; October 21-26, 1974
Kaza	3	July 26-30, 1983; June 25-28, 1978; October 26-27, 1974
Pin	1	May 8-12, 2004
Narkanda		August 20-21, 2007
Kinnaur	1	August 21-26, 2007
Sangla	1	June 7-8, 2006
Kalpa	1	June 8-12, 2006

contd...

contd...

Keylong	1	July 12, 1994
Puh	1	July 11-12, 1983
J&K		
Gulabgarh-Paddar	1	June 5-6, 2010
Ladakh	12	August 21, 2013; July 18-August 13, 2012; August 20-28, 2010; July 9-29, 2009; July 31-August 20, 2007; August 17-September 7, 2005; July 21-August 1, 2003; August 7-25, 2002; July 2-August 6, 1987; August 17-September 15, 1980; October 24-27, 1970; August 25-30, 1966
Jammu	1	December 27, 1998
Zanskar	2	August 9-13, 1997; July-August , 1988
Kargil	2	August 13, 1997; August 27-28, 1976
Leh	4	August 5-9, 1997, August 13-14, 1997; July-August, 1988; August 29-September 13, 1976
Gulmarg	1	1976
Srinagar	2	July 12-18, 2012; July-August 10, 1988
Sikkim		
Gangtok	5	March 26-27, 2013; December 19-23, 2010; October 22-24, 1997; March 27-April 8, 1993; October 16-27, 1981
Pelling	1	December 15, 2010
Tashiding	1	December 15-18, 2010
Ravangla	2	December 18-19, 2010; October 22, 1997
Namchi	1	October 21-22, 1997
West Bengal		
Salugara	4	March 27-29, 2013; December 23-24, 2010; November 2-10, 2001; December 16-27, 1996
Kalimpong	3	December 12-15, 2010; November 10-13, 2001; October 27-30, 1981
Darjeeling	3	April 8-12, 1993; October 30-November 3, 1981; May 23-June 3, 1975
Mirig	1	December 14-16, 1996

Source: The Office of His Holiness the Dalai Lama.

Appendix A-4.4(b)

Kalachakra Initiation by His Holiness the Dalai Lama in the Himalayan Region

S. No.	*Date*	*Place*
1	September 1976	Leh, Ladakh, India
2	August 1983	Tabo, HP, India
3	July 1988	Zanskar, J&K, India
4	April 1993	Gangtok, Sikkim, India
5	July 1994	Jispa, HP, India
6	June 1996	Tabo, HP, India
7	August 2000	Kyi, HP, India and it is proposed that another Kalachakra will be held at Leh, next year in July.
8	July 2014	Leh, Ladakh, J&K, India

Source: Souvenir: His Holiness the 14th Dalai Lama of Tibet, DIIR, CTA.

II

Peoples and Linkages

5

CLAUDE ARPI

History of the Dispute Between Tehri State and Tibet

A Himalayan Case

Introduction

One of the recent historic upshots in the relation between Tibet and the Himalayan region has been the Sino-Indian border dispute along the 4,000 km mountainous range.

As in most cases, the present 'dispute', what is today the Sino-Indian border, has its origin in disagreements between the Lhasa government and the administration of Himalayan princely states (and by extension, British India).

Our case study relates to Nilang/Jadhang area in today's Uttarakhand. It is particularly interesting due to the large amount of correspondence between Tibet (the Kashag in Lhasa and the Dzongpen in Tsaparang) and the princely states of Tehri-Garhwal, Bashahr as well as the provincial governments of the United Provinces and the Punjab, and of course, the Foreign and Political Department of British India in Delhi.

The 'negotiations' lasted some 12 years, at the end of which no mutually acceptable solution could be found.

The entire story is extracted from a couple of files in the British Archives.[1] A few years ago, I had the good fortune to come across

1. File Title: Tibet: Tehri-Tibet Boundary Dispute; dates: February 1923-May 1940; physical description: 338ff; file number: L/P&S/12/4172; Pol Ext Coll 36 File 9; Scope & contents: Report of the Commission appointed to make recommendations with regard to the territory in dispute between Tehri-Garhwal and Bashahr darbars in the neighbourhood of Nilang, 1934; Shimla: Foreign Dept, September 1935, [25]p 'Note on Tehri-Tibet boundary dispute' F. Williamson, 31 October 1932, Delhi: Foreign & Political Dept, November 1932, 7p, Confidential.

Figure 5.1

Tehri-Tibet Boundary Map

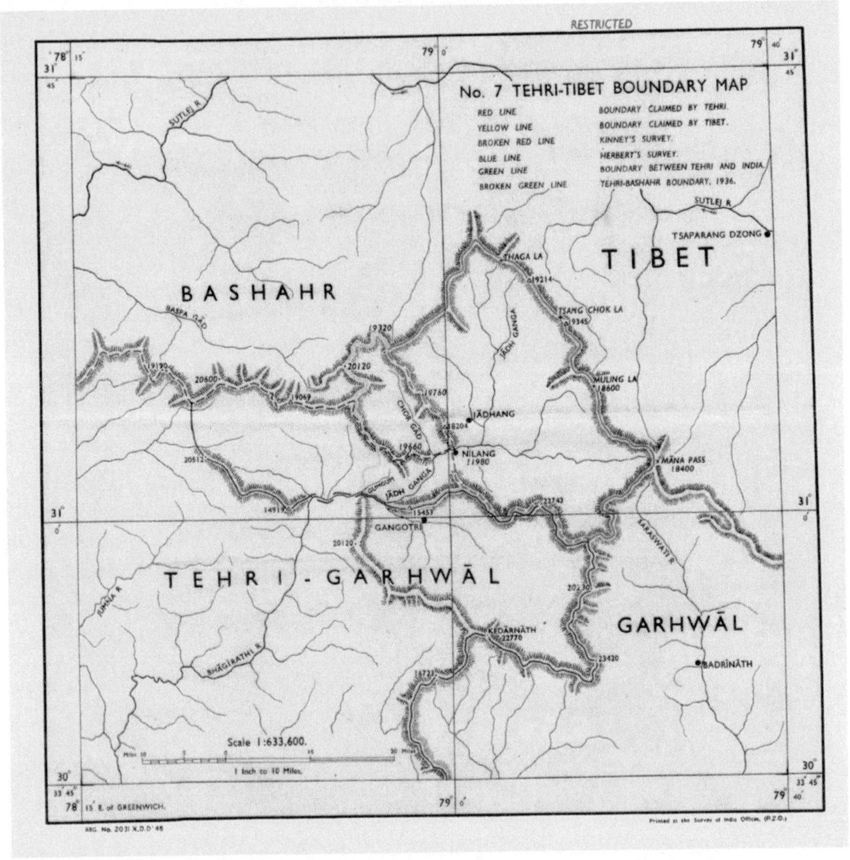

them and I thought it would be interesting to share this unknown aspect of Himalayan relations.

Location and Description

The area disputed by Tibet and Tehri-Garhwal state[2] lies between longitude 78.53 and 79.25 East and latitude 31 and 31.26 North (Figure 5.1).

2. Hereafter called the Tehri state or in some cases, the Tehri Darbar, when we refer to the state administration.

For the sake of the different commissions which looked into the dispute between 1926 and 1935, different colours have been assigned to the respective claims on a map prepared by British surveyors:

- The boundary between Tehri-Garhwal state and Garhwal district of the United Provinces is shown in green.
- The boundary claimed by Tehri-Garhwal state is shown in red. It is the watershed between the western sources of the Bhagirathi river and the valley of the Sutlej river, known in Tibet as Langchen Khabab.
- The boundary claimed by Tibet is shown in yellow; their frontier claim is unclear at several places as the Tibetan representatives often claimed 'a single point as the boundary', that is the junction of the Gumgum Nala[3] with the Bhagirathi (one mile west of the Jangla Forest bungalow).

A Brief History of the Dispute

The dispute seems to have arisen when the Dzongpen[4] of Tsaparang, the nearby Tibetan district, visited the Gumgum Nala in 1914. He publically announced his decision to set up a boundary pillar near the bridge. When the local villagers objected, the Dzongpen left without any further action.

In 1918, Tehri state decided to erect three pillars on the top of the Tsang Chok La[5] (31.30 North and 79.16 East). Some versions claimed that the pillars had already been there in the past and were only 'repaired'.

Two years later, Tehri state surveyed the area and, for the first time, prepared cultivation maps of Nilang region (31.7 North and 79.4 East). The Jadhang Valley (31.11 North and 79.6 East) was also included in the maps.

3. A *nala* is a small stream.

4. The Dzongpen or Dzonpon can be called a district (Tibetan, Dzong) Commissioner. The *dzong* is an administrative area in Tibet. In Western Tibet, *dzongpens* were posted in Tsaparang, Daba and Purang (near the tri-junction Nepal, Tibet and India). After 1904, there was an Indian Trade Agent in Gartok looking after trade and related issues. A Garpon or Governor (for Western Tibet, known as Ngari Khorsum in Tibetan) was posted in Rutok.

5. 'La' is the Tibetan name for 'pass'.

In 1921, the Tsaparang Dzongpen visited Nilang again. This time, he sent a letter to the Raja of Tehri requesting him to send an official to sort out the boundary issue; at that time, it was not yet considered a 'dispute', it was more a 'difference of perceptions' between neighbours. The Raja answered that the issue had to be raised through the Government of India (GoI), as it involved a problem with two foreign governments.[6]

During the next warm season, the Dzongpen visited Nilang again and collected a tax of ₹1 from the local people of Nilang and Jadhang.[7] He thus collected a total of ₹300.

In 1924, it was finally proposed by British India to appoint a boundary commission, but due to poor communications and the fact that these areas could only be visited in the summer, the commission could meet only in the summer of 1926.

The Acton Commission

On 12 June 1926, T.J.C. Acton, an officer of the Indian Civil Service who had been nominated as the British representative, met Tibetan officials near the Gumgum Nala. The Tibetan representatives were Pishi Sunam Kunga, Postmaster General of Tibet and the Dzongpen of the Shekhar, a district near Mount Everest. They met near the small bridge over the *nala*.

Although the Tibetan representatives had no authority to negotiate any sort of compromise, they had received strict instructions from Lhasa to go to the Gumgum Nala and claim the bridge as the frontier of Tibet.

Later, Acton wrote in his report: "I had tea with them and talked the matter over, and offered to go back with them the next day to the Gumgum Nala and see the place claimed as the frontier. I did this."

The Tibetans claimed that the Tehri people had removed their boundary marks after they returned to Tibet. The two parties inspected an inscription in red paint on a cliff face, as well as some marks of an obliterated inscription (also in red paint), and a roughly

6. In this case, Tibet and British India.

7. Known as Jadhs.

rectangular crevice (about 9 inches by 6 inches) in the rock. One of the Tibetan witnesses affirmed that it had contained the base of a boundary pillar. However, there was no trace of the pillar.

Acton explains: "The existing inscription on the cliff was *Om na ma si dhang*[8] in Hindi[9] over a hieroglyphic in the form of a seven-pointed star." The British Commissioner commented that this could be an invocation to a deity, "it is commonly used by the people of these hills".

Both inscriptions on the rock were exposed to weather conditions; "it could not have lasted for more than a few years," thought the British representative, who added:

> Scratches on the four corners of the crevice in the rock seemed to show that a stone had been inserted in the crevice, but there was no sign of the stone and the place was in the middle of the path leading to the bridge and a small stone in such a position could not have been an ancient boundary pillar.

Acton thought that it was probable that a stone had been fixed during the Dzongpen's visit in 1914, it was then claimed as the boundary, while the obliterated inscription dated from a year before Acton's visit,[10] when a junior Tibetan official[11] of Tsaparang district came from Tibet. The Rupen affirmed that he saw the pillar at that time.

The British Commissioner commented: "Their attitude, I think, was that His Highness [His Holiness] the Dalai Lama had said that the boundary was the Gumgum Nala, and that any criticism of that decree would be a dangerous form of blasphemy."

Acton returned to Lamathatha (31.4 North and 79.1 East) the same day, and on 14 June, he went on to Nilang. The Tibetans joined him on 15 June.

---

8. *Om Mani Padme Hum*.

9. In Hindi or in Tibetan scripts.

10. In 1925.

11. The Rupen of Sarang.

The Proceedings of Acton Commission

From 16 June to 19 June 1926, the commission took evidence at Nilang and examined witnesses and documents on behalf of both the parties.

At first, the Tibetans produced only two witnesses; they said that they considered this sufficient, but later asked that 53 Jadhs should be examined. Then they further produced 6 more Tibetan witnesses.

The latter asserted that the frontier was at Gumgum Nala. They were unable to say how it ran from that point onwards and give a logical reason for their assertion. Acton noted that there were no boundary marks beyond the Gumgum Nala (towards Nilang) and it was not even alleged that such marks had ever existed. The Tibetans produced two witnesses from Bashahr who were termed as "false witnesses" by the commission: "The Bashahr State has a boundary dispute with the Tehri state and these witnesses are contradictory and undoubtedly biased."

The Tehri Darbar examined 12 witnesses, and 3 more were called by the commission.

The Tibetan government also produced a written statement stating their case. The atmosphere was cordial: "At Nilang, the Tibetan representatives came to tea with me twice and were most friendly," wrote Acton.

The Tibetan Position

On 20 June 1926, the Lhasa government addressed a letter to the Representative of the British government. We shall quote large portions of this letter as it shows the position of the Dalai Lama's administration in the dispute.

It has to be noted that Lhasa sent several letters to British authorities on this issue. The tone and content of the missives is more or less the same.

The Kashag in Lhasa wrote:

> This letter is being sent by [through] the Tibetan representatives. Nowadays as the British and Tibetan governments are on such friendly terms that they seem as if they are the brothers of the same

> parents, they have decided to settle the boundary dispute after consulting each other. And now, it is evident, that representatives have been sent from both sides for this purpose. So, if they desired that the dispute should be settled so as to prevent reoccurrences of disputes of this nature, Sang (Jadhang) and Tsong (Nilang) should continue to pay tax to the Tibetan government as before. And they should be kept under the administration of Chaprang [Tsaparang] Dzongpon. And in addition to these, an agreement promising that neither the Headmen nor the people of Sang (Jadhang) and Tsong (Nilang) will be troubled by any of the officers of the Tehri and Tibetan governments should be signed....Hoping a reply to this letter will be favoured. Sent on the 10th day of the 5th month of the Fire Tiger year.

The British Representative, T.J.C. Acton acknowledged the letter in the same polite way: "Thanks very much for the meat you sent for me and others with salaams. As regards your proposal of talking about the boundary at Hop, I am ever ready. Sent with a scarf."

At Nilang, the Tibetan representatives came twice for tea (British or Tibetan is not clear); they were said to be most friendly.

The Findings of Acton Commission

The commission was of the opinion that the Tehri Darbar was able to prove its possession of the area till Nilang, by doing some work on the deodar forest up to Gangotri, by building and repairing the pilgrim route to Gangotri, as well as supporting, repairing and managing the Gangotri temple and a bridle path and bridges as far as Karche (10 miles south of Nilang) and opening a school at Nilang.

On 19 June, the officials of the parties involved held some discussions and finally the British Commissioner prepared a draft report; Acton was still hoping that he could get the seal of Tibetan and Indian governments on a compromise.

He suggested a frontier similar to the one described by Surveyor Kinney in 1878; this would leave Nilang village with its cultivation (and grazing grounds) with Tehri state while Jadhang would go to Tibet. But a complication soon cropped up, Jadhang (and even Nilang) were also claimed by Bashahr state. We shall come back to this later.

Acton reported to his bosses in Delhi:

> I made the suggestion in the hope of getting a first settlement by agreement, but the Tibetan representatives had really, I think, definite instructions not to consider a compromise, and on further consideration of the evidence and having now seen the country beyond Nilang and beyond the passes I consider that a compromise would be unfair to Tehri and that the watershed frontier should be claimed.

Acton says that there was no evidence of any claim having been made before 1914, and no objection had ever come from the Tibetan government about the forest work and road construction carried out by the Tehri Darbar.

The commission left Nilang on 20 June and crossed over to Tibet via the Tsang Chok La on 27 June. The representatives could see the cairns alleged to have been erected by Madho Singh Bhandari in the time of the Kumaon Rajas of Chandpur, and the three pillars alleged to have been built (or repaired) in 1918. They took pictures of what Tehri considered indubitable proofs of its possession.

A day earlier, Acton had written to the Dzongpen to ask him if he wanted to present any further witnesses. He also suggested a meeting on 28 June, for a final discussion at a camping ground on the north-east of the pass. The Tibetans immediately said that they would be glad to do so, but they left in the opposite direction (towards Puling), some 20 miles inside Tibetan territory. On 29 June, they sent a letter saying that they had no other evidence to produce and had to proceed due to the 'lack of grazing and water':

> As we had nothing more to say except what we three and our witnesses had given evidences at Nilang (Tsongsa in Tibetan) and the orders of the Tibetan government regarding the unreasonable construction of the tall pillars by the Tehri [at Tsong Chok La], we did not wait for you at the top of the pass. At first, we expected that you would discuss about the boundary at Puling Sumdhor or Mandi, but afterwards we received a letter from your babu saying that you would talk about the boundary at Hop. Although we gave an affirmative reply to the above, we could not stay there as there was no grass for the animals. We intended to stay at Menthang Serpo, but the

water was not good, so we had to come to Puling. We have finished discussing or producing documents at Tsongsa (Nilang).

The conclusions of the Acton Commission were:

- The Tibetan claim to a frontier on the line of the Gumgum Nala is 'clearly absurd': "That line would include within Tibet not only the head waters of both branches of Bhagirathi river, but a large part of the deodar forest of these valleys, the upper 10 miles of the pilgrim route, and the temple of Gangotri."
- The Tibetans have no evidence to support such a claim. They have never had any interest in the management of the Gangotri temple; they have never attempted to work the forests, and they have never built or repaired any roads.
- The Gumgum Nala itself is a small and insignificant ravine on the right bank of the Bhagirathi. It cannot mark the frontier of a country. It is inconceivable that such a place should ever have been chosen as a frontier line between India and Tibet.
- There is however good evidence to show that the villagers of Nilang and Jadhang have for 120 years been much more under the control of the government of the Tehri state than under that of Tibet.

On 26 August 1926, the political agent for the Tehri-Garhwal state, wrote to the Chief Secretary to the Government of the United Provinces: "I had not much hope that the Tibetan representatives could or would agree to any settlement of the dispute", the United Provinces Government was happy that Acton's "very clear report leaves no doubt that we can back the Tehri claim with entire confidence in its justice."

He further commented: "The Tibetans claim is entirely vague: a particular point on the Nilang road is claimed." In this case however, "a frontier at the Gumgum Nala would apparently place the Gangotri temple in Tibet, a result which cannot even be considered."

The political agent mentioned a 'third alternative' of keeping Nilang in Tehri state and offering Jadhang to Tibet; he said that it would be a possible compromise, though it would result in putting Jadhang under Tibetan authorities, something "which the inhabitants do not desire".

The United Provinces government therefore suggested that Delhi should put pressure on the Tibetan government to accept Acton's conclusions.

In October, the Chief Secretary of the United Provinces while forwarding Acton's report said that the United Provinces' government agreed to the conclusions of the report and suggested "that his services should be suitably acknowledged".

Again he repeated that the Tibetan representatives only relied,

> on the assertion of superior authority[12] for the claim to a boundary at the exit of the Gumgum Nala.... They were unable to specify anything in the nature of a continuous boundary, they produced no evidence worth the name, they either could not or would not negotiate for a settlement by compromise.

He again listed the actions of Tehri Darbar to improve the facilities in the area and concluded:

> Mr. Acton has marshaled and discussed the Tehri evidence in sufficient detail, and it is unnecessary to recapitulate. He has also analyzed the ethnological, geographical and topographical aspects of the problem in its wider bearings and has in consequence recommended that negotiations with the Tibetan government be undertaken for the acceptance of the watershed boundary. This boundary would require no demarcation.

This obviously did not settle the issue as the government in Lhasa was not in a mood to drop its claim to Gumgum Nala so easily.

The Saga Continues

Two years later, on 14 November 1930, Colonel J.L.R. Weir, the Political Officer[13] Sikkim informed the Foreign Secretary in Delhi that he had received a letter from Lhasa about the Tibet-Tehri boundary question. Weir commented:

12. The Dalai Lama.

13. Known as PO.

> This Tehri boundary is one to which much importance is attached by the Tibetan government so much so that they paid me a special visit to discuss the matter the day before I left Lhasa.... Such a visit is contrary to Tibetan precedent and would only have been made in the matter of supreme importance in their eyes.

The Tibetan government which had done some homework in the meantime, produced three maps on which their claims were based:

- The Harmsworth Atlas and Gazetteer published in 1907.
- Map of the Manual of Colloquial Tibetan by C.A. Bell published in 1905.
- Philips New Series of Imperial Maps for Tourist and Travellers, India North Sheet (unknown publication date).

Weir admitted that though on a very small scale, the maps distinctly showed Nilang and Jadhang in Tibetan territory, the PO's commentary was that the Tibetan government was "not sufficiently advanced" to differentiate between maps published by the government and those published by other agencies: "Their reliance on the maps put forward by them can be readily understood. Their claim up to Gumgum Nala has been steadily maintained since the inception of this boundary dispute and I found it impossible to move them".

The fact remains that the map had been drawn by the British. The Tibetans had a point.

The letter from the Kashag[14] is dated the 25th day of the 8th month of the Iron Horse Year (17 October 1930). It states: "As this is a border question in accordance with ancient usage, the matter was put before the Tibetan National Assembly. The joint resolution, being that Jadhang and Nilung [Nilang] can be proved without a shadow of doubt to be within Tibetan territory."

It argues further: "Firstly our revenue dated Water Bird Year and kept at Tsaparang Zong [Dzong] has an account of the number of houses at Jadhang and Nilang and details of land tax to be paid in goods are as follows:

- 20 native bushels of barley.
- The complete bear's biles (used as medicine).

---

14. The Tibetan Cabinet.

- 400 maunds of areca tree leaves.
- 1000 bamboo sticks.
- Two confection of the barberry each larger than a hen's egg (yellow eye medicine).
- 800 sheets of small size white paper.
- 200 sheets of large size white paper.
- Necessary timber for a room with four pillars (size 23' x 23') including wooden pillars, 80 beams for making long and short cross beams.
- 80 planks including four large size planks for making doors
- 10 front and 10 rear panels for wooden pack saddles suitable for donkeys.
- 10 halters, etc."

The missive continues thus: "Therefore we maintain that the western border between Tehri and Tibet is the yellow boundary mark as shown in your recent map sent to us until the mark comes to Gumgoong [GumGum] bridge and Jangla Forest Bungalow."

It further defines the border: "From Gumgoong ridge the southern boundary runs up the river Jadahganga to Lamathatta, the territories being divided by the river, thence eastwards till it meets the red dotted line suggested by the Government of India and from that point the boundary is the same dotted line."

The Lhasa government announced a small compromise from its side: "If the boundary is determined as stated above it would be satisfactory as there would be no occasion for dispute in connection with the Hindu temple and Gangotri and Gaumuk because then they will both come within Tehri territory."

The Kashag requested the PO to communicate their new proposal to GoI to settle the issue "immediately".

For Colonel Weir, the PO: "The solution now offered by the Tibetan government is one which I think might reasonably be accepted by all parties. The area now claimed is mountainous in the extreme and presumably of little value and all claims to Gangotri and Gaumukh, which are sacred to the Hindus, are renounced by the Tibetans".

This is probably one of the reasons why Delhi decided to send Frederick Williamson to find out about the situation on the ground in Nilang.

The Frederick Williamson Inquiry

Colonel Weir was replaced by Frederick Williamson as the PO in 1932. During a tour in western Tibet from August to October 1932, Williamson was requested by GoI to look into the 'Tehri-Tibet' dispute. During his tour, he was accompanied by Frank Ludlow, an old Tibet hand. They met the Dzongpen of Tsaparang in Gartok and the latter accepted to accompany them to Nilang.

Although the Tehri Darbar was informed, they did not send a representative. Why? It is not clear, but Williamson said: "This was not a great consequence, as I was able to discuss the matter later with His Highness the Raja and his Dewan at Narendranagar."[15]

In his report, the PO mentions the Acton Report which "reported in favour of the watershed boundary claimed by Tehri, but the GoI considered that the evidence showed that Tibet was entitled to a frontier further to the west." He noted that even the Tibetan revised claim "leaves still in dispute a tract of country measuring 12 miles from north to south and some seven miles east to west."

Williamson commented, "with the exception of the north-west corner, this tract appeared to my untrained mind to be practically valueless. But the south-west corner contains valuable deodar forest."

The new PO was obviously very keen to find a solution and was ready to push for a compromise:

> The Tehri claim to the watershed frontier passing through Tsang Chok La has no more justification than the Tibetan claim to a frontier at Gumgum bridge. Any boundary pillars which Tehri may have erected were put up without the knowledge and consent of Tibet and cannot possibly have any validity.

The PO went through the same exercise that Acton did six years earlier; he met a number of witnesses who presented him their 'evidence'.

15. The summer capital of Tehri-Garhwal state.

His report says: "The Tibetans showed me the two old books which they had showed Mr. Acton, regarding the collection of certain revenue from these villages, and this revenue is still being collected in the form of a cash payment of 74 rupees a year."[16]

Although the Tehri Darbar's representative was not present, he could collect some information from the local Jadhs: "I understand that Tehri also has, for many years, collected 24 rupees a year from these villages. The Tehri Darbar claim that the Tibetan tax is a trade tax. It seems to me, however, that both taxes are exactly on the same footing and that one is a land tax just as much as the other."

He however admitted that: "The Tibetans have not been able to produce any evidence showing that they have actually administered Nilang and Jadhang but, under their system of Government, records are not regularly kept in the way they are in Tehri."

Frederick Williamson elaborated further on the Tibetan compromise: "when it was pointed out to the Tibetan government that their original plan, as understood, would include within their frontiers the shrines of Gangotri and Gaumukh, they dropped this part of their claim and stated that they would accept a frontier following the yellow line on the map from its northern extremity to Gumgum bridge or Jangla forest bungalow."

There is no doubt that Williamson was keen to find a compromise which could be acceptable to Lhasa. He wrote: "Even, however, if this is true[17] (and there is a strong suspicion, though no real proof, that this is true) that does not make it a boundary pillar any more than the Tehri pillars on the Tsang Chok La."

It is correct, though in those days there was not a single place on the Indo-Tibetan border where the abornment process had been done by both parties. Customary borders were an accepted arrangement.

This sometimes led to dispute like in the case under study.

What is more interesting for a study of the Himalaya is Williamson's observation that the people of Nilang and Jadhang look more Garwahlis than Tibetans. Williamson adds: "This is mainly due

16. See list given in the letter from the Kashag.

17. That the Tibetans had planted a pillar in 1914 near Gumgum bridge.

to their dress. If they were to be put into Tibetan clothes, many of them would easily pass as Tibetans. They are of course a transition people. ... The country down as far as Nilang is Tibetan in aspect. The question of administrative control is not, I think, very important."

An important point was that the Jadhs spent 7 months in a year in Garwahl: "The passes are closed for only 5 months in the years. During these five months no inhabitants are left at Nilang and Jadhang except one or two old men. The rest all move down to Tehri territory," the PO wrote.

Further, they wore Garwahli dresses; for Williamson: "They seem to speak Hindi, Tibetan and some dialect of their own, which is rather allied to Tibetan, with equal facility. But they always write Hindi. None of them called the Tsang Chok La by its Hindi name of 'Jelukhaga'."

The Jadhs' seasonal migration is interesting: "When they move down to the lower valley they call in Brahmins and give any children born there Hindu names. It is most important that these villagers who are peaceful and amiable people, should not be troubled by either side."

It is the case of several communities from the Himalaya which often belonged to two worlds: the Tibetan and the sub-continent.

What was of utmost importance in the PO's mind was the welfare of the local people who had lived for centuries without bothering about the two governments' more recent claims. Williamson says: "It is most necessary that the Tehri Darbar should continue to permit them to go down the valleys in the winter as they do at present and where, of course, they will be entirely under Tehri's jurisdiction".

The 'Tibetan aspect' did not mean much, as it could be argued that Ladakh too has a 'Tibetan aspect'. Does that make it a part of Lhasa territory?

Once again Williamson pleaded Tibet's cause:

> Tibet really has a system of administration and these very amenable people can easily be controlled by Tibet during the time they stay at their higher villages. In these days when everyone is over-administered, they will not be so fortunate as to be left without administrative control.

However, the Tibetans continued to stick to their position, though, after a meeting with a senior Tibetan official, Williamson wrote in his report:

> I did not think I should be able to get the Tibetan government all they wanted, and asked how he would review a solution on these lines. His reply was non-committal. He had of course no power to agree to anything himself and did not know what his Government would say. He reiterated that the frontier was at Gumgum bridge.

Most of the objections from the Tehri state were brushed aside:

> Tehri have stated that they would have to abandon a school and a customs post at Nilang if it were given to Tibet. The school is not there now and was, I understand, not maintained for long. The customs post was a trade registration post maintained at the expense of the Government of India. Such a post does not necessarily imply that its site is within the frontiers of India, as we maintained one for many years at Yatung in Tibet.

The situation of the Yatung post was entirely different in the sense that since 1904, British India was entitled to three trade agencies in Tibet and Yatung was one of them. It cannot be compared to Nilang.

Williamson rightly remarked that "feeling on both sides is at present a little hostile and it is necessary that this dispute should be ended in order to restore local friendly relations."

This probably explains his keenness to find a quick solution. His final conclusions were:

- We should adhere to Kinney's frontier line, with a slight deviation so as to include in Tibet the whole of the fields irrigated by Kinney's frontier stream. We should inform Tibet that, as they admit themselves, an annual tax of ₹24 has been taken from the villages of Nilang and Jadhang by the Tehri Darbar for many years. This being an old tax and a matter of immemorial custom, should be allowed, to continue.
- I do not think there will be any objection to asking the Tibetan government not to collect more than their old customary tax of ₹74 a year from the Jadhs.

- My whole object in this suggestion is to see that these unfortunate people do not suffer. Tibet will certainly not oppress them, generally speaking, but they might occasionally demand another exceptional tax such as they collected in 1921.

Once his tour completed, Williamson returned to Lhasa and Gangtok.

The issue then got further complicated by the hardening of the dispute between Bashahr and Tehri over Nilang. Delhi decided that it had to be tackled first.

Objections from Tehri State

While the Tibetan stand remained the same during the following years, Tehri state was not happy with Williamson's conclusions.

The United Provinces' Chief Secretary, J.K. Clay wrote a note of objection after getting the Williamson report. As Clay put it:

> Throughout this note Mr. F. Williamson shows himself to be biased in favour of Tibet and the Governor in Council observes with regret that he has given scant attention to the arguments contained in Mr. Acton's report, arguments which appear to the Governor in Council to be at least as convincing as those used by Mr. Williamson.

Perhaps more importantly, Clay raised the issue of precedence for the rest of the Indo-Tibet border:

> It is also very necessary that the Tibetan government should agree not to use any precedent created by the settlement of this dispute at any other point on their frontier. More especially they should agree not to make the settlement a pretext for re-opening the dispute about the frontier between Tibet and British India in the north of the Garhwal and Almora districts. This dispute reached an acute phase about 30 years ago when it was actually necessary to send a small body of British troops up to the Tibetan frontier.

Retrospectively, keeping in mind the difficulties solving what has become the Sino-Indian border, it was a wise point made by the Chief Secretary of the United Provinces.

Had the Government of India agreed to Williamson's proposal, the Chinese People's Liberation Army would today be based a few kilometres from Gangotri. One can imagine the strategic and other consequences of its presence.

Clay pointed out further:

> Though this dispute has not since been heard of it may be conjectured, from the experience of the present dispute with Tehri, that the other dispute with the British Government is merely in a state of suspended animation and, given a favorable opportunity, may possibly be raised once more in the future. It seems therefore desirable that it should be clearly agreed by the Tibetan government, if and when the present dispute is settled, that it should not be taken to be a pretext or precedent for re-opening the disputed boundary question on the Almora and Garhwal border.

This was indeed a serious objection. In 1960, during the border talks between India and China, the Indian negotiators for the first time realised the wisdom of these remarks.

A New Commission

To complicate the matter further, the dispute between the Tehri and Bashahr Darbars in the neighbourhood of Nilang took a bitter turn. There was no question of settling the boundary dispute with Tibet as long as the internal issue between the two princely states was not solved. A commission was therefore appointed to make recommendations about the 'ownership' or at least the possession of these remote mountain areas.

Two officers were nominated to jointly decide the issue. They were E.A.R. Eustace, Superintendent, Hill States, Shimla and R.H. Williamson, Political Agent for Tehri-Garhwal. The latter has no relation with the PO in Sikkim (Frederick Williamson), who had visited the area two years earlier.

On 28 September 1934, the commissioners first met in Narendranagar, the winter capital of the Tehri-Garhwal state. The Superintendent of the Shimla Hill States, who had left Shimla at short notice, was not accompanied by the representative of Bashahr; he was himself unaware of the details of their claims. The Tehri-Garhwal Darbar refused to depute a representative to accompany the commissioner unless he was told of Bashahr claims.

On 7 October, both officers were finally joined half way to Nilang by Mian Daulat Ram, the Bashahr representative. The Tehri-Garhwal Darbar then agreed to depute a representative by 22 October with all the documents supporting his state's claim.

The commission reached Nilang on 10 October. They stayed there for a week, studying the maps and the topography of the place and returned to Uttarkashi on 18 October. The formal enquiry was conducted at Uttarkashi on 25 and 26 October, but after the Bashahr Darbar argued that they had not been given sufficient time to prepare their case and also due to the fact that the Tehri representative did not have all documents with him, the final enquiry was only conducted on 27 and 28 February 1935.

The terms of reference given by the Foreign and Political Department in Delhi were: to find out whether "in view of the change of site (of the village of Nilang) the Raja of Bashahr is still in position to claim that the present site is within his territories".

For GoI, it was clear that: "Any attempt to raise the international issue before a decision has been reached as to the Indian State which may be entitled to claim jurisdiction over this tract would necessarily weaken the position of the Government of India in negotiations with Tibet".

The commission had therefore to decide the ownership and possession of the tract of land between Tehri-Garhwal and Bashahr in the neighbourhood of Nilang.

The commissioners knew that the two states claimed not only Nilang village but also "the whole of and the other a portion of the Jadh Ganga valley." They decided: "We, therefore, propose to adjudicate on the conflicting claims in their entirety and not merely on a dispute as to the ownership of Nilang itself".

One first strange finding was that Nilang was not on the side of the river as it appeared on the maps. The report of this commission says:

> Every survey map which we have seen places the village on the right bank. Mr. Kinney, a surveyor, who visited Nilang in 1878 stated that the houses were on the right bank of the Jadh Ganga while the field of the village were on the left; Mr. Acton in his report of 1926 was

> informed by certain Tehri witnesses that the *abadi* [population] had been moved some years earlier to the left bank from the right bank on account of the danger of falling stones.

The report further asserted that the Government of India "is disposed to accept the above theory".

However on the spot, the commission's observations (supported by photographs) tend to prove that:

> it is improbable that Nilang *abadi* was ever situated on the right bank. There is no visible trace of any *abadi* on the right bank and the bank itself is precipitous cliff except at one point where it shelves slightly before falling again steeply to the river. The river itself cuts deep into the rock, and clearly cannot have changed its course.

Like Acton and Frederick Williamson had done earlier, Estache and R.H. Williamson described the inhabitants:

> The Jadhs, who are a small but distinct tribe of frontier graziers and traders, have 2 villages named Nilang and Jadhang in the Jadh Ganga valley; these villages contain *pucca* houses, and are considered by the Jadhs as their regular home. They are however only occupied for about 3 months in the year, and during the remaining months the tribe moves down slowly grazing through the lands of the other villages in Thaknor, which in summer graze in the Jadh Ganga valley, to 2 other settlements which they have at Harsil in the Bhagirathi valley about 20 miles below Nilang, and at Dunda about another 30 miles further down the same valley.

Regarding the claims, the Tehri-Garhwal claim included the entire valley of the Jadh Ganga and its tributaries on both the banks, while Bahsar claimed the western part of the area.

They studied the different maps of the area, particularly a map attached to an Emerson-Barker report of 1912 based on a survey conducted in 1859 by Mulherson, Shelverton, Dyer, Peyton, Johnson and Brown.

They also presented the map prepared by Kinney in 1878, which gave the same north and south international boundary with Tibet as does the Atlas sheet of 1859 passing through Nilang. It shows Nilang on the right bank of the Jadh Ganga river. Bashahr state produced the maps of Nilang and Jadhang villages prepared at the settlement of 1892.

The commissioners added: "The Tehri settlement map has been checked by us as regards its general features with conditions on the spot, and we have no doubt that it correctly represents the present position."

That was to be taken into account.

The Copper Plate

Another document had a direct bearing on the 'ownership' of the area. It was an engraved copper plate which was presented to the commission by the Bashahr Dabar. The report said:

> This purports to be an agreement dated S. 1723 [1667 A.D.] bearing the seal of Raja Prithwi Pati Shah of Garhwal, and the names of 10 Tehri witnesses. In recites a treaty between the two states for purposes of mutual defense, and goes on to say that the northern boundary of Tehri shall in future be at a point below Harsil.

Tehri refused the evidence on the ground that the dating of the plate was doubtful, "though to the layman there seems nothing suspicious about it," wrote one commissioner who added that if the decision had to be taken on the basis of the copper plate "it would be useful if the opinion of the proper officer of the archaeological department [could be ascertained]" about the map's apparent genuineness. Moreover, the plate was dated S. 1723 with the seal of Raja Prithwi Pati Shah of Garhwal, while in the United Provinces' official 'manual of titles', the same raja is supposed to have died five years earlier.

Although the Tehri Darbar had 'no opinion' on the date, the existence of the plate complicated the issue even further.

On 5 March 1935, R.H. Williamson gave his conclusions. He believed that:

> On the evidence before us the claim of Tehri state to sovereignty over the Jadhs and the area in dispute must be considered in every way stronger that have not been able to produce that evidence of past administration which is detailed in the Acton report, but even so it must be held that the long record of revenue assessment of the

> Jadhs and their village Nilang the use by other Tehri subjects of the Jadhganga valley as a grazing ground, the residence of the Jadhs for more than half the year in Tehri territory, the mass of records of jurisdiction by Tehri Courts, the maintenance of communications along the Jadhganga valley up to Nilang by Tehri state—all this must override the claim of Bashahr which is based mainly on periodical levies and fines such as a trading community might well be subject to from more authorities than one.

E.A.R. Eustace, the Superintendent, Hill States, Shimla, based his conclusions on the Hodgson and Herbert's map and other evidence such as the Tehri map of 1902 as well as the political boundary between Bashahr and Tehri-Garhwal 'settled' by Emerson and Barker in their report of 20 June 1912 (this was accepted by the Punjab government) and finally, the engraved copper plate put forward by Bashahr relating to an agreement dating 1667 AD with the seal of Raja Prithwi Pati Shah which would leave Nilang/Jadhang to Bashahr.

The Superintendent of Hill States separately gave his conclusion, in view of his differing arguments:

> By virtue of the copper plate of A.D. 1667 (if genuine) and in view of Hodgson and Herbert's map and the Tehri state map of 1902, it does seem that Bashahr may originally have had a good claim to Nilang and Jadhang. I also think that the correspondence of 1872 between the Raja of Bashahr, the Superintendent Hill States and Sir Henry Ramsay, the Commissioner of Kumaon, does suggest that the title of Bashahr over Nilang and Jadhang was at that time admitted. There is however no doubt that since 1892 Bashahr have really taken no interest in Nilang and Jadhang which since 1920 have definitely been administrated by Tehri, and I agree with Mr. Williamson that the interest of the Jadhs are now entirely bound up with Tehri in trade as in everything else. In the circumstances I can see no sufficient ground for assigning these villages to Bashahr and I consider that they should be assigned to Tehri.

On 14 March, the Political Agent for Tehri-Garhwal state, Bareilly wrote to the Chief Secretary of the Government of United Provinces about the joint report. He commented:

> The findings, though separate, have a single result, namely, a recommendation that all the territory in dispute with the exception of a small area known as the Chor Gad on the right bank of the river Jadhganga, opposite to Nilang itself, be awarded to Tehri-Garhwal State. The area in dispute is taken to include the whole valley of the Jadhganga from its source of Gartaga and not merely the village and adjoining cultivation of Nilang and its hamlet Jadhang.

One part of the dispute was now settled. Unfortunately, as we shall see, the two parties (British India and Tibet) did not pursue the issue further due to other reasons.

The Following Years

The 13th Dalai Lama passed away in 1933, two years before the internal dispute between Tehri and Bashahr states could be settled. After the demise of their leader, the Tibetans' priorities changed. The Lhasa government was now busy with the search of the new Dalai Lama (who took birth in 1935 and was discovered a couple of years later). During this period, the Tibetans continued their 'tax collection' incursions in the Nilang area and even issued *parwana*.[18]

At the end of 1935, Frederick Williamson fell sick while on an official tour in Tibet and he passed away on 17 November. The person who knew best the 'dispute' was no more.

A year later, Williamson was replaced by Basil Gould as the PO. When he visited Lhasa in 1936, the main issue was Tawang and the North East Frontier Agency (NEFA). It would occupy the Tibetan Kashag and the British authorities in Sikkim for the next 10 years. It was a far more serious issue for both the parties which culminated with the visit of Hopkinson to Lhasa at the end of 1945.

Later, during World War II, the British had more urgent matters to deal with than the ownership of Nilang/Jadhang. The issue was left to be tackled by the government of independent India.

---

18. An official document; in this case, requesting *corvee* and other services.

Some Conclusions

The dispute is interesting at several levels.

First, the dispute is typical of a border dispute in the Himalaya for the simple reasons that a number of areas/places belonged to two separate worlds, the Tibetan and the Indian. However facts such as ethnicity and customs, tend to prove that the villagers of Nilang and Jadhang were Bhotias.[19] For centuries, they moved freely from and to Tibet; the trade was still unhindered.

Another observation is that during the time of our main study,[20] Tibet was an independent state dealing with another independent state (Great Britian) as an equal without referring to the Chinese government. During this period, there was not even a Chinese representative in Lhasa; the Nationalist Government probably never got informed of the 'dispute' and the subsequent talks between Lhasa and Delhi.

For the Tibetan government, Nilang was a question of prestige, mostly because the Dalai Lama had stated that the Gumgum bridge was the border. There was therefore no question of compromising on this issue.

Williamson was probably wrong when he believed that the Tibetans were only interested in securing trade. It need not have changed much for the trade between Tehri and Tibet had the border been one side or another. In fact the status quo, allowed both states to have a convenient place of exchange both for Indian and the Tibetan traders and both local administrations could have continued to tax the local grazers and traders.

---

19. According to Wikipedia, the Bhotias (or Bhotiyas): "are groups of ethno-linguistically Tibetan people living in the trans-Himalayan region that divides India from Tibet, and were originally a hill tribe. Their name, Bhotiya, derives from the word Bod (Bodyul), which is the Classical Tibetan name for Tibet. The ancient language of Bot people is Boti. The Bot people are closely related to the Sikkimese Bhutia, the main ethno-linguistic group of Northern Sikkim that speaks the Sikkimese (Bhutia) language. They are also closely related to the Uttarakhand Bhotiya, several groups in the upper Himalayan valleys of the Kumaon and Garhwal of Uttarakhand Himalaya. These include the Shaukas of Kumaon and Tolchhas and Marchhas of Garhwal." The Jadhs of Nilang should be added to this list.

20. Between the early 1920s and 1935.

Epilogue

The *rapport de force* changed after the Chinese invaded Tibet in 1950-51. India had a new neighbour. Although it took some years for the Communists to get acquainted with the intricacies of the border area, India knew that it had to move fast.

The occupation of Nilang remains shrouded in secrecy. It is probably an outcome of the Himmatsinghji Committee[21] which prepared a report sent in two parts to GoI.

The first part consisted of its recommendations regarding Sikkim, Bhutan, NEFA and the Eastern Frontier bordering Burma; it was submitted in April 1951. The second part contained the recommendations on the borders in Ladakh, Punjab, Uttar Pradesh (UP) and Nepal and was submitted in September 1951. One of the actions suggested by the committee appears to be that areas such as Tawang and Nilang should be immediately occupied by the Indian forces.

Already in May 1950, the Ministry of External Affairs has sent a note to the Ministry of Defence asking the latter to comment on the feasibility of occuping the Nilang/Jadhang area. The PO in Sikkim had said: "the guiding principle in the new circumstances[22] must however be the Government of India's ability to vindicate what they would regard as the appropriate frontier, since it would be idle to claim territory which could not be effectively protected or controlled."

On 4 April 1950, the Ministry of Defence answered:[23]

> We are required to comment in the proposal with reference to the remark made by the PO.... The area under dispute is an extremely difficult country physically and climatically with hardly any communications. It therefore follows that operations in the area will have to be confined to short periods and undertaken by specially trained infantry organized on an ad hoc basis with very scanty artillery support and no support whatsoever from either tanks or

21. Also known as the North and North East Border Defence Committee.

22. Does it mean that the PO (Harishwar Dayal) knew that China would occupy Tibet a few months later?

23. National Archives of India: Ministry of External Affairs, file no. 2-2689-NEF/50.

aircraft. The administrative problems connected with an operation would be considerable. Even if the defence area were narrowed down to the protection of the villages Nilang and Jadhang, with the present resources of the army, it would be well nigh impossible to guarantee the integrity of the above villages. It will be equally difficult to afford hundred per cent protection to the small inhabited localities lying with the Indian frontier within the Indian frontier in this area.

The Ministry of Defence's conclusion was: "Whatever solution the E.A. [External Affairs] Ministry adopt, it would be subject to the conditions set out above so far as the defence of the frontier will be concerned."

A few years later,[24] Beijing started claiming five areas in the central sector of the now Sino-Indian border.

On 2 May 1956, the Ministry of External Affairs wrote to the Counsellor in the Chinese Embassy in Delhi about a Chinese intrusion in the Nilang area. It protested:

> We have learnt with surprise and regret from the Commander of our Border Security Force at Nilang that 12 Chinese soldiers including one officer equipped with tommy and sten guns and telescopes were sent half a mile east of Nilang at 12.30 hours of 28th April [1956].[25]

The Ministry clarified:

> Nilang at the area right up to Tsang Chok La pass is clearly within Indian territory and has always been in our possession. We have, therefore instructed the Officer Commanding our Border Security Force in Nilang to inform the Chinese officer to leave Indian territory immediately.

On 8 September 1959, Zhou Enlai the Chinese premier took the issue with Jawaharlal Nehru, his Indian counterpart:

> Concerning the section of the boundary between the Ari [Ngari] Area of China's Tibet and India. It can be seen from your letter that you also agree that this section of the boundary has not been formally

24. In the mid-1950s.

25. Notes, Memoranda and letters Exchanged and Agreements signed between the Governments of India and China 1954-1959 (White Paper I—1954-1959), Ministry of External Affairs, Government of India. *http://www.claudearpi.net/maintenance/uploaded_pics/WhitePaper1.pdf.*

> delimited by the two countries. Not only so, there have in fact been historical disputes between the two sides over the right to many places in this area. For example, the area of Sang and Tsungsha, southwest of Tsaparang Dzong in Tibet, which had always belonged to China, was thirty to forty years back gradually invaded and occupied by the British. The local authorities of China's Tibet took up this matter several times with Britain, without any results. It has thus become an outstanding issue left over by history.[26]

During the 1960 talks, the issue of Nilang came back several times on the table, but India stuck to its position that Tsang Chok La was the border, therefore its occupation of Nilang was fully legal.

It is still the position today.

---

26. Notes, Memoranda and letters Exchanged and Agreements signed between the Governments of India and China. Correspondence Nehru-Zhou (White Paper IV—Sept. 1959-March 1960). *http://www.claudearpi.net/maintenance/uploaded_pics/Correspondence_Zhou_Nehru_Sept-Nov59.pdf.*

6

SUNANDA K. DATTA-RAY

Sikkim can be put in India but Tibet can't be Taken out of Sikkim

But for the fortunes of the Great Game in the eastern Himalaya, Sikkim might have been a part of China today. On 16 October 1947, two months after India became independent, the Dalai Lama's government cabled New Delhi asking for what it called the restoration of a wide swathe of territory from Ladakh to Assam. The list included Sikkim. As Percy Brown (1944) wrote in *Tours in Sikkim and Darjeeling District*:

> In religion, in politics and in social matters, the people of Sikhim have been guided by the authorities of Lhasa, and all the institutions of the state were based largely on those of Tibet. The Sikhim Buddhists refer to the Dalai Lama on all important secular matters, and the aristocracy, having allied themselves matrimonially with Tibetan families, have accordingly vested interests in the larger country.

The opportunistic economics of 19th century colonialism weakened Sikkim's historical umbilical chord. Political developments aggravated the process. Politics may even have influenced economics. Whatever the sequence and despite a heavy dilution of traditional ties, the idea of Tibet (though under serious threat in Tibet itself) remains almost as closely wedded today to the idea of Sikkim as it was in the years of which Percy Brown wrote. Sikkim's non-Tibetan majority finds it more than ever necessary to cling to the Tibetan legacy for its own survival as a distinct entity in India. That is what Nar Bahadur Bhandari, the first Hindu, ethnic Nepalese Chief Minister, meant when he said, as quoted in *Smash and Grab: Annexation of Sikkim* (Datta-Ray, 2013), that Sikkim had "merged but would not be submerged." Only the notion of their Tibetan anchorage enables Sikkim's Nepalese to stand aloof from the aggressively sweeping tide of Nepalese nationalism that characterises the Gorkhaland movement south of the Rangpo border.

Until it became an Indian state in 1975, Sikkim was bracketed with neighbouring Bhutan. Bhutan's status is a separate subject but some discussion is unavoidable, as both kingdoms were regarded as fragments of Tibet's cultural empire. Although the institution of the Shabdrung (priest-king) may have recalled Tibet's incarnate lamas, Ngawang Namgyal, who arrived in Bhutan in 1616 and became the first Shabdrung (1594–1651), was a refugee from Tibet's sectarian persecution and endeavoured to create a distinctly Bhutanese identity. Undoubtedly, there were many cultural, social and religious similarities, but the dual system of government and the concealment of the Shabdrung's death for 54 years seem uniquely Bhutanese. The Druk kingdom's sturdy independence made for latent feelings of suspicion and mistrust so that "warfare remained the normal condition between Bhutan and Tibet during the 17th and 18th centuries" as Thierry Mathou noted in his essay, "The Growth of Diplomacy in Bhutan 1961-1991: Opportunities and Challenges" in Michael Aris and Michael Hutt's (1994) *Bhutan: Aspects of Culture and Development*. Bhutan's first essay in modernity—the hereditary monarchy created in 1907 under British auspices—was a major break from the Tibetan-influenced past.

Priding themselves on their exceptionalism, the Bhutanese do not talk of the iron-chain suspension bridges that Thangtong Gyalpo, a Tibetan saint who visited Bhutan during the 15th century, built. But they do show visitors the ruins of Drukgyel Dzong that Ngawang Namgyal built in 1649 to commemorate the rout of an invading Tibetan army. The embers of ancient hostility stirred again in 1974 when Bhutan's royal family accused the third king's Tibetan mistress, Yangki, of conspiring to set her son on the throne. She was supposed to have been in league with Tibetan refugees. Even the Dalai Lama's brother, Gyalo Thondup, was implicated.

As a sovereign kingdom, Bhutan had a practical reason for distancing itself from Tibet. Thierry Mathou reminds us that the Dalai Lama's cable was not Lhasa's first attempt to claim suzerain rights, although "there is no evidence of Tibet ever having practically implemented its rule in Bhutan." By repudiating Tibet's claims lock, stock and barrel, Bhutan's perspicacious Wangchuck kings and their astute pro-British Dorji aides ensured that China, whose position in the Himalaya rested on Tibet's, had no case either.

Playing down the Tibetan connection, Lyonpo Dawa Tsering, Bhutan's Foreign Minister from 1972 to 1998, one of the longest-serving in the world, emphasised that unlike Sikkimese royals and aristocrats, the Bhutanese did not seek spouses in Tibet. Prime Minister Jigmie Dorji, whose sister was the third king's wife, did marry a Tibetan aristocrat, Tsering Yangzom (Tess-la), but that was a love match. In contrast, every *chogyal* of Sikkim had a Tibetan *gyalmo*. John Claude White, British India's first Political Officer (PO) in Gangtok (1889-1908), with responsibility for relations with Sikkim, Bhutan and Tibet, blamed his problems with Thutob Namgyal, the 9th *chogyal*, on the influence of his Tibetan mother and wife, the latter entertaining an "exaggerated idea of the importance of Tibet and China." However, since both were declining powers, the connection suited the British who were not at all pleased when Thutob Namgyal's forward-looking son, Sidkeong Namgyal (also called Sidkeong Tulku), the 10th *chogyal*, wanted to broaden his horizons through a Japanese or Burmese bride. The beautiful Sangey Deki, first wife of the last *chogyal*, Palden Thondup Namgyal, was also Tibetan, a member of the family of the 7th Dalai Lama. His two sisters married into the families of the 8th and 12th Dalai Lamas.

His mother's Ragashar clan was so exalted that it did not need a title and was said to be the only family with unbroken descent in the male line since the Tibetan state was created. They enjoyed the unique privilege of honouring their dead with silver effigies. Gyalum's father, captain for life of the Dalai Lama's bodyguard, did not think Sir Tashi Namgyal, the 11th *chogyal*, good enough to be his son-in-law. Sikkim was too small, too far from the power centre of Lhasa, and too much under British influence. The marriage was arranged while he was travelling and there was no way he could break it on his return.

There was another peculiarly Sikkimese connection. The elder branch of the Namgyal dynasty had stayed on in Tibet where they governed the small principality of Taring near Gyantse. Tsotra, the line's founder, was Thutob Namgyal's eldest son. When he did not respond to the invitation to return and live in Gangtok, Claude White had him removed from the line of succession. His descendants continued in Taring (with the British title of *raja* bestowed in 1922) until Jigme Sumchen Wangpo Namgyal joined the 14th Dalai Lama in his Indian exile.

One feature common to Sikkim and Bhutan was that both owned enclaves in Tibet. They called them sovereign states but New Delhi described them as estates. Bhutan's eight enclaves in western Tibet, Darchen being the biggest, were all monasteries around Mount Kailash that the Ladakh kings (who ruled the region at one time) had bequeathed to the Drukpa Kargyupa sect. There was continuous friction between the Bhutanese and Tibetans over taxes and other administrative matters, with Bhutan's rulers appealing to British India for help. The position remained ambiguous until 1959 when Mao Zedong's People's Liberation Army seized the enclaves (as they did those that belonged to Ladakh too) without compensation. Historian, Parmanand, was probably referring to Zhou Enlai's talks with Jawaharlal Nehru in New Delhi when he wrote in *The Politics of Bhutan*, "On Bhutan's behalf India raised the question of the Bhutanese enclaves with China in 1960, but the latter refused to discuss the issue." It is not known whether the enclaves were discussed during the 19 rounds of direct Bhutan-China negotiations on Bhutan's 470 km northern border that have taken place since 1984. The circumspect Lyonpo Dawa asked me more than once not to write about the enclaves. He feared any mention might create the 'wrong impression' in Beijing and New Delhi.

The *chogyal* was never so tactful, and freely discussed Sikkim's enclaves whose status was similarly disputed. Although some British writers believe Lhasa recognised Gangtok's sovereignty over the enclaves, India regarded them as the royal family's personal estates. Chumbi with its palace and the two ancient monasteries of Bhakcham and Kirungtsal, administered by a Sikkimese headman designated Chumbi Adow, was always a bone of contention. It passed out of Gangtok's effective management when the Tibetans prevented the Sikkimese delegate from reaching Phari in time for an arbitration hearing, whereupon the *Amban*, imperial China's representative in Lhasa, delivered an *ex parte* judgement in Tibet's favour. The durbar demanded restitution after the Younghusband expedition, and Sidkeong Tulku pressed Sir Charles Bell, the PO, to take up Chumbi's status at the 1914 Shimla convention. But the British would not tolerate any change in the 1890 Anglo-Chinese convention which recognised Sikkim as a British protectorate and Chumbi as Chinese. That arrangement was made over the heads (behind the backs) of Tibet and Sikkim, the principal countries affected. To cite *Smash and Grab*, "the self-styled Kaiser-i-Hind (as Queen Victoria was proclaimed) and the tottering Son of Heaven might as well have agreed between themselves that Germany had no right to the moon."

Of the enclaves that remained, Sohar, "resting place of the patron lama," was the most important. But there was Taring too, and also about 150 square miles covering Chokar, Teling and Nyentse under Doptha's jurisdiction. The Phari Kutsap, as the durbar's representative was styled, administered this tract. Doptha-pas regularly and freely travelled to Gangtok to pay homage to the ruler and deposit their land revenues in the durbar treasury. In addition to being exempt from Tibetan land rent and customs levies on wool, salt and other items, Doptha-pas were not subject to military service or forced labour in Tibet. They enjoyed grazing rights in northern Sikkim.

Sikkimese history is far more closely woven than Bhutan's with Tibet. Legend has it that Tibet's first king Neh-Thi-Tsenpo (born circa 416 BC) descended from a Namgyal ancestor, Indrabodhi, who ruled what is now the Indian state of Himachal Pradesh. According to Claude White's (2008) *Sikkim and Bhutan: Twenty-one Years on the North-east Frontier 1887-1908*, Ti-son-desen, great-great grandson of another Tibetan king, Songtsen Gampo, founded the small kingdom of Kham in eastern Tibet in the 8th century. An offspring of this line, Khye-Bumsa, "the superior of ten thousand heroes," travelled to Sikkim in the 13th century. Other members of the family "found their way back to Tibet, where they rose to high positions." One branch went to Ladakh where descendants of Tibet's royal family survive to this day.

After Khye-Bumsa died in Chumbi valley, his third son, Mipon Rab ('leader of men') moved to Gangtok where he was acknowledged chieftain. He was succeeded by Guru Tashi whose great-grandson, Phuntsog Namgyal (born 1604), was consecrated as the first king of Sikkim in 1642.

Modern history begins with this monarch. It is said that three Tibetan lamas, Lhatsun Chempo, Sempah Chempo and Rigdsin Chempo ('the three superior ones'), met at Yoksam in the middle of the 17th century to convert Sikkim to Buddhism. "Here are we three lamas in a new and irreligious country," said Lhatsun Chempo. "We must have a dispenser of gifts (king) to rule the country on our behalf." Men of god being no less ambitious than laymen, Rigdsin at once proposed himself, being heir to a celebrated governor. Sempah promptly disputed the claim because he was of royal birth. Lhatsun then intervened:

> In the prophecy of Guru Rimpoche it is written that four noble brothers shall meet in Sikkim and arrange for its government. We are three of these come from the north, west and south. Towards the east it is written, there is at this epoch a man named Phuntsog, a descendant of brave ancestors of Kham in eastern Tibet. According, therefore, to the prophecy of the guru we should find him.

Phuntsog was given Lhatsun Chempo's family name of Namgyal and invested with the title of *chogyal* or the *gyalpo* (king) who upholds the *chhos* (righteousness). The Dalai Lama sent greetings to the "ruler of the sacred land of the southern slopes" and presented him with Guru Rimpoche's mitre and a valuable sand image. Tibet's claim of suzerain rights was possibly rooted in this source of the first king's title. Ippolito Desideri, the Jesuit priest who journeyed to Lhasa in 1716, called Sikkim a "province" of Tibet "subject to the emperor of China", like Phari, Haldibaari and Purnea in *An Account of Tibet: The Travels of Ipplito Desideri of Pistola, S.J., 1712-1727*. Tsugphud Namgyal, the 7th *chogyal*, submitted all his disputes with Lhasa to the *Amban*. He received a Chinese button of rank, and executed a document in 1880 promising that "in good and evil we will not leave the shelter of the feet of China and Tibet".

Relations were never as simple or clear-cut as the three-tier—Sikkim-Tibet-China—hierarchy implied. Tibet's political ties with China were not a constant factor, and might have been resolved differently in 1950. Lhasa's ecclesiastical jurisdiction over Sikkim was not disputed but Tibet's attempts to assert its suzerain claims fluctuated from pontificate to pontificate in Lhasa and reign to reign in Gangtok. They were also determined by the durbar's strength and its relations with Nepal, Bhutan and—increasingly—British India.

There was little sign of actual Tibetan control and none of Chinese authority despite Tsugphud Namgyal's obeisance. Thutob Namgyal, whom the British regarded as "a man of indolent disposition, whose inclination was to live in retirement and aloof from the worries and the government of his little state" was thought to be pro-Tibet. But he was probably more astute than people imagined. Menaced by the rising power of British India, he sought to preserve his independence through alliances with regimes he understood and could cope with.

Lhasa was content to leave Sikkim alone so long as it provided an effective barrier for Tibet's jealously guarded solitude. But alarm bells started ringing when the East India Company began to carve out a resort at Darjeeling. Tsugphud Namgyal's original cession was for an enclave of about 30 miles by 6 miles. Nowhere was it wider than 10 miles. The site was entirely surrounded by Sikkimese territory, entry and exit being restricted to a narrow path. Nevertheless, the vigour with which company officials set about clearing and developing the tract aroused Tibetan nervousness. When the mountainside was being blasted, a percipient old Tibetan told Darjeeling's Deputy Commissioner, "Sahib, the sound of that powder is heard in Lhasa." Tibet punished Tsugphud Namgyal by stopping his annual presents, restricting his visits to Chumbi valley to once in eight years, and cancelling Sikkim's grazing rights across the border.

Tibetan resentment continued to simmer until 1849 when the Superintendent of Darjeeling, Dr A. Campbell and Joseph Hooker, an English botanist, insisted on travelling in Sikkim in spite of the ruler's lack of enthusiasm. His son-in-law and minister, Dunya Namguay (the British called him 'Pagla dewan,' the mad *dewan*, but actually thought highly of his abilities), more actively resented the intrusion.

Ignoring hints, the two Europeans rode to the Tibetan border near Chola pass where a posse of Tibetan horsemen turned them back. Returning to Sikkim, Hooker and Campbell were roughly seized by the dewan's men. According to Sikkimese lore, Campbell, who was bound hand and foot, began yelling "Hooker! Hooker! The savages are murdering me!", whereupon one of his captors ordered: "If he wants a *hookah*, let him have one!" The unfortunate superintendent was forced to the ground and Dunya Namguay's *hookah* thrust into his mouth and held there.

The unwelcome guests were released only when news arrived that British troops were on their way. The company stopped paying rent for Darjeeling and seized the entire Morung district (Terai) and a large portion of the middle hills, "the whole southern part of Sikkim, between the Great Rungeet and the plains of India, and from Nepal on the west to the Bhutan frontier and the Teesta river on the east." The annexed 640 square miles carried Britain's jurisdiction into the heart of the Himalaya .

China and Tibet blamed Thutob Namgyal. In 1873 the *Amban* warned him in the emperor's name that "the Peling Sahibs (British) should not be allowed to cross the frontier" with specific instructions not to let John Ware Edgar, Darjeeling's Deputy Commissioner, enter Tibet. Although official British policy still sought to avoid provocations that might force Sikkim into Tibet's arms, the company was also looking for an opportunity to consolidate its hold. It came when the Sikkimese led another slaving expedition into Darjeeling.

There was also the matter of Campbell's wounded honour, which had been further injured when the Sikkim Guards repulsed a British force in 1860. Using slabs of stone as shields, the Sikkimese crushed to death some men of the Derbyshires at an encounter at Rinchinpong, forcing the rest to flee. Rinchinpong graces the Sikkim Guards' list of battle honours but British accounts gloss over the battle. One of the few official references—the subsequent demand that the durbar restore "all public property which was abandoned by the detachment of British troops at Rinchinpong"—confirms a hasty flight over which Dunya Namguay gloated from his perch on nearby Namche Hill.

The setback only whetted the appetite for revenge. Another force of about 1,800 men under Lieutenant-Colonel J.C. Gawler, with Ashely Eden as Special Commissioner, was sent into Sikkim in 1861. Tsugphud Namgyal being away in Chumbi, his son, Sidkeong, was forced to sue for peace. China and Tibet did not go to Sikkim's help, but neither did Nepal's Jung Bahadur take advantage of the conflict to take another bite at Sikkimese territory. The 1817 Titalya Treaty, which had governed relations until then, was revoked and a new treaty of friendship and alliance with the British Government was entered into at Tumlong on 28 March 1861. This arrangement continued to govern Sikkim's relations with India until 1950.

The year 1950 was a momentous one. Chinese troops 'liberated' (from whom, Nehru wondered) Tibet. New Delhi warned Beijing that "the recognized boundary between India and Tibet should remain inviolate." And a new India-Sikkim treaty was signed. This arrangement respected the kingdom's traditional relations with its neighbours but, increasingly, Sikkim's interaction with Tibet had become a minority interest confined to the durbar, royal family and aristocracy. But this passed unnoticed as events drifted to the 1962 war and the border marches became even more "the Asian Balkans" and "the Belgium of Asia" as H.H. Risley called them in *The Gazetteer of Sikhim*.

The consequences, for India, of Tibet's absorption in China are not central to the Sikkim story. However, the closure of the two passes, Nathu (4,310 metres) and Jelap (4,267 metres), dramatically symbolised the severance of Sikkim's traditional links. Instead of the brisk traffic of men and animals—more than a 1,000 mules and at least 700 people were involved in the 1940s—the only person permitted for 44 years to cross the barbed-wire frontier at Nathu La was a Chinese postman with an Indian military escort, who would hand over an empty mailbag to his Indian counterpart in a building at the border.

Because of its gentler gradients, Nathu La was Britain's preferred route to Lhasa; for that very reason, it was also "probably the easiest invasion route" from China into Tibet, according to senior Indian official, B.K. Nehru. This was the Old Silk Route connecting Lhasa with Kalimpong town in West Bengal. Its closure sounded the death-knell for Kalimpong, once the meeting place of *kalons* (ministers) from Sikkim, Bhutan and Tibet and the nerve centre of the Tibet trade up to the early 1960s. More than 10,000 men were employed in sorting mounds of dirty white, grey or black wool from Tibet into neat bales for export to Britain and the US. Thousands more provided fodder and maize for mules, and exotic entertainment for their masters enjoying a 10-day respite from the privations of a bleak and dangerous road. The daily turnover of more than ₹400 million persuaded the State Bank of India (SBI) to open a branch in Kalimpong.

Apart from wool and Kuomintang silver dollars, the caravans brought yaks' tails, musk, borax, curios and Chinese rice. They took back cement, kerosene and all the manufactures of Indian factories. A car for the Dalai Lama was dismantled and carted up piece by piece. Indian officials turned a blind eye when rations and equipment for Mao's forces, including jeeps from Calcutta, were similarly exported.

A massive set of carved sofas upholstered in yellow brocade in Raj Bhavan, as the PO's residence is now called, poignantly recalls that past. The suite had been specially made as New Delhi's gift to the Dalai Lama, but reached Gangtok too late to be sent by mule train through Nathu La. Tibet's Khampas had revolted, the pontiff was in flight and nearly 100,000 refugees gave the 'Tibetan question' a global dimension.

It isn't the only demographic problem in the border marches. The Nepalese present a more pressing challenge. Krishna Chandra Pradhan, one of the leading lights in the agitation against the *chogyal*, wasn't far out when he declaimed in 1973, "Our national language is a version of Tibetan. The state religion is Tibetan Buddhism. There is no such thing as Sikkimese!" But there were no takers for his answer of a Hindu Nepalese king for the majority.

There wasn't a single Nepalese in Sikkim in 1873. By Krishna Chandra's time they accounted for three-quarters of the population. Calculating that it would be easier to manage industrious Hindu economic refugees with a natural affinity to India than Mongolian Buddhists with Central Asian ties, the British sponsored migration with the support of some self-serving Sikkimese nobles who probably extracted bribes from the migrants.

About 225,000 of today's 300,000 registered 'Sikkim Subjects' (meaning they or their ancestors were bona fide residents of the kingdom) are ethnic Nepalese. Another 35,000 probably have fake certificates. Sikkim's Tibeto-Buddhist ethic has been watered down, and indigenes complain of existing on sufferance. Kazi Lendhup Dorji, the first chief minister whose anti-*chogyal* machinations played into the hands of Indian strategists, once chided me for not speaking Nepalese. "It's the language of the people," he said. In 1894, when his Gazetteer was published, Risley anticipated with satisfaction the long-term impact of the influx from Nepal on the Tibetan connection:

> Most of all will our position be strengthened by the change which is insensibly but steadily taking place in the composition of the population of Sikkim. The Lepchas are rapidly dying out; while from the west, the industrious Newars and Goorkas of Nepal are pressing forward to clear and cultivate large areas of unoccupied land on which the European tea-planters of Darjeeling have already cast longing eyes. The influx of these hereditary enemies of Tibet is our surest guarantee against a revival of Tibetan influence. Here also religion will play a leading part. In Sikkim, as in India, Hinduism will assuredly cast out Buddhism, and the praying-wheel of the lama will give place to the sacrificial implements of the Brahman. The land will follow the creed; the Tibetan proprietors will gradually be dispossessed, and will betake themselves to the petty trade for which they have an undeniable aptitude. Thus race and religion, the prime movers of the Asiatic world, will settle the Sikkim difficulty for us, in their own ways.

In solving Sikkim's Tibetan problem, the immigrants were the cause, wittingly or unwittingly, of the kingdom's ultimate abolition. They also helped to set the stage for the emergence of Gorkhaland, India's second Nepali-speaking state in the making.

The demographic flood has watered down Tibet's influence. But with China taking over Tibet's claims, New Delhi finds it necessary to be more circumspect about Sikkim than any other part of India even 37 years after the annexation. One reason could be that contrary to general belief, China has not explicitly recognised Sikkim as an Indian state. New Delhi acknowledged Chinese sovereignty over Tibet in the 2003 Declaration on Principles for Relations and Comprehensive Cooperation between India and China. But as an American scholar, David Scott, points out in his essay, "Sino-Indian Territorial Issues: The 'Razor's Edge?'", "the text shows a one-way agreement, one-way obligations and one-way concessions." As for the complacent Indian claim that China's acceptance of a border trade post at Nathu La means recognition of Indian sovereignty over Sikkim, Scott warns, "that was implied rather than explicit, de facto rather than *de jure*." As if to bear out his doubts, China contested Indian control of the 2.1 sq km Finger Area tract in northern Sikkim five years after the declaration.

Delivering the K. Subrahmanyam Memorial Lecture, "China in the Twenty-First Century: What India Needs to Know About China's World View" in New Delhi on 29 August 2012, Shyam Saran, former National Security Adviser, observed:

> In 2003, during PM Vajpayee's visit, China conceded Sikkim as a part of India but this was not explicitly recorded in a written formulation. In 2005, during Wen Jiabao's visit to India, China went a step further and handed over maps of China, showing Sikkim as part of India. Recently, some Chinese scholars have pointed out that the absence of an official statement recognizing Indian sovereignty leaves the door open to subsequent shifts if necessary.

As the physical reality of the old Tibet recedes, the idea of Tibet as the fountainhead of religion and culture remains as strong as ever. The Dalai Lama is a frequent visitor, never missing the opportunity when in Gangtok of going to the now empty and partially demolished palace and saying prayers there for Sikkim and its royal family. Those members of the *chogyal*'s clan who are in Gangtok always attend these low-key ceremonies.

The palace and its Tsuklakhang royal chapel hold many memories for His Holiness. He spent a long time there when he visited India in 1956 for the Buddha Jayanti celebrations and was reportedly reluctant to return to Tibet. With his usual sensitivity, Nehru had asked the *chogyal* to visit Lhasa on the Indian government's behalf and invite both the Dalai Lama and the Panchen Lama to the celebrations. So great was the Dalai Lama's trust in the *chogyal* that he stored a substantial quantity of the Potala's gold in a room underneath the palace garage that the *chogyal* later converted into his wine cellar. Old palace aides recall the muscular Tibetan soldiers who kept guard at the garage.

The other continuing link is through Ogyen Trinley Dorje, whom both the Dalai Lama and the Chinese government recognise as the 17th Karmapa Lama but whom the Indian government views with some reserve. The personable young monk heads Buddhism's Karma Kagyu sect and represents the world's oldest unbroken line of succession through reincarnation. He was born in 1985 in a nomad family in eastern Tibet, identified as the reincarnate in 1992, and installed in the traditional seat of the lineage at Tsurphu near Lhasa. New Delhi granted him official refugee status when he escaped from Tsurphu and arrived at the Dalai Lama's headquarters in Dharamsala early one January morning in 2000, but did not appear to know what to make of him. The foreigners who visit India to worship at his feet, the thousands of dollars they offer in homage, the worldwide network of fervently loyal Karma Kagyu centres and the many invitations to address congregations in Europe and America feed into Indian paranoia about the outside world. Other contenders for his throne take care to fan instinctive suspicion of a possible Chinese plant. Obviously, he cannot take over Rumtek Monastery or play any meaningful role so long as those misgivings remain.

Most Buddhists, however, see Ogyen Trinley Dorje as the Dalai Lama's natural heir. They believe that allowing him to assume the duties of his lineage would solve many present and future problems. The disappearance in 1995 of Gedhun Choekyi Nyima whom the Dalai Lama had recognised as the Panchen Lama and his substitution by China's nominee warns of Beijing's strategy of controlling Tibet through its traditional institutions. An even more divisive succession struggle is likely if the Chinese try to impose their protégé on Tibetans as the next Dalai Lama.

Bearing all this in mind, Pawan Kumar Chamling, Sikkim's ethnic Nepalese Chief Minister, has repeatedly asked New Delhi to let the Karmapa Lama take over Rumtek. The heads of Sikkim's 64 monasteries and the leaders of all the political parties in the state back the demand. The Sikkim Pradesh Congress Committee even made the Karmapa's return an election plank in 2004. But the Indian government keeps him like a prisoner of state at the small Gyuto Monastery near the Dalai Lama's headquarters in Dharamsala.

Although New Delhi has allowed him to visit the United States, it will not, for some unexplained reason, permit him to accept invitations from Karma Kagyu centres in Europe. Within India, he cannot set foot on Sikkimese soil. The nearest he was allowed was Mirik in Darjeeling district, just across the border with Sikkim where thousands of devout Sikkimese flocked when he presided over a mammoth public rally.

The future of this potential world leader of the Tibetan and Buddhist communities is inextricably linked with that of Sikkim where Rangjung Rigpe Dorje, the 16th Karmapa Lama who fled Tibet with the Dalai Lama and died in 1981, established the red and white Rumtek Dharma Chakra Centre which is also the global headquarters of Karma Kagyu Buddhists. It adjoins Rumtek Monastery which Wangchuk Dorje, the 9th Karmapa Lama, built in the 16th century. The 16th Karmapa officially inaugurated the Dharma Chakra Centre on Tibetan New Year's Day (Losar) in 1966 as "a place of erudition and spiritual accomplishment, the seat of the glorious Karmapa." Opposite is the Karma Shri Nalanda Institute for Higher Buddhist Studies.

The reality of contemporary Sikkim may not any longer be very connected to the reality of contemporary Tibet. Without the trading posts at Gyantse and Gartok, trade at Nathu La, where a mart was opened on 6 July 2006, the Dalai Lama's birthday, does not measure up to the old Tibet trade through the pass. Pemayangtse ('the sublime perfect lotus') Monastery, the first in 1982 to acknowledge Prince Wangchuck Namgyal as the 13th consecrated Denzong *chogyal*, must look elsewhere for novices since the supply of young Tibetans of good family is somewhat restricted. Yak herdsmen from the Lachen and Lachung valleys no longer graze along the border with Tibet and beyond. Few Doptha-pas can trek to Gangtok to pay homage to their sovereign lord. But the idea of Tibet continues to influence and inspire even those Sikkimese who cannot claim Tibetan antecedents. It is woven into the national consciousness. It is what gives Sikkim its distinctive identity and acts as a brake on the incipient demand for merger with Darjeeling. Tibet is what prevents 'merged' Sikkim from being 'submerged'.

7

SONAM JOLDAN

Historical Relationship between Tibet and Ladakh

Some Important Sustaining Factors

Introduction: Historical Background

Ladakh appears to have come into contact with Tibet in the 7th and 8th centuries, when the latter not only conquered western Tibet but went as far as Gilgit-Baltistan (Petech, 1977: 10-11).

But the real influences came with the establishment of the Ladakhi kingdom of Tibetan origin in the 10th century, when Ladakh shared with Tibet the development of some lamaic institutions. Tibetan cultural influence has been uniform. The influences, which continued for hundreds of years between Ladakh and Tibet, were felt in nearly every village in Ladakh. From the point of view of language, it has provided Ladakh with the western Tibetan dialect, which is still generally spoken to this day by Ladakhi Muslims as much as it is Buddhists. As far as literature is concerned, the regular style of literary Tibetan has remained current in Ladakh. Tibetan influence can also be seen in Ladakhi dress, customs, food and drink. The Ladakhi dress *goncha* is an adaptation of the Tibetan *chuba*. Both Ladakh and Tibet have the same staple food, *tsampa* or barley flour and *chang*, a mildly alcoholic drink made of fermented barley. As regards religion, the major sects and the several sub-sects of Mahayana Buddhism were developed in Ladakh. Besides, Tibetan influence can also be seen on Ladakhi architecture, astrology and paintings. The influences were two-way affairs, Ladakhis made their own contribution to the mainstream religious tradition of Tibet. One such contribution was Zanskar Lotswa's translation works. He translated many books from Sanskrit into Tibetan including part of the *bstan-gyur*, the Tibetan Canon (Rabgias, 1984: 87).

This relationship disappeared after the Chinese occupation of Tibet when the borders were closed. This paper traces some of the important sustaining factors in the relationship between Tibet and Ladakh, which, continued for hundreds of years. Some of these factors were the Ladakhi Royal patronage to Buddhism, monastic organisation and Ladakhi monks'monastic education in Tibet and pilgrimage and trade between Tibet and Ladakh. I will discuss or elaborate some of these factors focusing not only on the past but also on their relevance for the present and the future.

Monastic Organisation and Monastic Education of Ladakhi Monks in Tibet

Monastic organisation and monastic education of Ladakhi monks in Tibet was one of the important sustaining factors in the relationship between Ladakh and Tibet.

The name for a Buddhist monastery in both Tibetan and Ladakhi is Gonpa (*dGon-pa*), a solitary place or hermitage. According to Robert James Miller: "any unit where in there is a resident body of monks will be called Monastery" (Miller, 1959: 12).

The Buddhist monastery is a central feature of the Buddhist tradition and has been so since the early development of Buddhism. The origin of the monastery goes back to the time when Buddhist monks wandered around for knowledge and food. There is a problem with spending the whole year wandering in India. During the rainy season for about four months the roads and tracks are covered with water and it is very difficult to move around the country. There is also a moral question, which has been raised at times, that wandering around in water/floods may cause harm to living beings. Due to this, it seems that already in the time of Buddha, there was a tradition of staying in one place for the rainy season. So, it is likely that in many ways the origin of the Buddhist monastic tradition goes back to these rainy season retreat dwellings. Royal patronage, especially after King Ashoka, radically transformed the monastic structure.

Tibetan Buddhist monasteries were the cornerstones of Tibetan religion, culture, education and knowledge. For centuries, great monasteries with their renowned colleges become famous across Tibet and in neighbouring countries where Mahayana Buddhism took deep roots. Most of the major monasteries in Tibet have several colleges and many hostels called *K'am t'sam*. For example, Drepung Monastery with its 7,700 monks was divided into four great colleges (*grwa-ts'an*), namely: bLo-gsal-gling; sGo-man; bde-yans; and sNags-pa (Waddell, 1959: 188). The sGo-man, the largest of its four colleges, had 3,300 monks. Each college consisted of a number of houses (*K'am ts'an*) or a hostel; for instance, the largest college of Drepung had 23 houses or *K'am ts'ans* (Snellgrove and Richardson, 1968: 238). The monks were accommodated according to their nationalities and provinces in the *K'am ts'ans*. As Tsering Stobgais, a monk from Spituk Monastery in Ladakh, who studied in Drepung Monastery for about 11 years, mentioned that "all the monks from Ladakh who studied in Drepung Monastery stayed in Spituk K'am ts'an during that time" (Joldan, 2012: 44).

Many lamas from different countries went to Tibet for higher studies. Many monks from Ladakh also went to different monasteries in Tibet. It is difficult to say exactly when the Ladakhi lamas first started going to Tibet for their monastic education. According to the *Chronicles of Ladakh*, the tradition of sending monks to the dBus and gTsan region of Tibet began during the reign of King dnos-grub-mgon between 1300 and 1325 (Francke, 1926: 36). The *Chronicle* has mentioned that:

> Lha chen dNos-grub dei dus su rab du jung wa
>
> dBus, gTsan du iGro wai srol bTugs.

It means that during the reign of King Lha chen Lha chen dNos-grub, the tradition of sending monks for their study in the dBus and gTsan region of Tibet began. Later, they started going to different monasteries in Tibet. There were no records of how many lamas from Ladakh went to Tibet for education except those sent by the royal house, who were mentioned and recorded. As with Tibet, when Tibetans came to study in India, there were no records except for the

16 Tibetans who were sent to India with Thonmi Sambhota by the royal court. Thonmi Sambhota invented the Tibetan alphabets.

At present, there are more than 100 monks in different monasteries in Ladakh who have studied in different monasteries in Tibet. During my field survey a few years back in seven monasteries in Ladakh, I interviewed 96 monks who have been to Tibet (Joldan, 2012: 49). The seven monasteries are Lamayuru, Rigzong, Likir, Phyang, Spituk, Thiksay and Disket. In the case of Phyang Monastery, I could interview only one monk, though there are many monks there who have been to Tibet. I could not go to other monasteries in central Ladakh and Zanskar. These monks studied in various monasteries like Drepung, Sera, Dadan, Bri-gung and Tashi Lhunpo in Tibet for many years. Among the 96 monks, Lobsang Tomba had the longest stay in Tibet, about 22 years in Drepung and Tashi Lhunpo monasteries. He is about 88 years old and still regularly participates in the major ceremonies in Thiksay Monastery in Ladakh. On the other hand, Konchok Rigzen could stay only two years in Tibet. He had to come back after two years of study in Bri-gung Monastery because of the Chinese army's occupation of Tibet.

Out of 96 monks, 42 monks studied in Tashi-lhunpo Monastery, 30 stayed in Bri-gung, 20 stayed in Drepung and 2 monks stayed in Gandan Monastery. All the 30 monks who stayed in Bri-gung Monastery are from Lamayuru Monastery in Ladakh and belong to the Bri-gungpa, sub-sect of the bka-bgyud-pa sect. "It is not compulsory for the monks to go to the same sect monastery in Tibet for their study," said Konchok Namgail, who is from Phyang Monastery. Although the Phayang Monastery belongs to the Bri-gung-pa, sub-sect of the bka-bgyud-pa sect, he studied in Drepung Monastery in Tibet, which belongs to Gyalugpa. When the monks were asked why they wanted to go to Tibet for their education, they all had the same answer: the best monastic education is available in the great monastic institutions in Tibet. It was mainly because of two reasons that Ladakhi lamas went to Tibet: one, Mahayana Buddhism came directly from Tibet to the Himalayan areas and two, Tibet in due course of time became a centre of Mahayana Buddhism and the residence of leading lamas who taught Mahayana Buddhism.

The monks who were interviewed have been to Tibet through three different routes. Most of the older monks went to Tibet through the southern-eastern route, locally known as *dzung-lam* or the middle route. This was one of the main trade routes between Ladakh and Tibet. From Leh it followed the course of the Indus upstream till Karu, and then to Sakti over the Chang-la to Tangtse, Chushul, and then cut over to the Indus Valley via the Tsak-la and then to Demchok. From there, they would go to Gartok, a trading centre in Tibet. All the monks who followed this route were accompanied by trading groups. Lobsang Tonba, from Thiksay Monastery who went to Tibet through this route, mentioned:

> We went to Tibet with the trading party from lower Ladakh (Shamma), and after walking for many days reached a trading centre, the Ladakhi traders were going back from there and they requested their Tibetan counterparts to take us along with them to Tibet. So we went with the Tibetan traders and they were also very nice people, they not only guided us on those difficult and long tracks but also gave us food (Joldan, 2012: 51).

This route is the hardest among the three routes because it takes longer to reach and has to be walked the whole way.

The second route involved walking from Leh to Kargil and then to Kashmir, and from there, till Sikkim taking a bus and train, and then again walking till Lhasa. Majority of the monks followed this road. And the last route, which was followed by a few monks, is from Leh to Lahul-Spiti to Shimla and then to Delhi. The distance from Delhi to Sikkim was covered by train and bus, and the rest by walking to Lhasa.

Ladakhi monks who were fortunate enough to study in Tibet remember those times with nostalgia. Yeshe Jamyang from Nurla who studied in Bri-gung Monastery in Tibet said:

> I love the monastery where we studied in Tibet and never thought of coming back. I was interested in rituals and started learning from my Tibetan teacher and I became an expert in making ritual objects, especially butter painting etc. and I was one of the famous students in the monastery.

He had to come back against his wishes in 1959, when the Chinese occupied Tibet. After coming back from Tibet, he became a dance teacher (*Cham-spon*) for a few years and was very active in teaching dance to young monks at Lamayuru Monastery in Ladakh. Besides, he contributed to monasteries like Phaying, Gonpa Soma Leh, Lamayuru, Shashikul, Spituk and Timosgang in Ladakh and Ayang Gonpa at Belakupi in Karnataka, paintings of various religious objects like masks, Thangkas etc. He has also painted the Dalai Lama's *Photang* or a temple at Bod-Karbu, a village between Leh and Kargil.

While several Ladakhi monks made Tibet their home, many others like Yeshes Jamyang, after getting education in different monastic centres in Tibet came back to their native place and played a major role in spreading Mahayana Buddhism in Ladakh. A few royal princes became monks and went to Tibet for higher studies; after coming back from Tibet, they became heads of important monasteries and played an important role in spreading monastic education in Ladakh. For example, King Deldan Namgyal's second son, Lobsang Puntsog, became a monk and went to study in Tibet. He studied in Drepung Monastery (Petech, 1977: 84). After nine years of study in the slo-gsay-glin college at Drepung, he obtained the high degree of dge-bses-rab-byams-pa (Petech, 1977: 85). Upon his return from Tibet, he was appointed the abbot of Thiksay Monastery, which headed seven Ge-lug-pa monasteries in Ladakh at that time (Petech, 1977: 85). Ladakhi monks were intelligent and several monks were able to achieve higher degrees like dge-bses, which is equivalent to a doctorate degree in modern education in Tibet. Nawang Tsering (1992: 209) mentioned that:

> A few Ladakhi monks were able to obtain the degrees of Lha-rams-pa or bka-chen in Tibetan monasteries. The Five-fold philosophical subjects: the Pramanasatra, Madhyamikasastra, Prajnaparamitra-satra, Abhidharmaand Vinaya, were difficult to master. Sras Rinpoche of Ridzong monastery, and bka-chen bZod-pa of Thiksay, are few who have achieved thorough knowledge of these philosophical subjects in Tibet.

The tradition of Ladakhi monks to go for higher studies in different monastic institutions in Tibet has continued for hundreds of years. Ladakhi monks' higher studies in Tibet and lama missionaries have played an important role in the construction of monasteries and spread of Mahayana Buddhism in Ladakh. The four major sects and several sub-sects of Mahayana Buddhism have developed in Ladakh. Monasteries in Ladakh are the cornerstones of religion, education and spirituality for the Buddhist people of Ladakh. Monasteries as religious establishments cater to the religious and spiritual needs of the people. Besides their contribution in the field of education, their role in the cultural and social needs of the people is no less significant. The lamas play an important role as linkages between the monastery and the villages. The monks carry out all functions of the monastery. Quite a few events in Ladakhi Buddhist life are based on the achievement of religious merit, and the importance of religious merit is transmitted through monks and nuns. The existence of monkhood enables the laity to acquire merit (*bSod-nams*) ensuring a satisfactory or improved rebirth in the next life. A villager can add to his stock of merit through services to the monastery in the form of donation, work and the sponsorship of rituals.

The monastic organisations and monastic education played an important role in the development of a close cultural relationship between Ladakh and Tibet. This relationship disappeared after the Chinese occupation of Tibet when the borders were closed.

Pilgrimage and Trade

Another important sustaining factor between Tibet and Ladakh was trade and pilgrimage. In the olden days, Leh, the capital of Ladakh due to its strategic location in the western Himalaya, had developed into an active and important centre for commercial intercourse with Tibet, Persia, Yarkand, China and even Russia on the one hand, and Kashmir, the Punjab and the plains of Hindustan on the other (Moorcroft and Trebeck, 1971: 346). The origins of this trade are undocumented. But it seems to have started long ago.

Trade relations between Ladakh and Tibet are old. It is quite possible that the inhabitants of Ladakh felt Tibetan influence as early as the mid-7th century, for the nomadic Tibetans of Changthang would have good reason to have contacts with the Mons and Dards, exchanging grains for animal products. Tibetan nomads occupied the higher pasture ground for their animals and the Aryan tribes (Mons and Dards) irrigated in the lower plains. According to Francke (1907: 27), the products of the fields were as welcome to the Tibetans as were the produce of the flocks to the Dards and the peasants. During this period, the Tibetan nomads of Changthang probably intermarried with the Mon and Dard population and allowed a trading or bartering system to develop between the two groups of people. This trade developed for years. Luciano Petech mention that, "about 900 A.D., Ladakh, still inhabited by a Dardi-speaking population, was no longer connected politically with Tibet, at the most it maintained trade relations with it" (Petech, 1977: 13).

With the establishment of the first Ladakhi kingdom of Tibetan origin in the 10th century, religious and commercial relationships between Ladakh and Tibet were well established. The most important commercial relations between Ladakh and Tibet were the two missions known as 'Lapchak' and 'Chapa', which were set up in 1684 as a result of the Treaty of Tingmosgang (Francke, 1926: 42). This treaty brought to an end the three-corner conflict between Ladakh, Tibet and the Moghul empire (Joldan, 2012: 96).

The annual trade caravan from Lhasa to Ladakh was known as Zhung-tsong (government mission). It was also known as Chapa (tea man) consisting of 200 loads of tea, and it was only to cross the frontier at Demchok (Francke, 1926: 42; Petech, 1977: 78). The *Chronicle of Ladakh* (Francke, 1926: 42) mentions that if the government failed to come every year, then the stipulations of the treaty should no longer be binding:

> Pod nas gzyung Tsong khal ma ney bgyai cha tang
> chas yong Gry tang/cha pak du jee di Ladags ma
> thogs/gdzan mtha la gdong mi chog/gzyung-tsong
> lo tar ma yong chey/Ngar gi chad don la mi gnas pa chas.
>
> *Translation:* From Tibet, the government traders shall come with 200 loads of tea and the rectangular brick-tea will be brought only to Ladakh. Should the Zhung-tsong trader fail to come annually, then the agreement shall no longer be binding.

The head of the Chapa mission was the Dalai Lama's personal trader to Ladakh, and was always a Tibetan official, either lay or monastic, of some importance. The Chapa mission left Lhasa each June and arrived at Leh in December (Lamb, 1960: 57). It remained in Leh the entire winter months until the following April, when it left Leh for Lhasa, taking with it dry apricots, saffron and sugar, etc. (Datta, 1973: 65-66).

In exchange, Ladakh sent a mission known as Lapchak (Lamb, 1960: 57). The Lapchak mission went from Leh to Lhasa every three years, with offerings to Tibet for the Smon-lam and for the blessing of the Dalai Lama (Petech, 1977: 78). According to Captain H. Ramsay, the mission started from Leh every September and arrived in Lhasa in January or February. This has been mentioned in John Bray's article on Lochak mission (Bray, 1990: 85). The triennial mission would bring a specific amount of presents to the Bla-bran (treasury) in Lhasa and an unspecific amount of presents to other lamas (Francke, 1926: 42).

A prominent Ladakhi headed the Lapchak mission and was accompanied by a leading Ladakhi Muslim (Arghun) merchant of that class who had, by a long tradition, been permitted to trade in Tibet (Lamb, 1960: 57). The Lapchak mission while in Tibetan territories received all facilities available including free transport (*ula*), and the Chapa mission while in Ladakh also got the same facilities (Datta, 1973: 65; Francke, 1926: 42).

The two missions were the most important manifestation of the close relationship between Ladakh and Tibet. It gave rise to a number of smaller missions, and the feudatories of the king of Ladakh and several of the larger monasteries both from Ladakh and Tibet sent lesser missions. The Raja of Stok usually sent annual trading missions to Gartok (Lamb, 1960: 57). Certain Muslim traders possessed special privileges to trade in Chinese brick-tea between Ladakh and Lhasa (Rizvi, 1999: 160). In this respect, the history of Rangdu family recounted by Abdul Wahid Rangdu in his *Caravane tibetaine* is exemplary. Cited by Pascale Dollfus (1995: 43) in his article on Muslims in Ladakh, he says, "The first to settle in Ladakh was a religious man, Sheikh Asad." His son Faruq became a caravan merchant, maintained close ties with the Ladakhi kings and received land in the village of Stok, in Leh. His eldest son settled in Leh. The well-respected and high ranking Rangdu family owned handsome properties and important warehouses in several places. In recognition of their services, the Rangdu family received several titles from both the Maharaja's court and the British resident in Srinagar (Dollfus, 1995: 43-44).

The governors of Gartok, the Kharpons, as well as the Tibetan Commander of the fort at Rudok visited Leh annually to trade. Several of the larger Buddhist monasteries in Ladakh periodically sent combined religious and trading missions to Lhasa, and at about 10-year intervals a similar mission came to Leh from the great Tashi Lhunpo Monastery (Lamb, 1960: 57). For instance, during his lifetime, sTag-tsan-raspa (1574-1651), the head of Brug-pa sect in Ladakh, who founded several monasteries including the famous Hemis Monastery in Ladakh, sent several religious missions to many monasteries in Tibet. Following were some of them:

> In 1626, sTag-tsan-raspa sent a mission to the Brug-c'en incarnate and to the monastery of rNam-rgyal-thun-po and Ri-bo-rtse-brgyad (on the Manasarovar).
>
> In 1628, he sent a mission to the Brug-c'en and bDe-c'en-c'os-k'or.
>
> In 1629, he sent another mission to Brug-c'en, the Zva-dmar-pa incarnate and bDe-c'en-c'os-k'or.
>
> In 1630, he sent again a mission to Brug-c'en. The mission was headed by the king's brother Dzam-gling-graps-pa (Petech, 1977: 53).

Each of these missions carried several hundred ounces of gold, many more of silver, besides turquoises and shawls (Petech, 1977: 53). Dr Cayley, on British Special Duty in Ladakh, reported in 1871 that there were a dozen families in Ladakh who had the privilege of going as traders to Changthang and Lhasa.[1] He also mentioned that the old arrangements were still in force, that a trade mission of the Lhasa government came to Ladakh and a return trade mission from

1. *Ladakh Trade Report*, Foreign Department, Political. A. Branch, nos. 560-597, Consultation, June 1871, National Archives, Delhi.

Ladakh proceeded to Lhasa, and they were allowed free carriage in their respective areas.[2]

Several references in the 16th and the 17th centuries supported the fact that in the western Himalaya through Ladakh was well established not only with Tibet but also with other neighbouring areas. The people of Nubra petitioned King Ts'e-dban-rNamgyal (1530-1560 AD) to refrain from undertaking a campaign in the north of Leh against the Khan of Yarkand, as it would have seriously damaged the trade through the passes, which was of vital importance to Nubra. The king saw the point and decided in favour of the petition.[3]

Many travellers in the 17th and 18th centuries have also documented trade through Ladakh. The first most comprehensive analysis of this trade was by W. Moorcroft who was on his way to Yarkand. He reached Leh in September 1820 and remained there for a period of two years, until September 1822 (Moorcroft and Trebeck, 1971: xxxvi). He also mentioned that Leh, because it was centrally situated, became the great thoroughfare for an active commercial intercourse between Tibet, Turkistan, China and even Russia on the one hand, and Kashmir, the Punjab and the plains of Hindustan on the other (Moorcroft and Trebeck, 1971: xxxvi). Another reference by R.B. Shaw, the British Joint Commissioner on special duty, Ladakh, in 1872. He mentioned that the town of Leh had become an important point, where the great majority of traders from both sides were always coming but not going beyond Ladakh, and that they were present at Leh, bartering their goods with other merchants and returning to their homes.[4]

The trading caravans gradually declined. The last caravan from Leh or the Lopchak was carried to Lhasa in 1942. After the Chinese occupation of Tibet, border trade between Ladakh and Tibet came to an end when the borders were closed. Thus, such extensive and long

2. Ibid.: 8.

3. Ibid.: 32.

4. *Ladakh Trade Report*, Foreign Department, Political. A. Branch, nos. 126-130, Consultation, May 1872, National Archives, Delhi.

trade and pilgrimage between Ladakh and Tibet not only sustained the relationship between them but also further helped in developing close ties between the two.

Monasteries and Monastic Education at Present

After the Chinese occupied Tibet, the tradition of Ladakhi monks going to Tibet for higher monastic education came to an end. Soon, three important developments took place with regard to monastic education in Ladakh. First, the monks who came back to Ladakh after the Chinese occupation of Tibet played a major role in teaching young monks in Ladakh, and a Buddhist institute named the Central Institute of Buddhist Studies was established in 1959 at Choklasar, Leh, where novices from different monasteries in Ladakh came for their education. Second, the major monasteries in Ladakh set up their own schools. Lastly, with the establishment of the Tibetan government-in-exile in India, they set up some Tibetan monastic institutions in India. Some of these institutions are in Karnataka and in a few other places in India, where many well-known teachers from Tibet are teaching.

At present, there are 38 major monasteries in Ladakh. This figure does not include the medium and small monasteries. All the major monasteries have their own schools. In these schools, besides monastic education, they teach subjects like mathematics, social sciences and languages like Hindi and English. After the completion of their courses in these schools, many go for higher studies in monastic institutes in southern India and a few other places in the country, where the Tibetan government-in-exile has established monastic institutions. Thus, many Ladakhi monasteries have been re-connected with exiled Tibetan monasteries and teachers in India and the old sustaining factors continue.

Besides, many monasteries in Ladakh are also exchanging religious and spiritual ties with monasteries of their sect within the Cis-Himalayan states. One example is religious and spiritual exchanges between the Brug-pa sect monasteries in Ladakh and the monasteries of Bhutan. For the last several years, the Brug-pa sect of the Cis-Himalayan states have been organising religious teachings in different places in the Cis-Himayan states, wherein, many leading lamas of the sect from different monasteries of the Cis-Himalayan states participated.

The infrastructure of monasteries in Ladakh are improving. The governments are providing financial support to many of the old monasteries for their renovation and restoration. In addition, entry fees from tourism has also financially helped many of the bigger monasteries in Ladakh. Therefore, for the last several years, physical infrastructure of major monasteries of Ladakh has improved considerably. But there are two real concerns: one is declining enrolments in monastic institutes and second is that dropouts from the institutes are increasing. There are several reasons for declining enrolments in monastic institutes. One of the main reasons is people's preference to have smaller families compared to earlier times. Also, in earlier times, monastic education was the only education available in Ladakh. Secondly, many modern, both primary and senior secondary, educational institutions have been established in Ladakh. These institutions were established both by the government and the private sector where people now prefer to send their children. Lastly, quality of teaching in the monastic institutions is not up to the mark. Most of the novices in monasteries today come from remote areas of Ladakh, where family sizes are still large and access to affordable quality primary modern educational institutions is poor. When the children from remote areas are able to access quality modern institutions, enrolment in monastic education may drop further. In addition, people's preference for smaller families is also slowly catching up in the remote areas, which may further reduce enrolments. The main reason for dropouts from monastic institutes is lack of quality teaching. It is the quality that matters the most to survive in the competitive environment. As David L. Snellgrove and Tandeusz Skorupski (1977) mentioned some years back, "monks in Ladakh can recite liturgies that they have learned by heart but a few of them are capable of following the text." Therefore, if Buddhism in general and monastic education in particular is going to survive in Ladakh, the first requirement is improving in the standard of both monastic and modern subjects that they are offering. This is the only way to stop dropouts and to increase the enrolments. For that, institutes needs very 'learned and competent' leaders and well-qualified teachers so that they not only survive, but flourish on their own.

Re-opening of Border Trade: Future Prospects

Like monastic higher education of Ladakhi monks in Tibet, border trade between Ladakh and Tibet was also closed when the Chinese occupied Tibet.

At present, there is no formal border trade, but Chinese goods are found and sold in most of the shops in Leh. These goods come illegally across the borders. Many shopkeepers in Moti Market in Leh said that on the other side of the border there are no restrictions and people can freely exchange their goods with Indian traders. In fact, they had constructed a customs house near the border.

The people of Ladakh are consistently asking for the opening of the border through Demchok on the Ladakhi side and Tashigang on the Tibetan side for trade and pilgrimage. Of late, India and China have made progress in boosting economic ties, prompting both sides to look at opening up new routes to encourage cross-border trade. In June 2003, India and China agreed to open border trade along the eastern part of the Himalayan border between Sikkim and Tibet. In this changed environment, the people of Ladakh are optimistic about the re-opening of old trade. There is no reason why the old trade route should not be re-opened. There are three important benefits if the route between Tibet and Ladakh through Demchok is re-opened. The first is economic benefits; the re-opening of border trade will not only help the local economy but will also help governmental incomes. Ladakh's trade was good in earlier times. The documentation of trade from Ladakh and its value was started by the British Joint Commissioner in Ladakh in the 19th century. One such documented report from 1885-86 to 1894-95, prepared by Captain S.H. Godfrey, assistant to the Resident in Kashmir for Leh-Ladakh, shows that the total trade value in 1894-95 at Leh was more than ₹60 lakh.[5] Table

5. Foreign, Secret. F, 374-383, September 1895, National Archives Delhi.

7.1 shows the yearly details of value of import and export from 1885-1886 to 1894-95.

Table 7.1

Value of Imports and Exports from 1885-86 to 1894-95

(in ₹)

Year	*Imports*	*Exports*	*Total Value*
1885-86	18,31,501	15,69,321	34,00,822
1886-87	16,52,413	12,32,229	28,84,642
1887-88	17,16,245	17,12,328	34,28,573
1888-89	13,53,845	12,12,030	25,65,875
1889-90	16,00,580	15,13,626	31,14,206
1890-91	15,25,483	14,40,906	29,66,389
1891-92	15,65,278	14,47,840	30,13,118
1892-93	17,95,141	15,91,544	33,86,685
1893-94	21,54,252	18,37,375	39,91,627
1894-95	31,65,218	28,50,102	60,15,321

Source: Foreign, Secret. F, 374-383, September 1895, National Archives Delhi.

The total trade value in Ladakh in 1885-86 was about ₹34,00,800 and it increased to ₹60,15,000 during 1894-95. The trade value of ₹60 lakh rupees in the 19th century in a remote place like Leh-Ladakh meant huge business. In the present context too, it will be a huge benefit for both the local economy and the governments of both the countries if the old route is re-opened. It is common knowledge that informal trade between Ladakh and Tibet has blossomed in Leh-Ladakh. C. Raja Mohan has stated that "Some estimates suggest this trade could easily amount to couple of hundred crores of rupees." He further says that, "Formalization of this trade would effectively regulate commercial flows, generate customs revenue and prevent undesirable activities" (*The Hindu*, 2004).

In addition, re-opening of this old route will promote pilgrimage to the Kailash-Mansarovar Lakes and other holy places in Tibet. The Kailash and Mansarovar Lake are not only holy for Buddhists but also for Hindus. Many pilgrims, both Buddhist and Hindus, visited these sacred places through Ladakh. This route was used in the 19th century by pilgrims and traders. The British Joint Commissioner in Ladakh witnessed and reported in the 19th century that both Buddhists and Hindus pilgrims and traders came to Mansarovar Lake:

> Every autumn, a large fair is held at Gartok. People from all sides assemble and purchase pashmina wool, sheep wool, tea, and ponies. The Hindus and Buddhists also came as pilgrims to the sacred Mansarowar Lake and the holy mountain of Kailash (Gangri). In every six-year, a great festival is observed, wherein, thousands of devotees came from all quarters and ascended the sides of the mountain to pay homage at the Hindu and Buddhist shrines and bathe in the holy waters of the Lake. One of such festivals was held in 1870 and the road leading to Rupshu in Ladakh and Gartok was crowded with people and traders with their families and flocks, and herds, Lamas, Brahmins and beggars, all progressing towards the holy Mansarowar Lake (*Ladakh Trade Report*, June 1871).

There are several advantages for pilgrims going to Kailash-Mansaravor through Demchok-Ladakh. One of the advantages is that it is the safest route, as there are no chances of landslides and other risks. Secondly, the whole area is more or less plain and can be reached by jeep; thirdly, it is the shortest and more economical route compared to the present trekking route through Uttarakhand which takes many days on foot. The road between Leh and Demchok, the last Ladakhi village near the border, can be open throughout the year. It is reported that on the other side of the border, the Tibetan towns of Tashigong and Gorzong are located 35 and 150 km away from Demchok respectively (Joldan, 2012: 175). Another advantage of the route through Ladakh is that there is a motorable road on both sides of the border; one can drive all the way up to Kailash. This is ideal for older people and women. Lastly, Ladakh and Tibet have extensive tourism potential, especially adventure tourism like trekking, jeep safaris, religious and cultural tourism, in a relatively unexplored rich cultural circuit.

Therefore, the hope for Ladakhis is that there will be the restoration of normal border trading and cultural relations between India and Tibet. C. Raja Mohan (*The Hindu*, 2004) mentioned that, "New Delhi has taken up the issue with the Chinese leadership at the highest levels in recent years." He further stated that, "the Chinese have cited a variety of reasons—including lack of infrastructure—for their inability to open the Demchok route to Manasarovar, but the real reason might be the substantive differences on where the LOC stands in the Demchok area."

India needs to take up the re-opening of the border route through Demchok by diplomatically negotiating with the Chinese government, focusing on the potential of geo-economics rather than geopolitics.

References

Bray, John (1990). "The Lapchak Mission from Ladakh to Lhasa and the Government of India's Foreign Policy in the Second Half of the Nineteenth Century", *Tibet Journal* 15(4): 75-96.

Datta, C.L. (1973). *Ladakh and Western Himalayan Politics 1819-1948*. New Delhi: Munshiram Manoharlal Publishers Pvt. Ltd.

Francke, A.H. (1907). *Ladakh: A Mysterious Land, the History of Western Tibet*. London: n/d. New Delhi: Cosmo Publication (1907, reprinted).

————. (1926). *Antiquities of Indian Tibet: The Chronicles of Ladakh and Minor Chronicles*. A.W. Thomas (ed.) New Delhi: S. Chand & Co. (Pvt.) Ltd.

Joldan, Sonam (2012). *Ladakh's Traditional Ties with Buddhist Tibet*. Delhi: Kalpaz Publication.

Lamb, A. (1960). *Britain and Chinese Central Asia: The Road to Lhasa 1768 to 1905*. London: Routledge and Kegan Paul.

————. (1973) *Sino-Indian Border in Ladakh*. Canbera: Australian National University Press.

Miller, Robert James (1959). *Monasteries and Culture Changes in Inner Mongolia*. Wiesbaden: Otto Harrassonwitz.

Moorcroft, W. and George Trebeck (1841). *Travels in the Himalayan Provinces on Hindustan and Punjab; in Ladakh and Kashmir; in Pashawar, Kabul, Kunduz and Bokhara, from 1819-182*. Vol. 1. London: John Murray.

————. (1971). *Travels in the Himalayan Provinces on Hindustan and Punjab—In Ladakh and Kashmir in Pashawar, Kabul, Kunduz and Bokhara, from 1819-182*. Vol. 1. New Delhi: Sagar Publications and Karachi: Oxford University Press (1979).

Pascale, Dollfus (1995). "The History of Muslims in Central Ladakh", *The Tibet Journal* (Autumn).

Pectec, Luciano (1977). *The Kingdom of Ladakh, C.95—1842 A.D.* Roma: Istituto Italino Per IL Medio Ed Estreno Orient.

Rabgais, Tashi (1984). *Maryul La dvags kyi Snon rabs kun gsal melon Zhes bya ba zugso*. Leh- Ladakh: n/d.

Rizvi, Janet (1983). *Ladakh: Cross-roads of High Asia*. Delhi: Oxford University Press.

————. (1999). *Trans-Himalayan Caravan: Merchant, Princes and Peasant in Ladakh*. New Delhi: Oxford University Press.

Snellgrove, David L. and Hugh Richardson (1968). *The Cultural History of Tibet*. London: The Trinity Press.

Tsering, Nawang (1992). "The Fate of Traditional Education in Ladakh", in H.A. Osmaston and P. Denwood (eds.), *Recent Research on Ladakh*. Vol. 4 & 5. London: SOAS Studies.

———. (1979). *Buddhism in Ladakh*. New Delhi: Sterling Publishers Pvt. Ltd.

Waddell, L.A. (1959). *The Buddhism of Tibet or Lamaism, with its Mystic Cult, Symbolism and Mythology and in its Relation to Indian Buddhism*. 2nd edition. Cambridge: W. Heffer & Sons Limited.

Archival Materials

(1) National Archives of India, New Delhi.

Department Foreign, Branch Political. A, Consultation November 1868, Nos. 316-317.

Department Foreign, Branch Political. A, Consultation November 1868, Nos. 109-110.

Department Foreign, Branch Political. A, Consultation September 1869, Nos. 67-71

The Diary of British Joint-Commissioner, Ladakh, 18th June 1890, Foreign, Secret. F, 1-9, January 1892.

Dr. Caley's Report Relating to Trade of Ladakh. Department Foreign, Branch Political. A, Consultation October 1868, Nos. 140-141.

Foreign Department, Political. A. Branch, Nos. 560-597, Consultation June 1871.

Foreign Department, Political. A. Branch, Nos. 126-130, Consultation May 1872.

Department Foreign, Branch Secret. F, September 1892, Nos. 491-495.

Department Foreign, Branch Secret. F, Consultation September 1893, Nos. 425-495.

Department Foreign, Branch Secret. F, Consultation July 1894, Nos. 613-619.

Department Foreign, Branch Secret. F, Consultation September 1895, Nos. 374-383.

(2) Archive, Jammu

C. S. Old Record, File no. 271/17-C, Year 1916, Grand permission to leave Ladakh for Lhasa in favour of certain lamas, year 1916.

Lapchak (Lhasa) deputation of Lapchak to Lhasa with specification–articles for sale in conformity with custom. Persian Record, File. no. 980-C, Year 1886 A. D.

Persian Record, File no. 1209, Year 1839-40, Ladakh to Lhasa, statement of the stages on the road from Ladakh to Ladakh Lhasa.

News Papers

Hindustan Times, New Delhi.

The Hindu, Delhi

8

SANGEETA THAPLIYAL

Trans-Himalayan Cultural Linkages

India-Nepal-China

Culture and ideas originate in a historical context. People have a sense of history and do have a way of keeping remnants of that history alive. With time cultural boundaries traverse far and wide. These cultural boundaries, at times in friction with territorial or political boundaries, help us understand the relations between state and society, relations amongst states as it existed in the past and cultural components in defining and determining relationships. The interaction at the level of people and states has defined and shaped narratives of these cultural linkages. While analysing cultural linkages between India, Nepal and China, the present paper highlights Buddhism that has travelled from the plains of India to the highlands of Nepal and Tibet bringing a shared cultural heritage.

Nepal: The Cultural Transit Zone

Nepal is at the cusp of Indic and Tibetan civilisations. It has acted as a melting pot for the cultures of India and Tibet and as a transit point for facilitating cultural contacts between the two. Movement of population across the borders and commercial interests of traders kept the cultural boundaries fluid. Buddhism further brought cultural interconnectedness and linked the three areas under study.

Siddhartha was born in Lumbini, in present day Nepal, and he attained enlightenment in Bodhgaya in India. During the time period of Buddha, Kiratas ruled in Nepal (c. 1336-536 BC). They were Mongoloids and nature worshippers but many of them had adopted Buddhism as their religion. It was, however, during the Licchavi period (536 BC-877 AD) that Buddhism spread in Nepal. Originally from Vaishali, the Licchavis had a strong republican state during the time of Buddha in the 6th century BC. Following the invasion of Kushans, the state disintegrated and one branch of the Licchavis went to Kathmandu as Shakyas and Koliyas in the 6th century BC. Supuspa was the first Licchavi king in Nepal. Even though they were followers of Hinduism, Licchavis propagated and popularised Buddhism. They constructed many *viharas*, patronised nuns and monks, and empowered them to look after the moral laws of the country. Buddha as Boddhisatva in the form of Lokeshwara and Avalokiteshwara was developed during this period (Shreshtha, 2008: 49). "The Maurayans had close connections with the area of modern Nepal, since the foothills were within the empire" (Thapar, 1990: 74). It is said that one of King Ashoka's daughters had married a nobleman from the mountains of Nepal (Thapar, 1990: 74). In 249 BC, King Ashoka erected Rummeindei pillar in Lumbini indicating his visit to the place (Thapar, 2011: 426). It is the first epigraphic evidence relating to the life and history of Gautam Buddha. He had sent Dhamma missions to Nepal to popularise and propagate Buddhism. These missions brought in Theravada Buddhism to Nepal (Shreshtha, 2008: 147). However, it was during the rule of Kushans that Mahayana Buddhism came to dominate Nepal.

It is said that Nepal's links with Tibet through Buddhism began in the 7th century AD, when Songsten Gampo, King of Yarlung dynasty who had unified Tibet, gave royal patronage to Buddhism. His marriage to Nepali Princess Bhrikuti[1] (633 AD) and Chinese Princess Wengchen (641 AD) influenced him to give patronage to Buddhism. Both his wives had faith in Buddhsim. Princess Bhrikuti took along with her images of Akshabhya, Maitreya, Tara and Avlokiteshwara indicating the spread of Mahayana-Vajrayana Buddhism in Tibet. It is said that she built the Jokhang Palace (Shreshtha, 2008: 162-63). During King Gampo's time, Tamangs, who were part of his cavalry, settled in the bordering areas with Nepal to protect Tibet. They also cultivated land there. Similarly, Magars, Sherpa, Thakali and Gurungs

1. It is said that Bhrikuti was the daughter of Udaya Deva and sister of Narendra Deva of Licchavi dynasty. Narendra Deva took asylum in Tibet after his ministers revolted against him. He established marital alliance with Songsten Gampo by marrying his sister Bhrikuti to him and with his support regained his power in Nepal. See, Shrestha (2008: 164).

migrated from Tibet and settled in Nepal (Lal, 2004: 87). Hence, the northern region of Nepal became the zone of Lamaistic Buddhism, which is very similar to Tibetan Buddhism. The lower Himalayan valleys in the south are influenced by Hinduism. In some parts of the southern region, Buddhism and Hinduism have become more or less fused and no sharp lines can be drawn between the two.

Songsten Gampo sent scholars to study Buddhism in India. One such scholar, Thonmi Sambhota, considered an incarnation of Manjushree, was sent to India to study the script with Pandit Devavid Sinha. Sambhota took various books to Tibet and created alphabets and grammar for the Tibetan language. He also translated Buddhist scriptures (Shreshtha, 2008: 164).

Nepal acted as a meeting point for scholars from India and Tibet. Indian scholars travelled to Tibet via Nepal where Nepali Buddhists acquainted them with the Tibetan way of life. The Tibetans also learnt Sanskrit and basic knowledge of Buddhism in Nepal and prepared themselves for advanced learning in India. Thus, Nepal served as an interactive zone for scholars from north and south such as Shantarkshita (705-762 AD), an Indian scholar and Buddhist monk, who is said to have established the Samye Monastery and the Bhikhhu Sangha in Tibet. He preached the doctrine of Darshita, Ashtadasa Dhatu and Pratityasamutpada. He stayed in Nepal for six years (743-749 AD) and propagated his Vijnanavada doctrine. On his advice, Guru Padmasambhava went to Tibet via Nepal and worked towards synthesising Buddhism with the old Bön religion (Shreshtha, 2008: 179). Other Buddhist scholars visiting Tibet via Nepal were Kamalasila, Buddhasree, Ratnakirti, Kanakashree and Vairochana. Pharping in Nepal had emerged as the centre for Tantric Buddhism and many Tibetan scholars visited to study from 978-1026 AD. Tibetan monk Brog mi and his disciples studied Sanskrit from Nepali scholar Shanti Bhadra before leaving for India to study under the guidance of Acharya Ratnakar Shanti, who had composed Sadhana to worship Vajratara and Trilokya, a form of Heruka. Marpo-Do-Pa, Rwa-Lotsa-ba rdorje and Milarapa were some of the scholars who visited Nepal and India in pursuit of knowledge and philosophy (Shreshtha, 2008: 216).

From 3rd to 6th century AD, Buddhism was the dominant religion in India but it started losing its social and political patronage by the 6th century AD. To begin with, the rise of 18 sects proved divisive for the religion. Also compromise on ascetic life and Buddha's teachings by the monks did not go down well with the people who then hesitated to give patronage and support to the monasteries. This brought resurgence of Shaivism and Vaishnavism in India. By the 7th century AD, Shankracharya had revived Hinduism by incorporating many doctrines of Buddhism. With the advent of Islam in India, Buddhism lost state patronage and support. Later, the British were more interested in pursuing their strategic and commercial interests rather than cultural linkages with the Himalayan and Trans-Himalayan countries.

Simultaneously, political changes were taking place in Nepal, which had an impact on state patronage of Buddhism and the state's relations with its neighbours. Prithvi Narayan Shah had unified Nepal by 1769. His forces expanded to the north and south. In its north, when Tibet imposed private duties on merchandise, Nepal's commercial interests received a setback. In 1788, Nepal invaded Tibet. The Chinese *Amban* (resident) Shu Lien informed the emperor Chien Lung, who sent his army into Tibet. Through the Chinese mediation, Nepal and Tibet signed the Treaty of Kerong on 19 July 1789 (Manandhar, 1999: 11-14). This treaty was signed to safeguard Nepal's commercial interests in Tibet. By 1854, Buddhism had lost state support in Nepal when Jung Bahadur Rana, the then Prime Minister of Nepal, gave emphasis to staunch Hinduism and banned conversion to Buddhism in his legal code.

In the 18th and 19th centuries, Nepal was engaged in armed conflicts with British India and Tibet for expanding its territory and protecting its trans-Himalayan political and commercial interests. Pursuits for expanding political and commercial interests often led to clash of interests and armed conflicts.

Since then, academic writings on India, Nepal and Tibet relations have been analysed through the prism of geo-strategy and geopolitics. This statist approach has emphasised and highlighted the conflictual issues in the relations. The preponderance of politics and strategic interests is a modern political construct. The present paper takes 1769 as the marker in defining the relations between the three countries because, from this year onward political Nepal, as we see it today, came into existence after the unification of the principalities by Prithivi Narayan Shah, and its boundaries with India and Tibet were defined.

Political Relations Overshadow Socio-cultural Links

The expansionist policy of the Gorkhas brought them in conflict with Sikkim, Tibet and India. Nepal's army had captured Garhwal, Kumaon and had expanded its territory till Sutlej. It culminated in an armed conflict between British India and Nepal in which Nepal lost one-third of its territory and was compelled to sign a treaty of peace at Suguali on 2 December 1815.

Political boundary in the south of Nepal was defined by the Treaty of Sugauli. The East India Company tried to restrain the westward expansion of Nepal by following the principle of limitation which limited Nepal to the hills while the plains belonged to the British. The treaty incorporated provisions which took away territory from Nepal that had been taken over through armed aggression. This defined the territory of Nepal in the south. Nepal gave away its lowland (Terai) in the south, Garhwal and Kumaon in the west to the British and to the east of Mechi river to Sikkim. It was also agreed that if any differences arose between the rulers of Nepal and Sikkim then the matter had to be referred to the British.[2] To contain expansion of the Gorkhas towards the Indian plains, the British followed the 'forward policy' which implied that the frontiers of India's neighbours were to be integrated with the then existing defence system in a manner that they enjoyed internal autonomy but their external relations were subjected to British interests (Lamb, 1960: 260).

The geography in the north of Nepal was difficult, rugged with the high Himalaya and its passes. The 1414.88 km long border had high mountains and passes, ravines, gorges and river valleys, which made it difficult for people to cross the border. The Nepal Tibet Treaty

2. For the text of the treaty, see Narharinath and Basnayet (1964: 13-18).

Peace and Friendship signed on 24 March 1856, defined Nepal's border with Tibet till the Himalayan range. Nepal relinquished its rights over Kuti, Kerung, Jhangagadhi, Takldakhar and the territory up to Dhaking Pass. It also relinquished its rights over Khasa and fixed its border till Tatopani which is the present border of Nepal. These treaties defined modern Nepal's territory with its northern and southern neighbour and it emerged as a buffer.

Highlighting British India's interests Lord Curzon had said:

> It would be madness for us to cross the Himalaya and occupy it. But it is important that no one else should seize it, and that it should be turned into a sort of Buffer between the Indian and Russian empires....Tibet itself and not Nepal must be the buffer state that we endeavour to create.[3]

Nepal had fought wars with Tibet and kingdoms in India but the Chinese and the British Indian forces had contained and confined it to the Himalayan ranges. The forces of these two major powers did not meet in Nepal, Sikkim or Bhutan, and this was emphasised in subsequent agreements signed between Nepal and its neighbours.

The foreign policy of small states is defined and determined by big powers, and in the case of Tibet and Nepal, their immediate neighbours had signed treaties to make them neutral zones. Nepal had signed certain treaties with its neighbours defining it as a neutral zone. In 1904, British India had sent Colonel Francis Younghusband and his army to Tibet and succeeded in signing a treaty establishing bilateral relations and commercial trade between Tibet and the British empire (Roberts II and Roberts, 2009: 6). The Sino-British Treaty of 1906 agreed that:

> The Government of Great Britain engages not to annex Tibetan territory or to interfere in the administration of Tibet. The Government of China also undertakes not to permit any other foreign states to interfere with the territory or internal administration of Tibet (quoted in Duggal, 2012: 36).

---

3. Hamilton Papers, Lord Curzon's Private Letter to Hamilton, 11 June 1901. Source: National Archives, New Delhi.

In 1907, Britain and Russia had agreed that "in conformity with the admitted principle of suzerainty of China over Tibet, both nations engaged not to enter into negotiations over Tibet, except through the intermediary of the Chinese government" (Duggal, 2012: 36). In the meantime, the Manchu dynasty was overthrown and expelled from Tibet in 1911. In October 1913, at the Shimla Convention, the British government proposed division of Tibet as Outer and Inner Region where Outer Region was given full autonomy and Inner Tibet was administered by China. China accepted this proposal and claimed full sovereignty over Tibet. In the changing political dynamics, British India and Nepal signed the Treaty of Peace and Friendship in December 1923. The treaty stated that in case of any friction or misunderstanding with the states whose territories adjoin their common frontiers, the other signatory would be informed about it (Article 3). Article 4 bounds the signatories to prevent its territory from being used against the security interests of the other. In the Treaty of Peace and Friendship signed between Nepal and India on 31 June 1950, it was reiterated that both the signatories "agreed to inform each other of any serious friction or misunderstanding with neighbouring state likely to cause any breach in the friendly relations subsisting between the two governments".[4]

Nepal had entered into a similar arrangement with China earlier. The Treaty of Tibet signed on 5 October 1792 between Nepal and China, decided that if any dispute arose between Nepal and Tibet, then the Chinese ambassador at Lhasa would mediate. It was also agreed that if any foreign power attacked Nepal, then, "China would never lag behind in helping Nepal." These agreements amply testify that India and China did not want any political disturbance in the Himalayan and trans-Himalayan region, and wanted it to emerge as a neutral zone.

In the process, the entire discourse in understanding the relations between the three countries became state centric with emphasis on conflict and managing conflict. Subsequent governments in Nepal described themselves as 'landlocked', rather than 'land-linked', with

4. For the text of the treaty, refer Narharinath and Basnayet (1964: 35-37).

Tibet and India. The trans-Himalayan linkages that had existed since time immemorial were over-shadowed by geo-political and geostrategic issues.

Communist China Enters Tibet

Political developments in the north had alarmed India and Nepal. Chinese forces had entered Tibet in the early 1950s. Both India and Nepal were concerned with this development and considered it affecting their security interests. For India, security considerations were of utmost importance. The Indian government had considered India's security parameters to be in the north of Nepal, that is Tibet, but with China taking over Tibet, this line of security was infringed. Ideological differences with Communist China further influenced India's policy towards the Himalayan countries. Locating it in the Cold War context, India's preferred policy was to keep the neighbourhood free from the interference of extra-regional powers. Nepal was equally concerned with the southward expansion of China that brought it closer to its border. India and Nepal tried to strengthen their security in the north by signing the Treaty of Peace and Friendship in 1950 and agreeing to continue Gorkha recruitment in the Indian Army, and modernising the Royal Nepal Army by sending military missions to Nepal. The Treaty of Peace and Friendship highlighted reciprocity in security interests whereby India and Nepal agreed to share information on any eventuality or crisis and agreed to solve the problem through mutual consultation.

The treaty underscored security interests holistically by not only addressing the military strength and identification of threat but also through economic development and social stability that were essential in a politically unstable Nepal of the 1950s that was struggling to establish democracy. A socio-politically unstable Nepal would have found it difficult to contain the expansion of Communist ideology from its northern neighbour. Economically weak and politically unstable countries were considered perfect ground for breeding communism and locating it in the Cold War scenario; Nepal was considered vulnerable to such influences. India's security interests were compounded due to its open border with Nepal and its own weakness in managing it militarily.

Thus, the treaty addressed the socio-economic variables in bilateral relations. For instance, the citizens of one country could participate in industrial and economic development in another country without any discrimination (Clause 6). Similarly, citizens could enjoy right of residence, ownership of property, participation in trade and commerce and movement in each other's country (Clause 7). Geography had allowed easy accessibility with India and this was further strengthened and legalised by the Treaty of Friendship.

Political boundaries took precedence over cultural boundaries and the traditional meeting spaces for the people and communities shrunk especially towards Nepal's northern borders. The Nepalese did not have much link with Tibet after Communist China entered Tibet. Chinese forces entered Tibet in 1950 and this infringed the concept of buffer that was defined by British India and China. For instance, China had withdrawn facilities from Nepalese living in Tibet and the borders were controlled for its traders and pilgrims. Nepal and China had signed an agreement to maintain friendly relations and on trade and intercourse between Nepal and the Tibetan region of China on 20 September 1956. This treaty abrogated all the treaties and documents that were signed in the past by both the signatories (Article 3). China, however, did not breakup socio-cultural links completely at the people's level but redefined them. For instance, Article 4, para 3, of the treaty allowed pilgrimage by religious believers of either country to the other according to religious customs. Personal baggage and articles used for pilgrimage carried by the pilgrims of either party were exempt from taxation by the other party. Further Clause 4, para 5, stated that:

> Pilgrims of either party who travel across the border between the Tibet Region of China and Nepal for the purposes of pilgrimage and need not hold passports, visas or other documents or certification, but shall register at the border check posts of the first encountered authorised government office of the other party, and obtain permits for pilgrimage there from.

Permit system and provision for registration were introduced (Bhasin, 1994: 3044-46).

In the late 1950s, China started asserting its territorial claims in areas bordering Tibet in India, Nepal and Bhutan. It followed different strategies to deal with border disputes with the three countries. With India, China refused to accept the border demarcation and became aggressive on the frontier. It withdrew all the privileges enjoyed by Indians in Tibet and suggested fresh negotiations to rebuild relations. After the Sino-India war of 1962, traditional relations between Indians and Tibetans were disrupted. The Kailash yatra was stopped by the Chinese when its forces entered Tibet in 1962. The yatra was restarted in 1982. A Joint Working Group was set up to negotiate on the border issue and till date 16 meetings have been held. With Nepal, China resolved the border issue and its negotiations with Bhutan are still continuing.

In 1965, China declared a part of Tibet to be the Tibetan Autonomous Region of China. The Cultural Revolution started in Tibet on 25 August 1966, destroying hundreds of sacred wall paintings and statues, and banned the practice of Buddhist religion and ceremonies associated with it such as burning of incense. More than 6,000 monasteries were destroyed and plundered (Roberts II and Roberts, 2009: 130). Religion was defined as part of four olds: old customs, old culture, old habits and old ideas, which had to be eliminated.

The Dalai Lama along with his supporters had taken asylum in India and many Tibetans came to Nepal and Bhutan in 1959. Due to its traditional links with Tibet, Nepal gave them shelter and also allowed transit to enter India. The Nepalese government followed a two-pronged approach on the issue of Chinese in Tibet. On the one hand, it allowed a Tibetan military base in Mustang in north-west Nepal, which was supported by the US Central Intelligence Agency. The militants, mainly from Kham province of Tibet, were given military training, arms and equipment to carry out guerrilla operations against the Chinese People's Liberation Army (PLA) in support of the cause of Tibet. Following rapprochement in the US-China relations in the early 1970s, American support to the guerrillas was withdrawn. On the other hand, Nepal tried to diplomatically deal with China.

Domestic politics within the country had an impact on Nepal's policy towards China. King Mahendra had dismissed the democratically elected government of B.P. Koirala and taken power in his hands in 1960. Noting that Indian policy was not very favourable towards the royal takeover, Mahendra found it prudent to move closer to China. China utilised this opportunity by recognising Mahendra's leadership and positive efforts in the development of Sino-Nepal relations. Speaking at a banquet, Chairman Lio Shao described King Mahendra as an "outstanding spokesman" and an esteemed friend of the Chinese people. China expressed its gratitude to Nepal "when the handful of reactionaries in China's Tibet staged their rebellion, Nepal firmly adhered to a correct stand of non-interference in China's internal affairs."[5] Subsequently, King Birendra followed his father's policy of supporting Chinese policies in Tibet and regarded Tibet as an integral part of China. He visited Lhasa in 1973 and sent forces to supress Khampa rebels in Mustang, the next year.

Tibetans in Nepal

One of China's major concerns is the presence of and support to Tibetans in Nepal. Mustang operation had already shown that the pro-Tibet movement could be carried out from the Nepali soil.

There are nearly 20,000 Tibetans in Nepal. Many of them are engaged in the carpet industry and have made it the biggest foreign exchange earner in the country. Over the years, Tibetans have been crossing the border to enter safer places in India and Nepal. It is estimated that approximately 2,500 to 3,500 Tibetans cross Nepal's territory to enter India.[6] By 1987, there was an increase in the number of Tibetans leaving Tibet due to increased Chinese repression. China sought Nepal's help in suppressing Tibetan activities. Due to Chinese pressure, Nepal took steps to close its border and stopped giving refugee status to Tibetans in December 1989. It, however, agreed

5. Speech of Liu Shao-Chia, Chairman of the People's Republic of China at a banquet in honour of King Mahendra in Peking on 29 September 1961 (Bhasin, 1994: 553).

6. Tibetan Refugees, *www.savetibet.org/resources/tibetan-refugees/*

to UNHCR's request to allow Tibetans to use Nepal as transit and move to India. In practice, Nepal's immigration law does not have provisions for refugees. Many of them are arrested, or deported to Tibet.[7]

Successive governments in Nepal have looked at the Tibet issue from the prism of its relations with China. It is worthwhile to mentioning here that anti-democratic governments in Nepal like monarchy during the Panchayat period and Maoists under Prachanda's leadership looked towards China for political support to their respective regimes as they perceived the Indian government to be supportive of multi-party democracy. In lieu of their diplomatic dealings with China, these governments in Nepal were not favourable towards Tibetans. When King Gyanendra took direct control of power in 2005, the office of the Representative of the Dalai Lama was closed.[8]

Pro-Tibet demonstrations in Nepal during the Beijing Olympics in 2008 highlighted its geostrategic importance. Committed to 'One China Policy,' the Nepal government took harsh actions against the demonstrators. Commenting on the situation, Prachanda said: "We cannot term the Chinese government's step to check violence unleashed by the separatists in Tibet as 'crackdown'." "We regard Tibet as inseparable part of China."[9] Irrespective of ideology, the governments in Nepal have consistently followed the One China Policy, ignoring old cultural linkages and sentiments of the people. It is in the interests of the political elite that have given primacy to developing closer political relations at the altar of old customs, ideas and practices.

Political instability in Nepal, especially due to the Maoist movement, brought American, British and other European countries in the country. China's security concerns heightened with the American presence in Nepal, especially in the backdrop of renewed

---

7. "Information on Treatment of Refugees", *refworld. http://www.refworld.org/topic,50ffbce5307,50ffbce56ee,414fe0704,0,,QUERYRESPONSE,.html*

8. Quoted in "Tibet's Stateless Nationals: Tibetan Refugees in Nepal", *http://www.tibetjustice.org/reports/nepal.pdf*

9. *Times of India*, 24 March 2008.

political activism in Tibet in 2008. It tried to increase its presence in Nepal through military, economic aid and cultural connect.

China's Soft Power Approach

Countries around the world have realised that it is difficult to concentrate only on hard power of military might and technological advancement and that the use of soft power approaches such as diaspora, culture, values and civil society could be used for enhancing their power. A smart power will include both hard and soft power. Nye (2004: 6) wrote:

> One may obtain the outcomes it wants in world politics because other countries-admiring its values, emulating its example aspiring to its level of prosperity and openness- want to flow it...This soft power-getting others to want the outcomes that you want- co-opts people rather than coerces them.

China's policies and approach towards Tibet and Tibetans has been a blot to its image on human rights and inclusiveness. Hence, the Chinese policy towards its own image has undergone basic changes. After gaining hard power in military, technological and economic arenas, China has felt the need to acquire soft power such as culture, religion, ideas and values to influence international politics. There are two main schools of thought for the discourse on soft power. One view is that the core of soft power is culture and the country should emphasise it. The other view gives prominence to political power as the mainstay of soft power (Glaser and Murphy, 2009). The Communist Party has also conceded to the essentiality of culture. In a speech to the China Federation of Literary and Art Circles in November 2006, former President Hu Jintao said, "the one who takes commanding point on the battlefield of cultural development will gain the upper hand in fierce international competition" (Glaser and Murphy, 2009). There has been a calculated move to emphasise soft power and on including Buddhism and culture in its fold.

China has invested in cultural resources at home and abroad. It set up China study centres (CSCs) in Nepal to promote Mandarin and Chinese cultural heritage in 2000. Presently, there are nearly 35 CSCs in Nepal, and China proposes to open one each in 75 districts. Most of these centres are close to Nepal's border with India. In 2007, the Confucius Institute was set up in Tribhuvan University for teaching Chinese as a foreign language and for the promotion of Chinese culture.[10]

China has identified Chinese Buddhism as another soft power resource. It has nearly 300 million Buddhists in the country and is trying to project itself as promoting Buddhism and establishing links with Buddhist countries. Chinese Buddhism is treated more favourably than other officially recognised religions. Unlike Tibetan Buddhism, Chinese Buddhism is a local religion, which does not have any religious authority outside the country. It also has no linkage with any separatist movement. Chinese Buddhism is identified as a political resource through which China is trying to project building a harmonious society at home and to promoting a policy of building harmonious, peaceful world for the international community (Angelskar, 2013). In fact, three meetings of the World Buddhist Forum were held in China in 2006, 2009 and 2012. China's own policy towards Tibet is contrary to its professed goal of developing a harmonious society at home. And it is this image that gets projected in the western world, which China is trying to refurbish by pursuing its own cultural diplomacy.

As said earlier, China is making an attempt to follow a soft policy approach towards Nepal. It has made an attempt to be actively involved in developing Lumbini as a major Buddhist centre. In November 2010, Nepal gave permission to the Beijing Zhongtai Jinghu Investment Company to construct a 100 metre Buddha statue. This ₹8 billion project includes building of Lumbini as an International Buddha Centre.[11] Recently, there has been a move to renovate Lumbini in Nepal. The Asia Pacific Exchange and Cooperation Foundation (APEC), with the support from the Chinese government, has been given the contract for this. APEC will raise

10. For details on the Confucius Institute, refer to its official website *http://www.ku.edu.np/ci/index.php?go=home*

11. "China to Invest Rs 8 b in Lumbini", *Republica*, 21 November 2010. *http://archives.myrepublica.com/portal/index.php?action=news_details&news_id=25422*

$3 billion to construct temples, an airport, highways, hotels and a Buddhist university in Lumbini. Interestingly, Prachanda, the Chairman of UCPN (M), is the Vice Chairman and former Prince Paras is a member of APEC.[12] Many in Nepal questioned these projects; as a result, the government in Nepal said that there was no formal agreement with China to develop Lumbini.[13] Prachanda said, "Nepal, China and India should come together and form a strategic partnership through this Lumbini project for peace, stability and development in the region and Asia" (Jha, 2011).

The Indian government does not get involved in supporting religious activities in any country in pursuit of its broad secular aims which are mandated by the Constitution of India as this can lead to complexities at home. Blarel says:

> In practice, India's soft power remains weak for two primary reasons. First, Indian diplomacy has neglected soft power as an important tool of statecraft and has only recently understood the relevance of 'cultural diplomacy'. Second, soft power cannot really exist without some initial hard power achievements (Prashar, 2012).

India has stepped up its cultural diplomacy. In 2006, the Public Diplomacy Division was set up to promote soft power in its foreign policy. It tries to foster "a greater understanding of India and its foreign policy concerns. Its mand ate enables it to organise and support a broad range of outreach activities, both in India and overseas" (Blarel, n.d.). Through films and seminars in collaboration with universities and think tanks abroad and its magazine *India Perspective*, it tries to promote better understanding of India's foreign policy. India has set up cultural centres through the Indian Council of Cultural Relations (ICCR) in 38 countries. It has set up 108 chairs in collaboration with universities abroad to have academic collaborations. In 2010, India established an academic chair in Tribhuvan University, Kathmandu. ICCR has also set-up a cultural

12. "China Plans to Develop Buddha's Birthplace", *Reuters*, 16 June 2011.
13. *http://in.reuters.com/article/2011/06/16/idINIndia-57729620110616*

centre in Kathmandu.[14] There is one cultural centre in Beijing and seven ICCR chairs in different universities in China.

In 2011, the Global Buddhist Congregation was held in Delhi. It was attended by 800 delegates from around the world. On the occasion, the International Buddhist Confederation was formed to foster Buddhist values and perspectives in the global discourse.[15] Two more congregations were held in 2012 and 2013 in India. Bodhgaya and Sarnath are two main Buddhist pilgrim centres in the country. Setting up Nalanda University with international collaboration is another step towards this direction.

There has been an emphasis on the study of Tibet and Tibetan language: Sarat Chandra Das wrote the Tibetan-English Dictionary in 1902 and Rahul Sankrityayan's travelogues to Tibet written between 1930 and 1950 are a reservoir of information about the region, its culture and traditions. Vishwa Bharati University began the Centre of Tibetan Studies in 1954. Since then Tibetan studies and Buddhism are taught in various other institutions and universities. However, the Indian government has not shown enough interest to use religion as a soft power or to reach out to people or countries on this basis.

Additionally, India is making an attempt to ease the difficulty in reaching Kailash-Mansarovar from Kumaon, by trying to open the route from Demchok in Leh, as it is the shortest route to reach Tibet. However, no breakthrough has been achieved on this. China turned down the Indian request stating poor road and infrastructure conditions, and frequent landslides. Omar Abdullah informed Rajya Sabha in 2002:

> Government has on several occasions proposed to the Chinese side an alternate route for the Kailash Manasarovar Yatra through Demchok in Jammu & Kashmir. In response, the Chinese side has conveyed that it would not be feasible to open an alternate route through Demchok on account of poor road conditions, frequent landslides, high altitudes and lack of infrastructure in that uninhabited remote region of Tibet. The Chinese side also conveyed that they had

14. For information on Public Diplomacy Division, Ministry of External Affairs, see *http://indiandiplomacy.in/AboutUs.aspx*

15. For information on Indian Council for Cultural Relations, see *www.iccrindia.net/*

examined other alternatives, but none of them had been found feasible due to rapidly changing natural and weather conditions.

During the visit of Chinese Premier Zhu Rongji to India in January 2002, the Indian side again requested the Chinese side to upgrade facilities for the Yatra on their side and for the opening of a second route. The Chinese side said that utmost efforts are being made and that China will continue to make such efforts in the future.[16]

In 2007, Pranab Mukherjee, the then Foreign Minister, informed the Rajya Sabha:

> Government have proposed to the Chinese side, the opening of an alternative route to Kailash-Mansarovar through Demchok in Jammu and Kashmir. During the visit of the Chinese President Hu Jintao to India in November last year, the two sides agreed to explore the possibility of opening an additional route for the Yatra.[17]

Even though China has tried to project itself as a supporter and promoter of Buddhism, its policies towards Tibet and India highlight that it is using Buddhism as a tactic to make inroads into the Buddhist world. Cultural heritage and links with Tibet or India are not of much significance. China is competing with India and other perceived sympathisers in Nepal by emphasising on cultural linkages apart from political and strategic inter-relationships.

Over the centuries, Buddhism has acted as a link between India, Nepal and China. This links was forged when political elite in all the three states supported and promoted cultural relations. With changes in state's identity, relations with each other changed. Territories are not static and changes in states' territorial identities influenced and affected their external relations with others. For instance, Nepal's various principalities interacted independently with Tibet till the Gorkhas conquered and unified the country, which in turn centralised relations with its neighbours. With waning state patronage, cultural

16. Information of World Buddhist Congregation *http://asokamission.in/event/global-buddhist-congregation-2011-new-delhi*

17. Omar Abdullah, Minister of State for External Affairs replying to a question on Kailash Mansarovar Yatra Ladakh Routein Rajya Sabha on 14. 3. 2002, *http://164.100.47.5:8080/members/Website/quest.asp?qref=63450* also see, "Alternate Route for Kailash Yatra Not Feasible: China", *Times of India*, 7 March 2002.

links dwindled. With changing times, contexts and circumstances, elites laid emphasis on their national interests either by giving patronage to cultural relations or by emphasising on strategic or commercial interests. At any given time, all aspects of relations exist but the elites, based on their ideology and personality decides which aspect will be given more emphasis in the relations. States have tried to either facilitate or hinder cultural contacts but they have not been able to completely block them. Despite the states' actions cultural popularity and commonalities have remained and have travelled far and wide through the efforts of individuals, religious groups or other non-state actors. States cannot ignore these cultural realities. The resurgence of emphasis on Buddhism is again a soft power approach to reach out to people and communities in other countries. These identities have been constructed to complement national interests defined and determined by time, place and context.

References

Angelskar, Trine (2013). *China's Buddhist Diplomacy*. Norwegian Peace Building Resource Centre. March. *www.peacebuilding.no*

Blarel, Nicolas (n.d.). "India's Soft Power: From Potential to Reality", *http://www.lse.ac.uk/IDEAS/publications/reports/pdf/SR010/blarel.pdf*

Bhasin, A.S. (1994). *Documents on Nepal's Relations with India and China 1947-1992*. Vol. 1. Delhi. pp.3044-46.

Duggal, P.N. (2012). *China's Tibet Invasion*. New Delhi: Sumit Enerprises. p.36.

Glaser, Bonnie S. and Melissa E. Murphy (2009). *Soft Power with Chinese Characteristics: The Ongoing Debate. www.csis.org*. 10 May.

Jha, Pashant (2011). "No Pact on Chinese Lumbini Project", *The Hindu*, 29 July.

Lal, Harishchandra (2004). *Buddhism in Nepal*. Kathmandu: Ratna Pustak Bhandar. p.87.

Lamb, Alaistar (1960). *Britain and Chinese Central Asia*. London. p.260.

Manandhar, V.K. (1999). *Cultural and Political Aspects of Nepal-China Relations*. New Delhi: Adroit Publisher. pp.11-14.

Narharinath, Yogi and Narendra Mansingh Basnayet (1964). *Itihas Prakasma Sandhi Patra Sangraha*. Kathmandu. pp.13-18.

Nye, Jospeh (2004). *Soft power: The Means to Success in World Politics*. USA: Public Affairs. p.6.

Prashar, Utpal (2012). "Prachanda wants Indian Involvement in Lumbini Project", *Hindustan Times*, 10 November.

Roberts II, John B. and Elizabeth A. Roberts (2009). *Freeing Tibet*. New York: Amacom. p.6.

Shreshtha, Khadga Man (2008). *History of Buddhism in Nepal*. Kathmandu: Kamla Devi Shreshtha. p.49.

Thapar Romila (1990). *A History of India*. Vol 1. New Delhi: Penguine Books. p.74.

————. (2011). *Cultural Pasts, Essays in Early Indian History*. New Delhi: Oxford University Press. p.426.

9

NANI BATH AND MAN NORBU

Tibet's Relation with Tawang

A Factor for Chinese Claim and People's Perception on it

Introduction

Historically Tibet has been an independent state with a history, language, culture and political system of its own. It also had bilateral trade relations and signed a number of treaties with other countries (Tibet Truth, 2009). From 1911 to 1950, Tibet successfully avoided undue foreign influence and behaved, in every respect, as a fully independent state. The 13th Dalai Lama reasserted Tibet's full independence internally by issuing a proclamation, and externally in formal communications with foreign rulers and also in a treaty with Mongolia. Even China's own historical records and treaties signed with Tibet refer to Tibet as a strong state with whom China was forced to deal on an equal footing (Free Tibet, n.d.).

The Tibetan government maintained independent international relations with all neighbouring countries and people of the Himalayas. In fact, there was a close historical, cultural, economic and religious affinity between Tibet and the Monpas of Tawang, and this age-old relation has become a key factor for Chinese claim over Tawang.

Tawang was actually a part of Tibet in medieval times until 1914 (The Economic Times, 2012) when British India signed the Shimla Accord with Tibet. Before that, Tawang was directly ruled by the Tibetan administration. It was a part of Tsona district in Tibet, and Tibetan authority continued up to 1950 (Verma, 2013). The Tibetan government collected taxes from the people of Tawang through tax collectors located at Tsona Dzong, Kongbu and Kham (Lama, 1999). Tibet collected everything from Monpas in the form of tax. The local land owning families were the Khraipa 'tax-payer class' who were obliged to pay taxes directly to the government. Most taxes were collected either in kind or in the form of agricultural and horticultural products mainly rice and other food grains. The most oppressive was the 'compulsory labour tax', typically a number of labour days that had to be contributed to transportation of tax loads or the construction of state-sponsored buildings (Bobt, 2012). According to Pema Gombu:

> The Tibetan officials in that time were corrupt and cruel. I am sure His Holiness did not know this. In those days, if a Tibetan stopped you they could ask you to work for them like a slave. They forced us to pay taxes. Poor farmers like me had to give over a quarter of our crops to them. We had to carry the loads 40 km (25 miles) to a Tibetan town as tribute every year (China Matters, 2011).

This makes it very clear that the condition of Monpas during Tibetan rule worsened.

There were trade relations between Tibetans and Monpas of Tawang. This is evident from an observation made by Tsewang Norbu (2008):

> The Monpas of Tawang had a flourishing trade with Tibet till the political upheavals in Tibet. Trade fairs used to be held at Tsona every year in the fifth, seventh and eleventh Tibetan months. The Monpas in large numbers used to go there with items like wooden bowls and cups, fresh and dry chillies, medicinal herbs, rice, handmade papers, bamboo pens, animal skins, vegetable dyes, tea-bricks made from the leaves of musheng (Alnus), yier (Xanthaxylum), turmeric, ginger, mushrooms, gall bladder of bear, musk, fresh and dried fruits like persimmon, peach, orange, amla and certain other items. From there, the Monpas used to bring down wool and woollen clothes, dried meat and fish, black salt, quality tea-bricks, cheese, butter, woollen carpets, swords, saddle, saddle bags, shoes, caps, walnuts, Chinese made crokeries, jewellery, ritual objects, mustard oil, horses, mules, ponies, and many other items.

Tawang was the most prosperous province of Tibet and accounted for a third of its economy. Most of the food consumed in Tibet was grown here as per the records at Tawang (The Economic Times,

2012). The Monpas of Tawang migrated from Tibet mostly during the times of the 4th and the 5th Dalai Lamas according to Tsewang Norbu. According to him, there were seven waves of Monpa migration to Tawang from Tibet (The Times of India, 2012).

The Tibetan-Buddhist saint Thangtong Gyelpo (1385-1464), who is known for the construction of an iron chain bridge (Chak-Zham), visited the Tawang area and it was during his stay that the bridge was constructed, connecting the south bank at Mukto village with the north bank at Kitpi village; this bridge still exists (Bobt, 2013: 99).

Further, he is also known for starting the Ache Lhamo, the famous Tibetan folk opera for collecting money and donations which would help him in his construction work. The Ache Lhamo dance is still practised on certain festive occasions by the people of Tawang.

The Monpas also had close religious contact with Tibet. They are generally adherents of the Gelugpa sect of Tibetan Buddhism. In the 11th century, the Monpas of Tawang came under the influence of Tibetan Buddhism of the Nyingma and Kagyu denominations. It was during this period that they adopted the Tibetan script for their language;[1] they are still using the Tibetan script and calendar. The missionaries of the Gelugpa sect of Mahayana Buddhism from central Tibet brought Monpas into their fold in the early 17th century (The Economic Times, 2012). The present Tawang Monastery, a centre of Gelukpa power, was built by Mera Lama Lodre Gyatso in 17th century (1680-81) in accordance with the wishes of the 5th Dalai Lama, Ngawang Lobsang Gyatso, who ruled over Tawang from Lhasa. The site of the present monastery is believed to have been chosen by a horse owned by Mera Lama. When Mera Lama Lodre Gyatso failed to find a suitable place to establish the monastery, he decided to meditate in Bramdongchung's cave; and during this time his horse ran away. He retraced the footsteps of the horse and finally found him at a place called Tana Madrelgang and thus the Ganden Namgyel Lhatse Monastery was constructed. In Tibetan language, 'Ta' means horse and 'Wang' means to choose and thus Tawang derived its name. The Dalai Lama then appointed the Dzongpon (governor) of Tsona

1. *Monpa People-Wikipedia*, the free encyclopedia. *http://en.wikipedia.org/wiki/Monpa_people*

as the secular authority over the Tawang area (Bobt, 2012). One can still find the sites and remains of Dzongs of those days in Tawang, Sange and Dirang which were used by Tibetan rulers. Tawang is the birth place of the 6th Dalai Lama, Tsangyang Gyatso, who was identified as a reincarnation of the 5th Dalai Lama and was taken to Lhasa from Urgelling village in 1697 when he was 14 years old (The Economic Times, 2012). Moreover, it was through Tawang that the present or the 14th Dalai Lama made his way into India when he fled Tibet in 1959, taking refuge at the Tawang Monastery for over a week (Ramachandran, 2008).

Direct Tibetan rule over Tawang was established in the 17th century which continued up to the early 20th century.[2] Tawang came under the British Indian administration in 1914 with the signing of the Shimla Agreement, when a new boundary was drawn between British India and Tibet. However, the British did not show much interest and Tibet continued to administer Tawang by collecting taxes from the people.[3] No attempt was made to administer Tawang until April 1938. It was only in 1938 that the British paid attention to Tawang when Captain Lightfoot, the then Political Officer of the then Balipara Frontier Tract, led an expedition to Tawang (Ghose, 2009). Tibet protested very strongly and Tibetan authority was restored after Lightfoot's brief stay at Tawang (The Economic Times, 2012). Even after independence, for quite some time, India did not establish its authority over Tawang. India asserted its administrative control over Tawang in February 1951, when Major R. Bob Khating led Indian army troops to relocate Chinese squatters (China Matters, 2011) and the Tibetan administration was removed from Tawang once and for all, and thus Tibetan rule over Tawang came to an end and Tawang came under Indian administration. At the same time, China's sovereignty over Tibet was established leading to serious issues between China and India vis-a-vis Tawang's historical relationship with China.

2. Ibid.

3. *Tawang district-Wikipedia*, the free encyclopedia. *http://en.wikipedia.org/wiki/Tawang_district*

Chinese Territorial Claim

China has continuously claimed Tawang as its territory on the basis of the relations that Tibet had with Tawang in the past. China bases its claim on the basis of the historical relationship that existed between Tawang Monastery in Arunachal Pradesh and Lhasa Monastery. The Chinese logic is that since Tibet is now part of China, Arunachal Pradesh should also be a part of it (Goswami, 2002: 3).

China not only claims Tawang district, but also lays claim to the whole of state of Arunachal Pradesh (Asia News Agency, 2009: 37). China claims around 90,000 square kilometres of territory, roughly the size of Arunachal Pradesh, and regards the area as 'disputed' (Wasim, 2010). In November 2006, on the eve of Chinese President Hu Jintao's visit to India, Sun Yuxi, the then Chinese Ambassador to India, stated: "In our position the whole State of Arunachal Pradesh is Chinese territory. And Tawang is one of the places in it. We are claiming all of that. That is our position" (Asia News Agency, 2009: 37).

Chinese claim to Arunachal Pradesh stems from the Five Fingers Theory of Mao Zedong, the first Chairman of the Communist Party of China, who termed Tibet as the palm of a hand with Ladakh, Sikkim, Nepal, Bhutan and the then North-East Frontier Agency (now Arunachal Pradesh) as its five fingers (Asia News Agency, 2009: 36). In fact, Chinese claim to Arunachal and more specifically, to Tawang, stems from Tibet's accepted historical or ecclesiastical ties with Arunachal Pradesh (Chellaney, 2007).

There has been no consistency in Chinese territorial claims. From 36,000 square miles claimed in 1959, it had increased its claims to 90,000 square kilometres by 1965. It made their sweeping territorial claims asserting that Arunachal Pradesh was established largely on the three ares of China's Tibet region i.e., 'Monyul, Loyul and Lower Tsayul', but were unable to produce necessary evidence to substantiate its claim and was also unable to locate where these areas was situated in the thousands of square miles constituting the North-East Frontier Agency (Banerjee, 1985).

China has become visibly aggressive with regard to its territorial claim (Goswami, 2011). It denied visas to many people of Arunachal Pradesh claiming the entire state as its territory and that the indigenous inhabitants of Arunachal Pradesh are its own people and thus do not require a visa to visit their own country. In 2007, China refused to grant a visa to Ganesh Koyu, an Indian Administrative Service (IAS) officer from Arunachal Pradesh citing that he is a citizen of China by virtue of being from the state of Arunachal Pradesh and therefore needed no visa to visit his own country. Ganesh Koyu was to visit China as part of a 100-member IAS delegation, but Chinese refusal of visa to him led to the cancellation of the visit of the entire delegation in protest (Asia News Agency, 2009: 38).

Similarly, Gegong Apang, the former Chief Minister of Arunachal, was also denied a visa (Asia News Agency, 2009: 38). Again in early January 2012, China denied a visa to Group Captain Mohonto Panging, a senior Indian Air Force officer from Arunachal Pradesh. He was to visit China as part of a 30-member Integrated Defence team under a bilateral defence exchange programme (Goswami, 2012: 17). And very recently, two young women archers from Arunachal Pradesh Mihu Maselo and Yumi Sorang, who were heading to Wuxi for the Youth World Archery Championship, were given stapled visas in October 2013 by the Chinese embassy (Arunachal Times, 2011: 1).

China raised strong objections to the Dalai Lama's proposed visit to the monastery town of Tawang in Arunachal Pradesh in November 2009. Jiang Yu, the spokeswoman for China's foreign ministry asserted that "China's stance on the so-called 'Arunachal Pradesh' is consistent. We firmly oppose Dalai visiting the so-called 'Arunachal Pradesh'" (Goswami, 2010: 2-3). However, India acted against China. In spite China's strong concern, India made it clear that no restrictions would be put on the Dalai Lama's visit in November 2009 to the border state of Arunachal Pradesh (Wasim, 2010: 92). The former Chief Minister of Arunachal Pradesh, late Dorjee Khandu termed the Chinese claim to Arunachal as absurd (Wasim, 2010: 80). He stated, "Chinese claim of Arunachal is baseless. So India should once for all settle the border dispute and clarify all doubts" (Hindustan Times, 2009).

China has repeatedly been objecting to the visit of Indian leaders in what they called "disputed territory" (Bath, 2009). China expressed strong dissatisfaction over Prime Minister Manmohan Singh's visit to Arunachal Pradesh to campaign for the Congress party during the state assembly elections in October 2009. The Chinese foreign ministry spokesman Ma Zhaoxu said, "We demand the Indian side address China's serious concerns and not trigger disturbance in the disputed region so as to facilitate the healthy development of China-India relations" (Wasim, 2010: 86-87). But India rejected the Chinese protest against Singh's visit to Arunachal Pradesh (Wasim, 2010: 85).

China also reacted against the visit of A.K. Antony, the Defence Minister of India, to Arunachal Pradesh. On 25 February 2012, the Chinese foreign ministry spokesman Hong Lei stated that such visits create complications towards resolution of the border dispute (Goswami, 2012: 17).

Coinciding with President Pranab Mukherjee's two days visit to Arunachal on 29-30 November 2013, Chinese official news agency Xinhua reiterated Beijing's territorial claims on Arunachal Pradesh. In a report, Xinhua said China saw the state as being "currently under Indian illegal occupation." "The so-called 'Arunachal Pradesh' was established largely on the three areas of China's Tibet-Monyul, Loyul and Lower Tsayul currently under Indian illegal occupation," the Xinhua report said. The report further added, "These three areas, located between the illegal 'McMahon Line' and the traditional customary boundary between China and India, have always been Chinese territory" (Krishnan, 2013). Xinhua also referred to foreign ministry spokesman Qin Gang's statement in response to Pranab Mukherjee's visit. It quoted Qin as saying, "China's stance on the disputed area on the eastern part of the China-India border is consistent and clear" (The Times of India, 2013).

Apart from these, China had also objected to the Asian Development Bank (ADB) loan to be used for the development of Arunachal Pradesh. In June 2009, China tried to block \$2.9 billion loan to India from ADB because part of the loan that is, \$60 million had been earmarked for flood-control projects in Arunachal Pradesh, the state that includes Tawang (Wasim, 2010: 176). This was the first time that China sought to broadcast its claim on Arunachal Pradesh in a multilateral forum (Goswami, 2010: 2).

China began claim on Tawang during the border talks 1960s. Initially, it was more a form of bargain to exchange Aksai Chin with the then NEFA (now Arunachal Pradesh), but now lays a permanent claim on Arunachal Pradesh (Arpi, 2012). On two different occasions in the past (1960s and 1980s), China had offered to give up its entire claim in Arunachal Pradesh if India accepted Chinese claim to Aksai Chin in Ladakh.

The first solution was put forward in 1960 by Chou En-lai, the then Chinese Prime Minister during his visit to India. The second was suggested by Deng Xiaoping in 1980, who proposed a solution similar to Chou En-lai's offer of giving the areas south of the McMahon Line to India and Aksai Chin to China. But India did not accept this 'east west swap' offer. India's refusal to consider the proposal led China to press claims on Tawang on the plea that this is an area that had close religious ties with Tibet (Asia News Agency, 2009: 36).

It seems very interesting that while China demands Tawang on behalf of Tibetans, the Tibetans are not claiming Tawang as Tibetan territory. The Tibetan spiritual leader Tenzin Gyatso, the 14th H.H. Dalai Lama himself acknowledged the validity of the 1914 Shimla Agreement and the McMahon Line drawn between Tibet and British India several times (Ramachandran, 2008). He expressed surprise over Chinese claim on Tawang during his visit to Tawang in November 2009. He said the People's Liberation Army occupied Tawang during the 1962 war with India. But the then Chinese government declared a unilateral ceasefire and withdrew. "Now the Chinese have got different views. This is something which I really don't know. I am little bit surprised," he said in an apparent reference to Chinese claims over Tawang (The Financial Express, 2013). Similarly, many other Tibetan leaders have the same view and recognise the McMahon Line. Samdhong Rinpoche, the then Prime Minister of the Tibetan government-in-exile said, "we recognise it because we agreed to it (Wasim, 2010: 94).

People's Perceptions of Chinese Claim on Tawang

The Monpas consider the Chinese claim baseless and illegal. During a field survey conducted in 2013, 150 respondents from 10 circles of Tawang district were interviewed out of whom 100 had witnessed the war and 50 who had not. To know the perception of the people, certain specific questions were forwarded to the respondents regarding Chinese claim over Tawang.

In the beginning, respondents were asked what their opinion on Chinese claim over Tawang was. They expressed the view that the Chinese claim was totally illegal and absurd. People's perception about Chinese claim over Tawang can be better understood with the help of Table 9.1.

Table 9.1

Genuineness of the Claim

	Respondents' Responses						
	Yes	*%*	*No*	*%*	*Don't know*	*%*	*Total*
Witness to 1962 war	00	00	83	83	17	17	100(100)
Non-witness to 1962 war	00	00	47	94	3	6	50(100)
Grand Total	00	00	130	86.7	20	13.3	150(100)

Source: Field survey, 2013.

In response to a query whether the Chinese claim was genuine, 86.7 per cent of the respondents expressed the view that the Chinese claim was not genuine. If we take the percentage of the witnessed and non-witnessed respondents separately, we find that 83 per cent of the witnessed respondents and 94 per cent of the non-witnessed respondents said 'No'. They were of the opinion that the Chinese claim was totally wrong. Only 13.3 per cent of the total respondents gave the answer 'don't know' and if we take them separately, 17 per cent of the witnessed respondents and 6 per cent of the non-witnessed respondents said 'don't know' to the question. This small portion of respondents was ignorant of the validity of the Chinese claim mostly because they were illiterate and were not aware about historical facts. None of the respondents were of the view that the Chinese claim was genuine.

It is very clear from Table 9.1 that the people of Tawang have a negative response to the Chinese claim because not a single respondent favoured China.

When the researcher interacted with the respondents during the field survey, they reported that Tawang was never a part of China and thus the Chinese claim was baseless and illegal. They further reported that China's claims were based on the historical relations that Tibet had with Tawang. The common opinion amongst the respondents was that although Tawang was historically under the Tibetan administration, it became a part of the Indian Union through a peaceful agreement with the then Tibetan government. They further said that Tibet was an independent nation when the Shimla Accord of 1914 was signed and thus China should recognise the validity of the McMahon Line.

During the field survey, it was found that a number of respondents mainly, the educated opined that though China did not ratify the 1914 Shimla Agreement between Tibet and British India, their main concern was the boundary with Tibet not with British India, and hence China had no genuine reason for their claim. They strongly argued that China should also respect the McMahon Line.

During the discussion, the respondents said that neither had the British Indian government taken Tawang by force nor had Tawang agreed to the agreement under pressure. They further said that China's claim over Tawang was unrealistic. They argued that China had no right to claim Tawang because the Tibetans and even their spiritual leader, the Dalai Lama, recognise Tawang as a part of India.

The respondents clearly reported that China did not have any right over Tibet because it forcefully captured Tibet against the wishes of the people and compelled the Dalai Lama to leave Lhasa. They consider Tibet as an independent country and want their freedom. They further stated that China cannot lay any claim over Tawang on the basis of its historical relations with Tibet because Tibet was then an independent sovereign nation.

In an interview, Dorjee Norbu of Sakyur village said:

> Tawang was never a part of China. How can Chinese make claim over Tawang when the Tibetans themselves do not consider Tawang as their part? If the Chinese are basing their claim on historical relations, then they should not forget that Tibet was an independent nation then and thus they should give freedom to Tibet on historical

grounds. They cannot make any claim citing mere history rather they have to respect the reality and agreement signed.[4]

According to Nawang Chotta of Mukto village, "Chinese claim is totally baseless. Historically we had our border with Tibet and Bhutan, never in the history of Tawang there is any mention of our relation or being a part of China."[5] When asked the same question, Tsewang Norbu of Urgelling replied, "the Monpas had never seen a single Chinese before 1962 nor could they speak a Chinese word, how could China claim Tawang."[6]

Another respondent, Kesang Ngurup Damo of Gispu village stated:

> Our forefathers did not know China except Tibet. Neither they had seen nor heard of Chinese. If Arunachal Pradesh was a part of China then why did they leave when they managed to reach Assam foothills without much retaliation from the Indian army side.[7]

According to Rinchen Dorjee of Mukto:

> It is absolutely wrong on the part of Chinese to lay claim over Tawang. Historically, Tawang had no relation with China, no boundary, no economic, social, political, cultural and commercial and any other relation with China at any point of time.[8]

One of the respondents (Tsering Dakpa of Gispu) stated:

> The Chinese had never come to Tawang. The Monpas saw them only in 1962. India was under British rule and Tawang under Tibet but Tibet was never a part of China. Unlike Chinese, who forcefully captured Tibet, India did not take Tawang forcefully.[9]

Many were of the view that the Chinese claim to Tawang was absurd as China reached up to Bomdila and even beyond, but left without staking any claim. They further believed that the Chinese

---

4. Personal interview with Dorjee Norbu, on 17 August 2013, at his residence, Sakyur.
5. Personal interview with Nawang Chotta, on 26 July 2013, at his residence, Tawang.
6. Personal interview with Tsewang Norbu, on 27 July 2013, at his office, Tawang.
7. Personal interview with Kesang Ngurup Damo, on 13 August 2013, at his private residence, Tawang.
8. Personal interview with Rinchen Dorjee, on 10 August 2013, at his residence, Tawang.
9. Personal interview with Tsering Dakpa, on 24 July 2013, at his residence, Tawang.

were claiming Tawang because it has now become a world famous place, it has a rich hydro-power capacity and is a good tourist destination. All the respondents had similar views. On being asked whether India should accept the Chinese claim, 100 per cent of the respondents gave negative answers. All the 100 witnessed and 50 non-witnessed (1962 war) respondents, gave a negative answer. They were of the view that India should never accept the Chinese claim. Even those 13.3 per cent who were not aware of the validity of the Chinese claim gave 'No' as an answer.

Table 9.2

Should India Accept the Chinese Claim?

	Responses						
Respondents	*Yes*	*%*	*No*	*%*	*Don't know*	*%*	*Total*
Witness to 1962 war	00	00	100	100	00	00	100(100)
Non-witness to 1962 war	00	00	50	100	00	00	50(100)
Grand total	00	00	150	100	00	00	150(100)

Source: Field survey, 2013.

It is evident from Tables 9.1 and 9.2 that the people of Tawang are more than happy to be associated with India. All the respondents positively affirmed that India should never accept the Chinese claim because Tawang is an integral part of India. They clearly reported that the people of Tawang have been considering Tawang as an integral part of India from the very beginning and do not want the Indian government to accept any claim made by China. According to Pema Khandu of Gyangkhar, "Tawang is an undisputed integral part of the Indian union and thus India should never accept any Chinese claim over Tawang."[10] Thutan Tashi of Mangnam stated:

> The boundary between India and Tibet (China) is demarcated by the McMahon Line and Tawang falls under Indian territory as per the Line and as such the Chinese claim over Tawang is not justifiable. Thus, India should never accept their claim.[11]

10. Personal interview with Pema Khandu, on 14 August 2013, at his residence, Bomdir, Tawang.
11. Personal interview with Thutan Tashi, on 30 July 2013, at his residence, Lumla.

The respondents narrated that the Monpas were against the Chinese even in 1962 when China attacked India. They believed that the locals by virtue of their patriotism and their inclination towards India helped the Indian army in the 1962 war with China (see Table 9.3).

Regarding a question "what was the reaction of the people towards the Chinese PLA?" a majority of the respondents, that is, 92.7 per cent were of the view that the reaction of the people had been totally negative towards the Chinese PLA in 1962 war. Ninety-four per cent of the witnessed respondents and 90 per cent of the non-witnessed respondents had the same view. Not a single respondent opined that the reaction of the people was positive.

Table 9.3

Reaction of the People Towards the Chinese PLA

	Responses						
Respondents	*Positive*	*%*	*Negative*	*%*	*Neutral*	*%*	*Total*
Witness to 1962 war	00	00	94	94	6	6	100(100)
Non-witness to 1962 war	00	00	45	90	5	10	50(100)
Grand Total	00	00	139	92.7	11	7.3	150(100)

Source: Field survey, 2013.

The respondents were of the opinion that the locals left everything behind in their villages to save their lives. The whole village became empty. The villagers mostly hid in jungles, and some even went to Bhutan and Assam. Very few who were either old or handicapped stayed back.

However, only 7.3 per cent of the total respondents were neutral (6% of witnessed and 10% of non-witnessed). They said that the reaction was neutral in the sense that though the locals were against the Chinese they could not express their feelings freely out of fear of them and so had to remain neutral.

In contradiction to the people's reaction, the Chinese attitude was always positive towards the locals as reflected in Table 9.4.

Table 9.4 reveals that 86.7 per cent of the total respondents held the view that the attitude of the Chinese towards the local people was positive. Ninety-three per cent of witnessed respondents and 74 per cent of non-witnessed respondents responded positively. Eight per cent of the total respondents (5% witnessed and 14% non-witnessed respondents) said that the Chinese attitude was negative towards the local people. And very few, that is, 5.3 per cent (2% witnessed and 12% non-witnessed respondents) viewed the Chinese attitude towards the locals as neutral.

Table 9.4

What was the Attitude of the Chinese PLA Towards the People?

	Responses						
Respondents	*Positive*	*%*	*Negative*	*%*	*Neutral*	*%*	*Total*
Witness to 1962 war	93	93	5	5.0	2	2	100(100)
Non-witness to 1962 war	37	74	7	14	6	12	50(100)
Grand Total	130	86.7	12	8.0	8	5.3	150(100)

Source: Field survey, 2013.

Further, we posed a query to the respondents: what tactics did the Chinese adopt to impress the local people? Although China adopted harsh methods to express its claim and fought a war with the Indian army in 1962, they adopted a positive attitude towards the locals and tried to impress them. They opted various tactics to win over the confidence of the locals and tried to build affinity with them on the basis of race and physical features. They asked locals not to fear them, rather they helped them in their household and field work like fetching water, brooming and harvesting crops.

Moreover, they never entered the houses even though they were vacant. They mostly entered '*sarongs*', the lowest storey of the house used for keeping pigs and other animals. They did not take anything free of cost.[12] The Chinese rather tried to bring the locals back to their villages.[13] They also said, "Our complexion is same, we are alike from

12. Personal interview with Dawa Norbu, on 18 July 2013, at his village,Gonghar.
13. Personal interview with Ngawang Tsering, on 13 July 2013, at Tawang Monastery.

every angle unlike them, who are like *hang* (devil)."[14] The Chinese even invited the local people for a community feast. But the very next day, people came to know that the Chinese had served them dog meat.[15]

The respondents stated that despite all their tactics, the Monpas did not like the Chinese and were rather afraid of them. Sang Dakpa of Changprong said, "The Chinese always tried to impress but we knew their tactics. They pretended as if they were kind and good. They tried to be helpful but their intentions were not good."[16] The respondents argued that the Chinese compelled the locals to help them against the Indian army. They were also of the view that the they would have ended like Tibetans.

Table 9.5

The Dalai Lama Factor and People's Response to PLA

	Responses						
Respondents	*Yes*	*%*	*No*	*%*	*Don't know*	*%*	*Total*
Witness to 1962 war	100	100	00	00	00	00	100(100)
Non-witness to 1962 war	31	62	00	00	19	38	50(100)
Grand Total	131	87.3	00	00	19	12.7	150(100)

Source: Field survey, 2013.

The people of Tawang have not forgotten the way the Chinese compelled the Dalai Lama to leave Lhasa in 1959 and thus 87.3 per cent of the respondents believed that Chinese PLA did not get a positive response. Hundred per cent witnessed and 62 per cent non-witnessed respondents were of the same view. Not a single respondent said 'No' to the query. Only 12.7 per cent of the total respondents and 38 per cent of the non-witnessed respondents gave the answer 'don't know' (see Table 9.5).

The Monpas supported the Indian army during the war. According to them, the locals helped by carrying "*whoolas*" (loads) of the Indian

14. Personal interview with Ngawang Tashi, on 14 July 2013, at Pamaghar.

15. Personal interview with Pema Khandu, on 15 July 2013, at his village Blaiteng.

16. Personal interview with Sang Dakpa, on 24 July 2013, at Changprong.

army to various posts. Under each Tsorgan, every household sent one representative to carry loads and rations for the Indian army.[17] According to Khyong Tsering of Bongleng village, "the locals played the role of porters, guides and messengers." Khyong Tsering and Sang Dakpa went up to the main border at Pangchen (Zemithang) carrying *whoolas* but were taken prisoners by the Chinese and were freed after three months.[18]

The locals helped in every possible way and were later rewarded.[19] They helped by providing food, shelter, medicines and by dressing the Indian armed personnel in local costumes and showing them short-cut routes through Bhutan. The Tsorgan of Rho village informed the Indian army about Chinese staying in the *sarong*, the ground floor of the Gompa. The Indian army were able to attack the Chinese by locking them from outside.[20] Almost everyone supported the Indian army morally and physically. Many locals lost their lives and many were injured while helping the Indian army.

Another question had to do with whether the local people supported the Chinese PLA or Indian army during the 1962 war. It is observed from the data that a majority of the respondents, that is, 90.7 per cent believed that the locals helped the Indian army. Only 9.3 per cent of the respondents believed that the locals helped both Chinese PLA and the Indian army. But no respondent believed that the local people supported the Chinese PLA. On being asked whether the people supported the Chinese PLA or the Indian army, Rinchin Gombu of Mukto replied, "the Chinese compelled some of the locals to help and threatened them with dire consequences and some locals had no option but to help the Chinese out of fear." For example, Pema Wangdi of Yubu,[21] Lobsang Tashi of Mago[22] and Ngawang of Shoktsen[23] helped the Chinese out of fear; they were then severely

---

17. Personal interview with Thapkey, on 10 July 2013, at his village, Shakti.
18. Personal interview with Khyong Tsering, on 12 July 2013, at Bongleng.
19. Personal interview with Dorjee Norbu, on 17 August 2013, at his residence, Sakyur.
20. Personal interview with Lungtan Tsering, on 14 July 2013, at Khinmey.
21. Personal interview with Rinchin Khandu, on 25 July 2013, at his residence, Gyangkhar.
22. Personal interview with Dorjee Norbu, on 17 August 2013, at his village, Sakyur.
23. Personal interview with Tsering Dakpa, on 24 July 2013, at Tawang.

punished. The Chinese PLA compelled them and used them as local guides against the Indian army.

Table 9.6

Whether People Supported Chinese PLA or Indian Army

	Responses						
Respondents	*Indian army*	*%*	*Chinese PLA*	*%*	*Both*	*%*	*Total*
Witness to 1962 war	92	92	00	00	8	8	100(100)
Non-witness to 1962 war	44	88	00	00	6	12	50(100)
Grand Total	136	90.7	00	00	14	9.3	150(100)

Source: Field survey, 2013.

The people of Tawang have now become more critical of the Chinese claim over Tawang because of Chinese inhuman atrocities in Lhasa. In fact, the Monpas do not want India to accept any claim made by the Chinese, rather they do not trust them.

Thus, it is inevitable that the people of Tawang do not favour Chinese claim nor do they want India to accept any Chinese claim. They want that India, instead of accepting any claim, should instead develop the border areas of Tawang by developing communication networks and deploying more and better arms and army. The Monpas not only consider Tawang as an integral part of India but also perceive Tibet as an independent sovereign nation. They believe that the Chinese forcefully captured Tibet against the wishes of the people of Tibet.

On the one hand, the Monpas of Tawang are integrated and happy with the Indian Union and in spite of several strong Chinese efforts during and after the war they have been consistent in their approach. On the other hand, China is constantly staking its claim based on the historical relationship between Tibet and Tawang, but the reality is that China has yet to make peace with the Tibetans. Thus, Tawang and its historical ties with Tibet have become the centre of the dispute between the two Asian giants, India and China.

References

Arpi, Claude (2012). "When China Did Not Claim Tawang", in *claudearpi.blogspot.com. http://claudearpi.blogspot.in/2012/10/when-china-did-not-claimtawang*

Arunachal Times (2011). "Arunachal Archers Detained at Airport for Stapled Chinese Visa", *Arunachal Times*. Itanagar. 11 October. p.1.

Asia News Agency (2009). *Special Study: An Analytical Backgrounder, India-China Accords and Discords.* Haryana. p.37.

Banerjee, D.K. (1985). *Sino-Indian Border Dispute*. New Delhi: Intellectual Publishing House. p.27.

Bath, Nani (2009). "The Arunachal Factor in Sino-India Relations", *Echo of Arunachal*, 22 October.

Bobt, Timotheus A. (2012). *The New Lamp Clarifying the History, Peoples, Languages and Traditions of Eastern Bhutan and Eastern Mon. Wageningen.* The Netherlands: Monpassang Publications. p.145.

Chellaney, Brahma (2007). "Sino-Indian Relations: Tibet is the Key". *www.hrichina.org/sites/default/files/PDFs/CRF-2007-1_Indian.pdf*

China Matters (2011). "The Little Town of Tawang: The Dalai Lama's Headache", in *chinamatters.blogspot.com. http://chinamatters.blogspot.in/2011/04/little-town-of-tawang-dalai-la*

FreeTibet (n.d.). "The Legal Status of Tibet". *http://www.freetibet.org/about/legal-status-tibet*

Ghose, Arabinda (2009). "Tawang, Inhabited Mainly by the Cultured Monpas, was Not Under Tibet, Let Alone China", *http://organiser.org/archives/historic/dynamic/modules56e6.html?na*

Goswami, Namrata (2010). *China's Territorial Claim on Arunachal Pradesh: Crafting an Indian Response.* New Delhi: Institute for Defence Studies and Analyses. pp.2-3.

————. (2011). "China's 'Aggressive' Territorial Claim on India's Arunachal Pradesh: A Response to Changing Power Dynamics in Asia". *http://www.idsa.in/strategicanalysis/35_5/chinasaggressiveterritorialclaim_ngoswami*

————. (2012). *China's Territorial Claim on Arunachal Pradesh Alternative Scenarios 2032*. New Delhi: Institute for Defence Studies and Analyses. p.3.

Hindustan Times (2009). "China Cannot Do a 1962, say Border Villagers", *Hindustan Times. http://www.hindustantimes.com/News-Feed/India/China-cannot-do-a-1962-say-border-villagers/Article1-458281.aspx*

Krishnan, Ananth (2013). "China Reiterates Claim to Arunachal". *http://www.thehindu.com/news/international/world/pranabs-arunachal*

Lama, Tashi (1999). *The Monpas of Tawang: A Profile*. Itanagar, Arunachal Pradesh: Himalayan Publishers. p.4.

Norbu, Tsewang (2008). *The Monpas of Tawang Arunachal Pradesh.* Guwahati: Bhabani Offset & Imaging Systems Pvt. Ltd. p.153.

Ramachandran, Sudha (2008). "China Toys with India's Border". *http://www.atimes.com/atimes/South_Asia/JF27Df01.html*

The Economic Times (2012). "The Himalayan Blunder: Tawang's Age-old Connect with Tibet & China", *The Economic Times. http://articles.economictimes.indiatimes.com/2012-10-17/news/34525*

The Financial Express (2013). "Surprised Over Chinese Claims on Tawang: Dalai Lama", *The Financial Express. http://www.financialexpress.com/news/surprised-over-chinese-claims*

The Times of India (2013). "China Reiterates Claim on Arunachal Pradesh Through Mouthpiece", *The Times of India. http://articles.timesofindia.indiatimes.com/2013-11-30/india/445960*

Tibet Truth (2009). "Independent Tibet: The Facts". *http://tibettruth.com/independent-tibet-the-facts/*

Verma, Virendra Sahai (2013). "Sino-Indian Border Dispute: The Issue of Tawang". *http://virendrasahai.com/sino-indian-border-dispute-the-issue-of-tawang*

Wasim, Mohd. (2010). *China-India Border Conflict Recent Perspective.* Delhi: Prashant Publishing House. p.94.

Wikipedia (n.d.). "Monpa People", in *Wikipedia*, the free encyclopedia. *http://en.wikipedia.org/wiki/Monpa_people*

————. (n.d.). "Tawang district", in *Wikipedia*, the free encyclopedia. *http://en.wikipedia.org/wiki/Tawang_district*

10

BIJAY THAPA

An Identity in Flux

Tibetans in Sikkim and Darjeeling Hills

Introduction

The history of Tibetans in Sikkim-Darjeeling hills[1] has been embedded within the region despite significant changes since 1959. Tibet and Sikkim-Darjeeling hills share close links through their mountain passes.[2] These links were strengthened by religious and cultural exchanges, movement of people and ideas, trade and services and pastoral activities.

British influence in Sikkim-Darjeeling hills in the late 19th century and their subsequent involvement there, deteriorated the cordial relationship between Tibet and Sikkim-Darjeeling hills. The Younghusband Mission in 1904 is one such incident. However, the relationship revived through trade and cultural and religious exchanges. After a few decades, the India-China war in 1962 followed the closing of passes, which affected the cordial relationships between Tibet and Sikkim-Darjeeling hills (Wangchuk). The re-opening of Nathu-la in 2006 for cross-border trade has revived ties to a certain extent especially between Tibet (now Tibet Autonomous Region [TAR]) and Sikkim.

1. Here, Sikkim-Darjeeling hills are referred as one based in terms of traditional and cultural linkages exclusive of political connotation.
2. There are three passes along a straight line on the Chola Range: Cho-la, Nathu-la and Jelep-la. The Cho-la mountain pass was used by the royal family of Sikkim to cross into Tibet, mainly to the Chumbi valley where they had a summer palace. Nathu-la and Jelep-la were the hubs of yak herders from Tibet and used to access pastures on the Sikkim side. Since there was some traffic on these passes, they were also used for small-scale trading by the yak herders and graziers, but the real trade between Sikkim and Tibet was carried out over the passes in the North Sikkim—mostly through Kongra-la and also from Chorten Nyima La and some other passes (Wangchuk, 2013).

The fundamental aspect in this subject is the issue of refugees. Two major incidents—the Chinese invasion of Tibet in 1959 and the India-China war in 1962—led the Tibetans to flee their homeland in great numbers. This process continues as Tibetans under the Chinese command face oppression and injustice even today. Like many Indian states hosting Tibetan refugees, Sikkim and Darjeeling hills have received refugees since Sikkim shares a physical border with Tibet and there exist close ties accompanied by racial and cultural commonalities. This was further strengthened by the establishment of Tibetan settlements[3] both in Sikkim and Darjeeling hills. Today the settlements are located at Ravangla, south Sikkim, which technically falls under the agricultural-based settlement and in Sonada in Darjeeling, which comes under handicraft/industrial-based settlements. A large number of Tibetans also reside in scattered settlements in Darjeeling, Gangtok and Kalimpong (Central Tibetan Administration).

The Tibetan population varies every now and then because of new arrivals, local integration, third country resettlement and an inconsistent population (who move from host country to third country/one place to another, within a country). For the year 1976, identified altogether, there were 2,406 Tibetans in Sikkim and 4,475 in Darjeeling and 1,973 in Kalimpong areas of the Sikkim-Darjeeling hill region.[4] However, according to the Central Tibetan Administration, Planning Commission Demographic Survey (2009), there were 3,270 Tibetans in Gangtok, 1,180 in Ravangla, 3,001 in Darjeeling, 1,941 in Kalimpong and 546 in Sonada. The data over three decades indicates a different scale and a different movement. There is a gradual rise in the population of Tibetans in Sikkim, while on the other hand, there is a gradual decline in the number of Tibetans in Darjeeling hills. One has no clear explanation for this change as the process itself is a gradual movement and there are

3. Today, there are 46 Tibetan settlements in India, Nepal and Bhutan, home to most of the 100,451 Tibetan refugees in South Asia (Planning Council 1998 figures). According to Tibetan Justice Centre (2011), "Most Tibetans in India live in 37 formal settlements and about 70 informal Tibetan communities scattered throughout the country."

4. Data quoted in a study by Lynn Pulman (1983).

many associated reasons for the change. However, one factor for the population decline in Darjeeling is local integration, which is in fact a known aspect. Also, political unrest adds to a decline in population as the Tibetans rely on their business which gets affected in such a situation. Unlike Darjeeling, Sikkim does not give any citizenship rights to the Tibetans but offers ample commercial avenues to the business-oriented community (see Figure 10.1).

Figure 10.1

Tibetan Population in Sikkim-Darjeeling Hills

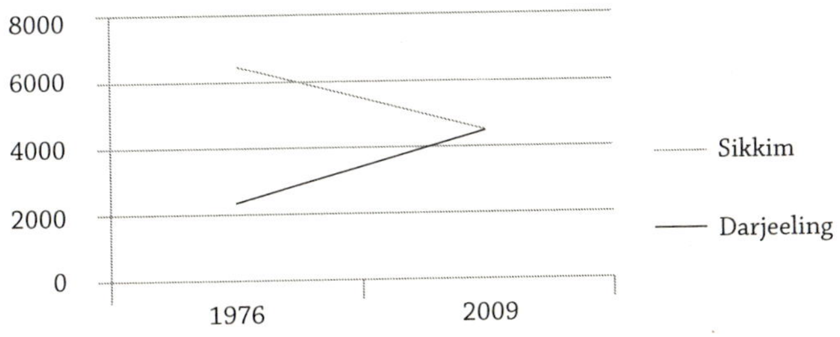

Source: Composed by author based on figures from: 1. Data quoted in a study by Lynn Pulman (1983), for the year 1976. 2. Central Tibetan Administration, Planning Commission Demographic Survey 2009.

Tibetans in Sikkim-Darjeeling Hills

Tibetans and Tibetaness prevail, represent and define the historicity and landscape of Sikkim-Darjeeling hills. In an entirely different setting with geographical barriers, the socio-cultural aspects of Tibetans retain their essence and preserve their domain distinctly in the region. Within these, the Tibetans have a varying degree of identity in Sikkim-Darjeeling hills. Theoretically, Tibetans who live around the world can be best defined as a refugee diaspora because they are not only refugees but also diaspora. Additionally, the term fits the Tibetans who fled their country and are today scattered around the world with their 'government-in-exile.' Within this holistic definition, it is important to study the changing status and varying degree of Tibetan identity that is mostly visible in the study area. Understanding the cosmopolitan identity of Tibetans in Sikkim-

Darjeeling hills will help in comprehending the transforming Tibetan identity in general.

Generally, Tibetaness exists in the eastern Himalaya, despite decades of border closure. However, a mosaic of Tibetan identity is evident as Tibetans have been adapting to unprecedented changes. Some of the variant levels of Tibetan identity are as follows.

First, the Tibetan presence in Sikkim-Darjeeling hills can be traced back to historical times. At that time, they migrated, settled and integrated because movement of people was not restricted across borders. This section of the population includes in particular those who moved to Sikkim-Darjeeling hills prior to the 1959 crisis. They are representatives of those Tibetans who have integrated into the host society. To be definitive, this section of Tibetans can be best defined as migrants who are today better known locally as Indian Tibetan or *bhutias*, that is, they are Indian citizens but prefer to be called *bhutias*. A *bhutiain* from Darjeeling explains, "We are Tibetans by root but Indians by nationality. We are called *bhutias* or Indian Tibetans." Therefore, this section of the population wants to be recognised as Tibetans and not clubbed with Tibetan refugees.

Second, with the Chinese invasion of Tibet in 1959 and the India-China war of 1962, Tibetans were forced to flee their homeland thus making them refugees. These refugees were and are confined to settlement areas and some are even scattered outside the camps. Although some of them have integrated into the host region, many have by choice abstained from obtaining citizenship of the host country and this resonates with cultural preservation of the government-in-exile. This variant therefore comprises Tibetan refugees who are primarily older people and have seen and faced the difficulties in the hour of crisis. Thus, their identity remains as to that of refugees and that to by choice.

Third, due to commonalities in terms of race, culture, religion, traditional and historical imprints, local integration has taken place, mainly in Darjeeling and Kalimpong hills. However, such local integration is restricted to Sikkim, as it follows protective measures to curtail illegal migration and local integration. But this does not mean that there is no evidence of Tibetan integration.[5] Among many other reasons, one fundamental reason behind their integration is easy access to the host community which means one can easily integrate with the host society. This section of the population forms another type of Tibetan identity that can be termed as 'new citizens'.

Fourth, among the Tibetan refugees, there are people who constantly juggle their identities. Those refugees who wish to sustain themselves and aspire to be self-reliant and independent leave the settlements to explore commercial avenues. With such temporality, if they sustain or are able to establish themselves, then they leave the settlement and integrate with local society. If unsuccessful, they rejoin the settlement. Such juggling is a unique feature of Tibetans in the Sikkim-Darjeeling hills. This variety of identity can be termed as 'juggling identity'.

Fifth, as settlements do not have sufficient area, for instance in the Sonada settlement camp, refugees settle in host communities but remain closely linked with the settlement. Beyond the businesses that they set up in the market, some are engaged in settlement areas for various purposes. Lack of physical area obliges them to maintain a different degree of identity which is uncommon among other places. They can be termed or defined as 'out stationed citizens'.

Tibetan Identity and its Political Essence

Tibetans, generally referred to as 'refugees' or 'diaspora' are discussed and debated among scholars. Their understanding varies on Tibetans' status as refugees, diasporas and asylums. But to be specific, politically the term 'refugee diaspora' fits in the debate because Tibetans are not refugees any more but they have also become diasporas. Tibetans who took refuge in India, Nepal and Bhutan are today scattered around the world and at the same time have maintained a functional government-in-exile in Dharamsala with a large number of Tibetans present in India. Yes, they are refugees but they have also acquired the characteristics of diaspora.

5. Initially, the king had offered integration for the Tibetans into the Sikkimese society as they were very similar in many aspects. However at that juncture, the Tibetans declined the proposal as this was against their morale and movement.

Thus, it is theoretically a combination of refugee and diaspora which defines the Tibetans holistically as refugee diaspora.

Tibetans in India are known as refugees but it is of course not applicable to all in the eastern Himalayan region of Sikkim-Darjeeling hills. As discussed earlier, there is a variant Tibetan identity in the region; most of them are Tibetans but this is not applicable holistically. One cannot differentiate who is a Tibetan and who is not, which basically helps in masking self with the other. Beyond such camouflaging (intentional/unintentional), Tibetans are known as refugees like in any other states in India. The term for many is a symbol of struggle, with the belief that they will soon repatriate to their motherland. Facing challenges and discrimination in exile, Tibetans have strived to uphold their political identity as refugees.

With the passage of time, issues related to Tibetan identity have also undergone changes in the course of the last decade or so. One of the most significant changes has been acceptance, accompanied by conferring citizenship by the Government of India (GoI) in 2010 after the case of Namgyal Dolkar. The case of Namgyal Dolkar versus Ministry of External Affairs on 22 December 2010 entitled Tibetans to citizenship but at the same time challenged Tibetan authority and harmony. The judgement of the High Court of Delhi stated that: "every person born in India on or after the 26th January 1950 but before the 1st day of July 1987 shall be a citizen of India by birth." The court held: "that Tibetans born in India, regardless of their parentage, during the aforementioned period, enjoy birthright citizenship comparable to that guaranteed by the Fourteenth Amendment to the U.S. Constitution" (Moynihan, 2012). Although the entitlement of such rights has minimised the identity crisis it has weakened and seriously challenged Tibetan unity and the government-in-exile per se.

Further, the validity of the 'Registration Certificate' (RC), the official document provided to Tibetans which is renewed after every year, has been extended to five years for those who have settled for more than 20 years. However, for those who have stayed for less than 20 years, the renewal period is unmodified, which is after a year. This has certainly gifted many Tibetans a sense of ease because renewing it every year was troublesome and frustrating.

The political essence of Tibetans in Sikkim-Darjeeling hills is unusual. This is partly explained by the degree of Tibetan identity in the region. Tibetans in Sikkim do have a political identity and have the identity of refugees. This is because integration in Sikkim is not easy due to restrictive measures to control illegal migration and integration. Largely their identity is dissolved in the larger crowd because of their cultural, racial and religious commonalities. Despite such facts, there exists a clear gap between Tibetans and Sikkimese. The distance between the two communities is maintained because of various issues. One such fundamental issue is that Tibetans are more conscious in terms of safeguarding their culture, tradition and religion. Thus, they discourage inter-marriages with host communities.

In addition, Tibetans in Sikkim are supported by the locals primarily because of their historical ties. Further, there exists close religious attachment despite many dissimilarities. Tibetans are supported by Sikkimese for their genuine cause of freedom. Therefore, Tibetans in Sikkim enjoy healthier freedom and rights despite the existing gap.

Unlike Tibetans in Sikkim, Tibetans in Darjeeling hills have a multifaceted political identity. The cosmopolitan character of Darjeeling hills absorbs the Tibetan identity in a friendlier manner. This is further supported by the historical and religious ties, which exist in Darjeeling hills. Indian Tibetans or *bhutias* support the Tibetan freedom movement but at the same time also vehemently support the Gorkhaland movement in the Darjeeling hills. They often talk more about Gorkhaland and local politics rather than Tibet's freedom movement. This group is joined by the recently integrated Tibetans who seek to project their existence as legitimate Indian citizens.

On the other hand, the settlement population is more passionate about their freedom, their culture and religion. Thus, they remain outside the purview of local politics and are engaged within the settlements. But, within this group, some sections swing as per the situation often acting as representatives of both the identities. Unlike this section, Tibetans who settle outside the camps and preserve their Tibetan identity abide to the local needs but strongly support the Tibetan cause. However, their involvement is an amalgamation of both political identities as they are settled outside settlement areas. Therefore, there clearly exists a division among Tibetans on the issue of political identity.

Another issue fundamental to Tibetans is the question of citizenship. Tibetans integrate into host communities by giving up their RC, as having both the identifications is an offence. Such steps are however discouraged by the Central Tibetan Administration (CTA) in order to preserve and maintain their unity and integrity. But this does not mean that there is absence of dual citizenship in practice.

Darjeeling has witnessed a number of integrations in various regions such as Kalimpong, Kurseong and other areas. This is partly facilitated by easy access to identity cards, local politics, racial, cultural and religious commonalities and historical ties. But such integration is restricted in Sikkim where they remain as refugees because to be a Sikkim subject, one has to be a Sikkimese and nothing beyond. And without the status of being a Sikkim subject or Certificate of Identification (CoI), one is not Sikkimese though one may possess other identifications such as voter's card, ration card and so on. Therefore, Tibetans in Sikkim-Darjeeling hills have a more complex political identity.

Economic Identity and Self-sufficiency

Cross-border movement of people and trade constituted the means of integrating Tibet and Sikkim-Darjeeling hills in the pre-1962 era. Large volumes of trade took place between these states through its mountain passes. But it stopped after the India-China war in 1962.The re-opening of Nathu-la in 2006 for cross-border trade has revived the traditional linkages to some extent.

T.B. Subba (2002: 139) highlights agriculture, pastoral economy and trade as the main economic sources of Tibet. But in the post-flight situation, land and pastoral economy are missing, whereas trade and business has remained constant. This is clearly visible even today as Tibetans are known for their business skills, progress and success. Norbu (2004: 190) writes: "Within a span of few years, the refugees from Tibet became self-supporting and emerged as one of the most successful refugee communities in the world." This self-estimate is corroborated by social scientists such as Melvyn Goldstein, an American anthropologist; Girija Saklaini, an Indian sociologist; and Tanka Subha, a Nepali anthropologist.

Tibetans in Sikkim-Darjeeling hills are no less different from the rest. They have exhibited their capabilities by taking over the market. They are among the most successful communities in the hills. Their strong business policies and discipline have challenged other business communities. They are famous for handicrafts (mainly carpets), restaurants and hotels, garments and food commerce.

The Tibetan settlement at Ravangla in south Sikkim, Sonada in Darjeeling and Darjeeling town, which were studied and surveyed December 2011, confirmed the achievements and self-sufficiency of the Tibetans. The Tibetan Refugee Self Help Centre at Darjeeling firmly asserted its self-sufficiency and independence. They stated that the centre helps refugees in several ways such as providing employment and through their profits the needy and old are taken care of. They pointed out that they make carpets largely on demand, mainly from abroad and customers wait for 5-6 years after their payment to receive their carpets. Their products are appreciated around the world and even the host state.

The Kunphenling Tibetan Refugee Multi-purpose Co-operative Society, Ravangla, reports similar success stories. They have embraced a wide range of activities ranging from traditional handicrafts to Internet facilities. Their effectiveness has been acknowledged by both camp dwellers and host communities. One of the unique features of this society is that its operation go beyond settlement areas. Further, their future plans are both ambitious and calculative. Like the Self Help Centre, the society provides both employment and social benefits to needy refugees.

The Tashiling Tibetan Co-operative, Sonada, is no less in its achievements. One of the unique features of this cooperative is the involvement of local people. It has an amalgamation of both the refugees and the local people. Their businesses range from hostels to Internet cafes, mills and dairies. They also help the needy and the poor, and at the same time generate employment both for Tibetans as well as locals.

In all these centre and societies, there is one inherent problem of declining human resources. The new generation is driven by easy money and is bestowed with good education therefore they look for employment opportunities outside the camps with better economic prospects. Similarly, the new generation has mostly accepted Indian citizenship and thus their population in the settlement is declining. A major impact of this shift has been felt in the carpet weaving sector. The previous generation of carpet weavers is now old and inefficient while the young are not interested in this industry. This is prevalent in all the places discussed earlier.

Tibetans are mostly self-employed, which includes both small and big businesses (including the *haats*), driving taxis and the seasonal sweater business. In Ravangla, young Tibetans are mostly employed in the Tibetan army as they are paid well and a majority discontinue their studies. In both the states, Tibetans are employed in self-help centre and cooperative societies. However, in Darjeeling area, most Tibetans are engaged in the garment business, restaurant and hotel industry. In general, the refugee and hosts have friendly relationships, except in a few cases as pointed out by Subba (2002: 141), where the *bhutias* in Sikkim accuse Tibetans of taking advantage of their similarities.[6] In Sikkim, the refugees argue that they face problems related to trade licences, as they are denied such rights. But they adopt different ways to secure such facilities.

One significant aspect of the Tibetan population in Sikkim-Darjeeling hills is their identity which is strengthened by their business and commerce. They are often regarded as champions of business and as business minded people. Their success has not only improved their living standards but has also helped the local population tremendously.

---

6. In Sikkim, the standing complaint of many indigenous tribal people, particularly the Bhutias, is that the Tibetans have taken advantage of their similarity with the Bhutias. Even the jobs reserved for the STs (scheduled tribes) of Sikkim, *viz*., the Lepcha and Bhutia, are alleged to have been appropriated by the more enterprising Tibetan refugees by surreptitiously acquiring ST certificates. These may be mere accusations but they show in a way a growing bitterness about the Tibetan refugees (Subba, 2002: 141).

Buddhism and its Bonding

Buddhism is embedded across the Himalaya. The religious culture of Sikkim-Darjeeling hills has not only strengthened its ties with Tibet but also provided asylum to Tibetan refugees. Religious commonality has facilitated the Tibetans to integrate and accommodate in the host society favourably. Additionally, the relationship between the hosts and refugees has been harmonious because of religious commonalities.

The one Tibetan institution believed to be still intact is that of the Dalai Lama. The institution in exile has become the very soul of Tibet, the nation, the culture and the religion. In Tibet, the Dalai Lama was formally the 'The Great Owner' of the country, still one of his names today. In religious and political ways, he was the head of the government and leader of his people. In exile, without a country and only a handful of people, without a legal mandate or a power base other than a globalised version of Buddhism, his tasks as head of state and government have become almost impossible. Yet he is everything to his people, the one true vestige of a cherished way of life that amounts to what is Tibetan for Tibetans. He has become the source of Tibetan identity per se (Bernis, 1996-1999: 5-6).

Subba (2002: 135-36) argues: "The sectarian conflicts, which had weakened the Tibetan society and polity to a considerable extent prior to their subjugation by the Chinese, seem to have been largely buried now." As the Dalai Lama is everything to his people in exile, he also has assumed that responsibility and trust from other sects, thereby making him a man of universal Buddhism. However, sectarian unity is still not visible in the settlement areas and outside Sikkim-Darjeeling hills. Sectarian conflict prevails albeit camouflaged in the larger domain.

With religious unity, the exiled community is successful in keeping up its struggle for freedom where the concept of 'home' has been maintained among the new generations. Their religious commonality has also gained support for freedom in Tibet from these regions. Generally the religious commonality has established an identity which goes beyond their bonding.

Culture and Cosmopolitan Identity in the Hills

Tibetan culture and traditions are deeply rooted in Sikkim and Darjeeling hills because of the close linkages built through cross-border trade, migration and religious and cultural commonalities. These regions epitomise cultural harmony among Tibetans and host communities in spite of discontinued linkages. The cultural adaptability of both the communities is also rooted in their histories.

Tibetans in exile, driven by a strong desire to preserve their identity, deeply embedded in the religion of the first generation refugees has apparently encouraged insularity but the new generation seeking to open up and grab the opportunities that the world has to offer (Subba, 2002: 137). This must be credited to the absence of experience about the values and ethos attached with Tibet. Neither the new generation was born in Tibet nor has it seen Tibet in reality. What they know about Tibet is what they have heard from other sources and hear in the news today. Thus, their absence from reality evokes or carries their interest more towards western liberal ideas and ideologies rather than towards their own freedom movement.

In Darjeeling and Sikkim hills, Tibetan culture is embedded in local society because of two fundamental reasons: (a) the cosmopolitan character of Sikkim-Darjeeling hills, and (b) the presence of variant Tibetan identity in Sikkim-Darjeeling hills. Sikkim-Darjeeling hills are now often regarded as a cosmopolitan region because of the presence of diverse cultures and religions. Similarly, there are different Tibetans especially in Sikkim-Darjeeling hills where their cultural identities are sometimes concealed or extra posed as per the situation and requirement. This also helps in shaping their culture in various ways.

Tibetan culture is embedded as the region has a special significance for Tibetans, for it was here that the 13th Dalai Lama spent his exile in India from 1910 to 1912 following the Chinese invasion of Tibet at that time (Basu, 2010: 1). This has an imprint on Tibetan culture in the Sikkim-Darjeeling hills.

Further, as language forms one of the important aspects of culture, Tibetan language in Sikkim-Darjeeling hills has been declining in recent days. Today Tibetans are visibly seen talking in Nepali and are more comfortable doing so. One of the major reasons for this is that Tibetans, instead of getting educated at the Central School for Tibetans (CST) where Tibetan language is compulsory, opt for private or missionary schools for better education. Here they are of course not taught the Tibetan language but English. This has certainly constrained the new generation and will further hamper movement and cultural preservation in the long run.

Institution and its Values

Institutions carry values that denote identity and culture of a particular group. Institutions are the source of culture and identity of a particular community. They also safeguard and maintain the identity and cultural ethos of a community. Thus, institutions are fundamental to a community. Accordingly, when the Tibetans fled and took refuge in India one of the foremost tasks planned by His Holiness and His Cabinet was to preserving and maintaining Tibetan values through institutions. As such, many institutions were built to safeguard and maintain Tibetan identity and culture in the host state. Today, the pay-off is tremendous as Tibetans have been able to preserve their culture and tradition even after many decades of living in the host state.

On the other hand, there are many dangers and challenges today as Tibetans face many changes with the passage of time, which many have accepted and others have not in their everyday lives. These are directly or indirectly a challenge to the institutions and their values as there have been no improvements in their quest for a free Tibet. One of the greatest challenges for the government-in-exile is the integration of Tibetans in the host society, as many feel that it is better to integrate rather than staying as a refugees. Such a step has not found favour with CTA which in fact discourages integration, though it claims to disagree about such measures. However, the rationale for doing so is objective as integration will weaken the quest for freedom and challenge the norms of the institutions.

One of the fundamental institutions is the institution of His Holiness the Dalai Lama. This institution has no borders if it is seen as a religious entity, though it is a fundamental part of Tibetans both politically and religiously. Sikkim-Darjeeling hills have always embraced the institution of His Holiness as the region shares religious and racial commonalities. Although the institution is no more political, it still remains a significant part of the Tibetan people, Buddhist followers and for the people of Sikkim-Darjeeling hills.

Beyond the institution of His Holiness the Dalai Lama as a religious guru, there are many institutions that were developed to uphold, preserve and maintain the culture and identity of Tibetans in exile. In Sikkim and Darjeeling hills, there are institutions which were established even prior to 1959 as the regions shared close linkages with Tibet. Region-wise, some of the prominent institutions are:

Sikkim:

- Namgyal Institute of Tibetology, Deorali, 1958.
- Tibetan Welfare Office, Gangtok, 1975.
- Kunphenling Tibetan Settlement, Ravangla, 1978, and
- Thumi Sambhota Tibetan School, Gangtok, 1980s.

Darjeeling:

- Tibetan Refugee Self Help Center, 1959.
- Central School for Tibetans, 1961.
- Tashiling Tibetan Co-operative Society, Sonada, 1965, and
- Manjushree Center for Tibetan Culture, 1988.

Kalimpong:

- The Indo-Tibetan Buddhist Cultural Institute, 1954.
- Central School for Tibetans, 1964.
- Gangjong Doeghar (Tibetan Performing Arts), 1995, and
- Shri Diwakar Vihara Buddhist Research and Educational Institute, mid-1990s.

A close observation of what is discussed earlier signifies the value of institutions. The major objectives of these institutions are to safeguard the culture and identity of Tibetans in the host state. Broadly, there are two types of institutions: educational/research and co-operative society/SHGs (self-help groups). An educational institute teaches, preserves and (re)discovers its history, culture, tradition, language and society and SHGs promote and maintain its tradition and culture.

Generally, both these institutions have been successful to a large extent in their quest for promoting, safeguarding and maintaining culture and values. However, it is important here to focus on the challenges being faced by Tibetans in the 21st century. Some of the common challenges in Sikkim and Darjeeling hills are:

- There is a decrease in camp populations which is now mostly habituated by older people. The new generation often lives outside the camps but many still remain associated with the community. The decrease in camp population has certainly become a greater risk for the community.
- There are many limitations in the camps such as infrastructure, rations, unemployment, non-fertile land and lack of space.
- Another major challenge is depleting human resources which include skilled, semi-skilled and unskilled labour. One of the industries severely hit by the lack of human resources is the carpet industry. However, others are also undergoing such experiences.
- With the passage of time Tibetans in the Sikkim-Darjeeling hills have started going to schools other than Central School for Tibetans. Their number today has increased tremendously and this is a drawback for two reasons: (a) students studying outside CST cannot speak proper Tibetan, and (b) their migration to other schools suggests the incapabilities of Tibetan school.
- Language has already become a major concern for Tibetans as many do not know the language, prefer the local language and remain ignorant about their own language. However, this is grave concern as language is an important aspect of culture and identity.
- Lastly, there is lack of support or funding because of which many things have undergone changes in the recent past.

Conclusion

After discussing issues which are related to the Tibetan identity, it is clear that there is a mosaic of Tibetan identities in Sikkim-

Darjeeling hills. These changes pose a challenge to the government-in-exile, which wants cultural unity and preservation. To their credit, the Tibetans are more integrated in Sikkim-Darjeeling hills than the host population.

Although their quest for identity is almost camouflaged in the region, their larger goal of achieving freedom has always propelled them to raise their voice against Chinese oppression and make people aware about their sufferings and their cause. Thus, even after obtaining all facilities and benefits in the host country, their heart always beats for a free Tibet.

Finally, Tibetan identity in Sikkim and Darjeeling hills is not just about identity but is a question of acceptance. It is a complex issue which cannot be better observed and studied any where but in Sikkim-Darjeeling hills.

Reference

Ahmed, Rafiul and Nagendra Thakur (2012). *Tibetan Settlements in Sikkim and Darjeeling Hills: A Contemporary Reflection on Society, Economy and Culture*. Report. Gangtok: Sikkim University. February-March.

Bernis, Ursula (1996-1999). "Condemned to Silence: A Tibetan Identity Crisis". Available at: *www.shugdensociety.info/pdfs/BernisResearch.pdf*

Hear, Nicholas Van (2009). "The Rise of Refugee Diasporas". April. pp.180-85. Available at: *www.compas.ox.ac.uk/.../VanHear/Rise%20of%20Refugee%20Diasporas*

Moynihan, Maura (2012). "Tibetans in India: The Case for Citizenship", in *The Tibetan Political Review*. Available at: *www.rangzen.net/2012/08/25/tibetans-in-india-the-case-for-citizenship*

Norbu, Dawa (2004). "The Settlements: Participation and Integration", in Bernstorff Dagmar and Hubertus Von Welek (eds.), *Exile as Challenge to the Tibetan Diaspora*. New Delhi: Orient Longman.

Phayul.com (2013). "Phayul in Conversation with Dr Dibyesh Anand"', February 25. Available at: *www.phayul.com/news/article.aspx?id=33084*

Basu, Sudeep (2010). "Organizing for Exile! "Self-Help" among Tibetan Refugees in an Indian Town", *Refugee Watch* 35. Available at: *www.mcrg.ac.in/rw%20files/RW35/1.Sudeep%20Basu.pdf*

Pulman, Lynn (1983). "Tibetans in Karnataka", *Kailash: A Journal of Himalayan Studies*: 119-73.

Subba, T.B. (1990). *Flight and Adaptation: Tibetan Refugees in Darjeeling and Sikkim Himalya*. Dharamsala: Library of Tibetan Works and Archives.

———. (2002). "One or Many Paths: Coping with Tibetan Refugees in India", in C.J. Thomas (ed.), *Dimensions of Displaced People in North–East India*. New Delhi: Sage.

Uhlin, Anders (n.d.). *Tibetan, but not from Tibet: A Minor Field Study on Tibetan Diaspora Identity in India*. Master Thesis. Lund University, Department of Political Science.

Wangchuk, Pema (n.d.). *India, China and the Nathu-la: Converting Symbolism into Reality*. Institute of Peace and Conflict Studies Available at: *IB202-CRP-Pema-NathuLa.pdf*

11

TSHERING DOMA KALEON

Border Trade Through Nathu-la

Reviving and Rebuilding Historical Trade Linkages

Introduction

Available historical evidence reveals a close relationship between the then independent state of Sikkim and independent Tibet. Such a relationship was maintained through cultural exchanges, common religious practices, trading ties, etc. Among all the linkages, trading practices acted as a firm bridge in building the relationship (till present) between the two states, even though the situations have drastically altered in the mean time. Both the regions are no more the masters of their own rule, yet the importance of their location has not lost its significance. In 1975, Sikkim has been merged with the greater Indian state. Since the late 1940s, Tibet was occupied by growing Chinese power because of which it is till now under the suzerainty of the Chinese government.

Trade from Tibet and through it was globally acclaimed to be very important even during early periods. And in the case of British India and Tibet, historically, regular trade between them was conducted through 13 trading routes: from Ladakh, Srinagar, Kulu and Lahul, Shimla, Tehri Garhwal, Badrinath, Almora via Darma and Gyanema, Almora via Milam and Uttadhura, Almora via Lankpya and Lekh, Almora via Lipu Lekh and Purang, Siliguri via Kalimpong, Siliguri via Gangtok, Nathu-la and Chumbi. Among all these trade routes, Nathu-la was reported to be the most vital route during those periods. Many reasons could be attributed to this importance, one of which can be because the 525 km route that passes through Nathu-la is considered to be the shortest route to Lhasa.

Tibet with its significant location and as the source of many natural resources conducted trade not only with British India but also with Nepal, Bhutan and other neighbours. Trade was one of the main activities adopted by the people of Tibet not only for export of its products but also because many products could not be found within Tibet and had to be imported from other regions. Such needs of Tibet are well reflected in George Bogle's work *Trade of Tibet*. He was the first Englishman to visit Tibet in the year 1774. In the opening paragraph of his work, Bogle mentions:

> The foreign trade of Tibet is very considerable. Being mountainous, naturally barren, and but thinly populated, it requires large supplies from other countries, and its valuable productions furnish it with the means of procuring them. It yields gold, musk, cow tails, wool, and salt. Coarse woollen cloth and narrow serge are almost its only manufactures. It produces no iron, nor fruit, nor spices. The nature of soil and of the climate prevents the culture of silk, rice and tobacco, of all which articles there is great consumption. But the wants of the country will best appear from the account of its trade.

Therefore, looking at such historical works and the experiences of the people, it becomes clear that during early periods Tibet experienced an active trading environment.

Historical Trade Linkages through Nathu-la

Nathu-la, 'pass of listening ears',[1] which is located in the eastern part of Sikkim, played a major role in developing relationships between Sikkim and Tibet and is currently playing a significant role in building the relationship between two growing economic powers of the world, India and China. Geopolitically, Sikkim occupies a very important position on the Indo-Tibetan frontier where it has Bhutan in the east, Nepal in the west, West Bengal an Indian state in its south and the Tibet Autonomous Region (TAR) towards its north (Arora, 2008). The importance of Sikkim was realised by the British in the early days, as is evident from their recommendation that the East Bengal Railway be allowed to extend its line from Kustia to Teesta Valley for promoting commerce between India and

1. Nathu means "listening ears" and La means "pass".

trans-Himalayan countries (Sen, 1972). Rail transport would have increased the volume of trade from Sikkim as it would have reduced the time taken for transportation and increased the amount to be traded. Such a development would have automatically increased the volume of trade through Nathu-la.

A traditional trade route through Nathu-la into Tibet was formally established by considering the report of John Edgar, the then Deputy Commissioner of Darjeeling in 1873. The report brought to the fore the great strategic and commercial potential of the route via Sikkim into Tibet which made the British India government explore trade linkages through it. Therefore, the trade route through Nathu-la, which has been active since then, made huge contributions to commerce for four long decades till it was closed after the 1962 war between China and India.

Along with Nathu-la, its sister mountain passers Jelep-la and Cho-la in the Chola Range were also traditionally used by the Sikkimese to trade and travel in Tibet. Likewise, Tibetans also travelled the same route to enter into Sikkim for trade and pilgrimage. However, the Cho-la mountain pass was used mainly by the royal family of Sikkim to travel to Chumbi Valley where they had their summer palace, which itself signifies the closeness of the relationship between the two regions. The other routes like Nathu-la and Jelep-la were crowded by yak herders who came there either for the purpose of trade or for grazing their animals. But the real trade between Sikkim and Tibet was carried through the passes located in north Sikkim, namely Kongra-la, Chorten Nyima La, etc. But, at present, the passes located in north Sikkim are not being used and it has become a hard border because of which it has lost its importance as a trading route unlike Nathu-la, which has been reopened for trading purposes.

Sikkim and Tibet are geographically close to each other, but for the concept of borders and demarcation. The geographical set-up of Sikkim and the area in Tibet which the Chola range leads to, are very similar to one another. Even the religious practices of Tibet (Buddhism) are popular in Sikkim. Traditionally, the major items which were exported from Sikkim to Tibet were timber, fruits, spices and goods that at times could be bought from British India. The items which were mostly brought back from Tibet were black salt, gold, precious stones, tea, wool and carpets. Therefore, a perfect blend of maintaining each others' needs and demands balanced the relationship between the two regions. But such a balanced relationship between the two neighbours could not last for long.

The prosperous commercial linkages between Tibet and Sikkim could not escape attention of the British who at that time were on the verge of world conquest. Sikkim was already a protectorate of the British during this period. Formal trade began with the signing of Sino-British convention of 1893, which led to the opening of Nathu-la and Jelep-la for trade. More than Nathu-la, Jelep-la was preferred for trade because it was the first pass into Tibet for traders from Kalimpong, which was the closest town of British India. British officials used the route through Nathu-la into Tibet more for political expeditions and official visits.

Sikkim witnessed trade activities along with a number of British expeditions into Tibet. This was part of the process of formulating policy for containing imperial Russia, which along with Britain at that time was emerging as the world's super powers. Even though the relationship between Tibet and Sikkim was hampered to a great extent due to the interruption by the British in the initial phase, in later years, the relationship was rejuvenated with growing religious and cultural exchanges as well as a prosperous trading relationship. However, this growing relationship could not sustain for long and was again fractured because of the outbreak of war between India and China in 1962, which resulted in the close-down of border trade between Tibet and Sikkim through both Nathu-la and Jelep-la.

The Significance of Nathu-la

Nathu-la is located 54 km from Gangtok, the capital of Sikkim and the road through Nathu-la is considered to be the shortest route to Lhasa from India. Compared to this, the trade route that passes through Kathmandu (Nepal) to Lhasa is about 1,000 km long. The route through Kathmandu, which at present occupies an important position for trade activities between China and Nepal, started prospering basically after the 1962 war between India and

China that led to the closing down of passes like Nathu-la and Jelep-la. Prior to this, even the people from neighbouring countries like Nepal came to India to trade with Tibet through the open passes. Trade paths through Sikkim were given much importance during that period because the trade path via Nepal almost came to a closure for British India, China and Tibet when the Gurkhas conquered Nepal in the 1770s. Any similar situation could once again hamper smooth economic transactions. But the closing of border passes after the 1962 war, altered the situation in favour of Nepal and its citizens.

But as history repeated itself, border trade between India and China which was closed in the year 1962 reopened, after almost three decades, benefiting the people of Sikkim and TAR, even though as compared to the earlier periods, the amount of profit and the total volume traded was very miniscule. The initiative for invigorating border trade between them came into action with the signing of a Memorandum of Understanding (MoU) in 1991. Since then, three border trading posts have been opened. The two countries opened the border passes for border trade via Tibet through Lipulekh pass in Uttrakhand where border trade markets were established at Pulan in TAR of China and Gunji in the Pithoragarh district in India. Another border trade pass opened through Shipki-la in Himachal Pradesh. Namgya in Kinnaur district of Himachal Pradesh and Jiuba in Zada country in TAR of China were designated as the border trade markets. In both these passes, trade takes place in the commodities approved by the Directorate General of Foreign Trade (DGFT), Government of India (GoI).

Despite the initiative taken by both the countries to rejuvenate border trading, trade was not very fruitful. Not much development could be achieved even after many years of opening of Ike Shipki La and Lipulekh passes. There was no marked difference even in the volume of trade. The need of opening a new gateway for intensifying the India-China relationship was felt and as a result Nathu-la, which is located in the eastern part of Sikkim, was (re)opened on 6 July 2006 after signing of a MoU in 2003 by the two governments.

The Re-opening of Nathu-la for Border Trade

Compared to the first two border trading regions, Nathu-la had the advantage of better infrastructure and comparatively better roads, which could remain open for longer periods. Along with these advantages, Nathu-la has historically been Tibet's ideal life-line to the outside world. Tibet's markets at places like Yatung, Gyantse, Phari, Garthok, Taklakot, Gyanima-Ebargo, Gyanima-Chakra, Ramura, Dongbra, Poling, Nabra, Xigaze and Tashigong had once been prosperous trading points and were well known for carrying out trade with much of South Asia through Nathu-la (Singh, 2010).

The re-opening of Nathu-la resulted in the first direct border trade between north-eastern India and south-western China. It has been a part of the ancient Silk Route which was traditionally recognised by Sikkim and later by British India as the shortest route to Lhasa. According to the 2003 agreement, the two sides accepted Sherathang in Sikkim which is located 47 km away from Gangtok (the capital of Sikkim) and 5 km away from Nathu-la, and Rinqingang in Tibet, which is located 17 km from Nathu-la, as trading posts. It was the opening of Nathu-la, that to a large extent resolved the pending dispute over recognition of Tibet by India and Sikkim by China.

Before the opening of Nathu-la for trade, the Indian Ministry of Commerce and Industry and the People's Republic of China made an agreement on various aspects. Details of the trading process were considered and along with it, the number of items to be imported and exported was decided upon. However, the commodities which were selected for trade were similar to the items which were already being traded through Shipki La and Lipulekh passes. The listed items to be traded were not of great importance because they were not as much in demand and were outdated. Therefore, as soon as trade began through Nathu-la, traders from both sides put forward repeated requests for bringing about development and revision of items which were listed during the time of the agreement, as the traders from both sides regarded the items listed in the schedule to be obsolete and without commercial value.[2]

2. *Tibetan Review*, June 2010. *http://www.tibetanreview.net/news.php?cat=10& cp=9&&id=1520*

It was only after six long years and repeated requests that changes in the list of items for trade were made. On May 2012, the Directorate General of Foreign Trade under the Ministry of Commerce and Industry added five new items to the import list and seven new items to the export list. With such changes, a massive impact was witnessed on the volume of import and export through Nathu-la. More than export activities, a great change in import activities took place where the import volume leaped from nil to more than ₹100 lakh. There is, therefore, a huge potential for the development and growth of trading activities through Nathu-la.

Role of Women Traders vis-à-vis Nathu-la

When it comes to the contribution of women in the local or national sphere, the total outcome is minimal. Such inequalities in terms of economic contributions between men and women have been witnessed because of more involvement of women in informal activities such as within their households and in small-scale units. Lack of women's contribution to economic activities has barred them from playing any significant role in decision making within their households and even in any public sphere. Economic security has acted as a major tool in determining the status and future of women not only in Sikkim but in other human settlements also.

Even in the present globalised era, in some parts of the world there still exist societies where discrimination and injustice towards women take place. They are not considered equal to men and are even paid less for the same amount of work done for equal hours of working. Looking into such injustice, Sikkim can be considered as one of the safe abodes for women where they enjoy every kind of freedom and are considered no less important than their male counterparts. Sikkim has provided immense opportunities for women to develop their economic status. Women in Sikkim have therefore taken up various jobs and economic activities that has led to their economic growth. Therefore, the participation of women in trading activities has been a common sight in Sikkim for a long time.

The re-opening of Nathu-la has opened one more gate for increasing the ground for trading activities. Prior to the closing of

India-China border, participation of women in border trade was basically indirect where they opened small hotels and *gaddis* helping their counterparts carry on trade smoothly. However, with the opening of Nathu-la in 2006, the participation of a large number of women, especially Tibetan women, has been witnessed. Women no longer participate just as mere hotel owners but are directly engaged in trade and are also owners of big garment shops. In Sikkim, a large number of shops are owned and run by women. They have opened a number of garment shops; they bring the products from Siliguri, Nepal and many other places. But with the opening of Nathu-la, these women traders along with their male counterparts have been bringing similar products directly through Nathu-la, which has resulted in lower costs and therefore more profit for them.

Trading is one activity where limitations like age, qualifications, social background, hardly have any significance. Interactions with traders in the Nathu-la trading region, reveals that there is no discrimination on the basis of gender, qualifications, etc. A person who has never got an opportunity to go to school as well as a person who is an MBA graduate, are both conducting similar business in the border trade conducted through Nathu-la. In some of the houses, the entire family is involved in trading through Nathu-la, including the mother of the family who was previously only engaged in household activities. She has now got an opportunity to come out of the house and earn a living for the entire family.

Participation of women in trading activities helps in increasing families income and also gives economic independence to them. Therefore, such economic activities have acted as a major tool in empowering women. The opening of Nathu-la for trade has been a boon for most women in Sikkim because it has given them more economic independence, as a result of which they have got to play an effective role in trade through decision-making processes within their family. The rejuvenation of Nathu-la has included large number of unemployed women of Sikkim in the trading business by providing them with proper trading licences. Therefore, the role of Sikkimese women, which was confined to households and in the agricultural sector, has shifted towards business and the production sector. Local products which are now being traded are mostly produced by women.

Conclusion

The re-opening of Nathu-la had made a significant impact on the relationship between India and China. The term 're-opening' indicates the functioning of border trade in earlier periods. Nathu-la has not only a border post that opened for trade, but prior to the sealing of the border post, it used to be a pathway for animals to graze, a bridge for family reunions and for royal families to visit their palaces in different parts of Tibet as well as in Sikkim. With the end of king's rule in both the regions, the situation is no longer what it used to be, but the significance of being connected cannot be ignored even today.

Analysing trading activities along the Nathu-la since its re-opening, it can be said that the main motive behind its re-opening i.e., the development of their political and economic relationship, seems to be getting fulfilled. However, an analysis of the total amount of profit and the total volume of trade conducted through Nathu-la pass indicates that hardly any concrete trade is taking place, despite predictions made by experts. According to Arora (2008: 4), just as facilitation of trans-border trade legitimised British Indian claims over Sikkim during the British rule, the re-opening of Nathu-la was instrumental in China recognising Sikkim as a part of India and India accepting TAR as a part of China.

However, by re-opening the closed border for trade, a bond of trust has been developing among old neighbours. This is evident in the practice of credit-based trade. Traders from both sides share gifts during the closing day of the trade, they even remain in contact through telephone and have even learned each others' languages.

Therefore, the initiative from both the sides for re-opening the border for trade has acted as an important tool for developing their relationship.

References

Arora, Vibha (2008). "Routing the Commodities of the Empire through Sikkim (1817-1906)", *Working Paper* No. 9. London Metropolitan University.

Edgar, J.W. (2005). *Report on a Visit to Sikhim and the Thibetan Frontier: in October, November and December 1873*. Varanasi: Pilgrims Publishers.

Lama, Mahendra P. (2005). *Sikkim-Tibet Trade via Nathu-la: A Policy Study on Prospects, Opportunities and Requisite Preparedness*.

Sen, Jahar (1972). "India's Trade with Central Asia via Nepal", *Tibetan Bulletin* 1.

———. (1981). "Sikkim and Himalayan Trade", *Tibetan Bulletin* 3.

Singh, Swaran (2010). "Significance of Nathu-la: Border Trade in China-India Relations", in Gurudas Das and C. Joshua Thomas (eds.), *India-China Trade and Strategy for Frontier Development*. New Delhi: Bookwell.

Tibetan Bulletin (1984). "Articles of Tibet Trade", *Tibetan Bulletin* 1.

III

Environment

12

TENZIN NORBU

Tibet: The Third Pole and the Himalaya

Overview

The world has one roof. It is the Tibetan Plateau, defined simply by the Tibetans as the land surrounded by mountains or the land of snow. Situated at the heart of Asia, Tibet is ringed by 14 high mountain ranges; the whole plateau has an average height of 4,500 metres. This vast plateau stretches for almost 2,500 km from west to east and 1,500 km from south to north. Despite its cold climate and intricately complex natural systems, the Tibetan people have occupied this plateau for thousands of years. They have created a cultural landscape based on the principles of simplicity and non-violence that is in harmony with the environment. It is in fact one of the most environmentally strategic and sensitive regions in the world, quite often referred to as 'The Third Pole' and 'The Water Tower of Asia'. These synonyms reflect the significance of its snow capped mountains, river systems and alpine grasslands. Since time immemorial, the plateau has held the Hindu Kush Himalayan Ice Sheet, considered the largest ice mass outside the two poles. The glacier-fed rivers originating from these peaks and the subsequent recharge from the underground aquifer make Tibet the largest river run-off from any single location in the world. This region also acts as the fountain-head for many rivers that flow into Asia (India, inner Mongolia, Nepal, Bhutan, Bangladesh, China, Pakistan, Thailand, Laos, Burma, Cambodia and Vietnam) creating a vast river basin area of more than 6 million sq km. During the last few decades, due to climate warming and human actions, the natural systems of this unique landscape and the adjoining Himalayan regions have been silently degrading, threatening the survival of millions who rely on its natural ecosystem.

The content of this paper has evolved through a series of discussions over the past few years to find a common ground for Tibet and the rest of the Himalayan region. In no way is this paper intended to politically divide the Himalayan states and compare government policies. It is an attempt to alert policymakers before they make any decisions and to encourage scientists and anthropologists to conduct social and scientific research within the study area. It is important to understand and bring forth the ground realities of what is actually happening, how our forefathers protected the ecology and how we must act together to protect the environment and ancestral cultures from degradation and neglect in the process of development.

Traditional Environmental Protection and Conservation in Tibet

The Tibetan Plateau is undoubtedly the most prominent and distinguishable feature on the face of the globe, rightly known as the 'Roof of the World'. It is the largest and highest plateau in the earth's geological history. It is surrounded by the Himalaya-Karakoram complex in the south and west and contains 14 major peaks of over 8,000 metres including Mount Everest. To the north, the plateau is bound by the deserts of the Tarim Basin and Tsaidam, while a series of alternating deep forested valleys and high mountain ranges mark its eastern periphery. The geological evolution of the plateau and the ensuing tectonic uplift has been a matter of interest, debate and deliberation among the scientific community. A series of tectonic deformations in the plateau have resulted in various types of active structures and sutures that are all zones of seismic activities of varying degree (Environment and Development Desk [EDD], 2012). (Figure 12.1).

Tibetans have always lived with nature, seeking to learn and understand its nuances and rhythms. Buddhism, which was introduced to Tibet in the 2nd or 3rd century, has played a vital role in this respect. A general taboo against exploiting the environment was a direct result of Buddhist knowledge and belief about the inter-relationship and inter-dependence between all plants, animals, as well as the non-living elements of nature such as sunshine, sky, mountains, valleys, lakes and rivers. The close relationship between religion and nature meant that the simple yet effective principles, which maintained a balance in the natural world, became a part of life. After ages of living like this, it is in fact difficult for a Tibetan to differentiate between the practice of religion and concern for the environment.

Rilung Tsatsig: Hill and Valley Decree

In the Water Horse Year of 1642, His Holiness the Great 5th Dalai Lama (Ngawang Lobsang Gyatso, the spiritual and political leader of Tibet) issued a royal decree in the 10th lunar month to protect the animals and the environment. This royal decree was widely known as Rilung Tsatsig or the 'Hill and Valley Decree' (EDD, 1992). According to research conducted by Huber (2004), the first comprehensive examples of territorial sealing to specifically prohibit hunting and fishing are found in those documents issued by the lay Buddhist king Rabten Kunsang Phagpa, between 1415 and 1440. He also mentions that in the article 21 (administrative code) of the 5th Dalai Lama's regent (De Sith Sangay Gyatso), the sealing section was immediately preceded by a quote, which sets out general duties of a king as an environmental steward.

The 'sealing of mountains and the valleys' was an expression sometimes used for political closures and controls over designated territories. It also expresses the practice of sealing in two contrasting spacio-temporal dimensions. The revival of the extensive period of blanket sealing or long-term sealing of mountains and valleys took place during the active rule of the 13th Dalai Lama. During his rule, a series of decrees were issued and officially circulated to all parts of his jurisdiction. Some of these were actually titled 'Hill and Valley Decrees' due to their content. One relevant clause in the 1932 decree ordered: "from the first Tibetan month up until the 30th day of the seventh lunar month, it is important to seal the hills and the valleys." After his demise, Regent Tagdra carried on this tradition till late 1944. Hundreds of copies of this decree were drafted by clerks in the private office of His Holiness and were then distributed to various regions and villages in the Tibet to be read out by the district head or the magistrate. This royal decree, in its own way, acts as a law that common people must obey in order to promote peace and prosperity. The decree also recalls the words of Lord Buddha to refrain oneself from committing sinful acts. It also reiterates legal rule and as such is regarded by the locals as a blessing from His Holiness (EDD, 1992; French, 1995; Huber, 2004).

On special occasions and upon the advice of the state oracle (Nechung) a special *tsatsig* would also be issued. For instance, Regent Tagdra issued a special Tsatsig in the seventh month of 1944 (wood monkey year). In short, the decree reads: "except for the predatory animals such as wolves, all the other animals, aquatic, boreal, or amphibians as long as they are endowed with the gift of life must be protected and should not be harmed." Clear directions were also given for the implementation of these decrees to all the governors and local officials (Atisha, 1990).

Similar *tsatsigs* or decrees were also issued from the local high priest or lamas and this tradition was prevalent throughout Tibet. These *tsatsigs* were considered the most effective ways of preserving religion, life, happiness and health for all sentient beings. For instance, in the Ngari region (western part of Tibet), periodic or territorial decrees, known to the locals as *kabdhus tsatsigs* that required local authorities to employ rangers to protect animals from hunters and poachers were issued. Those decrees that were issued during the spring season coincided with the birthing period of the Tibetan antelope calves and the migration of fish. Some decrees required the local authorities to employ special corps during the mating season of wild ducks in order to protect the eggs till the young hatchlings could swim freely with their mothers (Choephel and Tsephel, 2003).

From all these accounts, it is clear that these decrees or *tsatsigs* had a deep connection and reverence towards Buddhist philosophy of nature conservation and protection. These decrees were not only considered as direct commands but also referred to as a blessing from the Dalai Lama or the high priest. French (1995), described how this royal decree looked and the reactions of local Tibetans:

> The decrees that were issued from His Holiness's private office bear the full name of His Holiness the Thirteen Dalai Lama, the Tibetan year and date. The decree was always written on the finest paper, unrolled to almost a yard in width and two yards in length. The writing was exquisite; even those who could not read would marvel at the elegant shapes of the finest government duktsa script. At the top was a large red seal of the Dalai Lama's Office; it was followed by exactly forty five lines of even script, all perfectly spaced. The villagers went up to receive the blessing of the even larger red seal of His Holiness at the bottom, which was placed near his many-worded full name.

In a scholarly and well-researched article, Norbu (2009) indicates evidence of the successful implementation of such decrees in journal records of various western travellers, explorers and naturalists who visited Tibet before the Chinese invasion. These westerners also mentioned various bird festivals, certain areas being designated as bird sanctuaries for migrating birds and specific shrines that were assigned for the protection of these birds. For instance, Yarlung Jha-sa Lhakang, or 'the resting-place-of-birds temple', and the Jha-do gompa, or 'bird confluence monastery' a temple, located at the north shore of the lake Namtso. The author also elaborates that the location of these two bird temples was in tangent with the migratory routes of these birds from Arunachal Pradesh to breeding grounds in northern Tibet.

Since the occupation of Tibet, the Chinese government has not only restricted the practice of Buddhist traditions for environmental preservation but also embarked upon unsustainable development schemes in many parts of Tibet, adversely impacting most of its river systems, biodiversity and the pristine landscape. However, these restrictions have not deterred many monastic communities from actively protecting the wildlife and conserving the pristine environment, be it a result of continued religious beliefs or the influence of past decrees.

An article in the *Beijing Review* (Zhi, 2011) indicated that in Tibet, community reserves have become key frontiers in protecting wildlife and their habitats. The author mentions that: "these types of nature reserves are based on traditional cultures and religions. They demonstrate a combination of cultural values and natural values, and satisfy the communities respect for the nature." Another more recent journal article (NBC News Science, 2013) mentions that snow leopards are being protected by hundreds of Buddhist monasteries in Tibet. The monks actively patrol the forests to prevent poachers from killing these endangered cats.

Himalayan Water Demand: The Trans-Boundary Commons

Fast forwarding six decades or more of political repression and environmental destruction in Tibet, we are now at a point of reminiscing—had it not been or 'what if'. The fact is that those rivers that flowed from Tibet through the Himalaya still flow, but under a different guardian. These rivers are distinguished by their high silt loads resulting from the largely desert landscape from which they originate. These rivers enable Tibet to become the Water Tower of Asia. The following section focuses on the western rivers originating from Tibet and connecting the rest of the Himalayan regions (Figure 12.2).

In the southwest of Tibet lies Mt. Kailash, known to Tibetans as 'Gangkar Tesi' or the king of snow mountains, standing tall amongst the rest of the minor peaks. Kailash is considered a very sacred mountain by both Buddhists and Hindus. Four major rivers originate around it. The Yarlung Tsangpo (Brahmaputra river) flows from the east of Mt. Kailash through the most densely populated region of Tibet, irrigating most of the agricultural land in the historical Yarlung Valley of Tibet. The river then flows through the once forested Kongpo region before turning abruptly near Mt. Namchak Barwa to the south, cutting straight through the Himalayan divide to flow into India as Brahmaputra and then to Bangladesh. The Senge Khabab (Indus river) originates from the north of Kailash. It then flows west into India (Ladakh and Kashmir) and continues to become Pakistan's principal river. The Langchen Khabab (Sutlej river) begins from the west of Mt. Kailash, crossing the Himalaya into Himachal Pradesh in northwest India, passing through the Punjab region before joining the Indus in Pakistan. Macha Khabab (Karnali river) originates from the southern part of Mt. Kailash, crossing the Himalaya into western Nepal and then into India where it becomes one of the major tributaries of the Ganges river (EDD, 2000).

According to a report published by the National Research Council (2012), the combined river basin of Indus, Ganges and Brahmaputra supports more than 744 million people living within the contiguous arc from Afghanistan to Bangladesh. These rivers have played a vital role in irrigating agricultural lands that in turn feed millions of people. According to data for 2000, the use of water in the agricultural sector was 45 MHA (million hectares). The report also states that in Pakistan, the irrigation area mostly along the Indus river basin had increased by 1.3 per cent annually (from 1998 to 2008), with the irrigation area covering 20 MHA in 2008. If this trend continues, by 2030, Pakistan will use 25 MHA for irrigation and by 2050 it would use 30 MHA. This simply means more demand for irrigation water and will be a defining moment to test the applicability of the Indus water sharing treaty.

According to The Economic Times (2012), in India, over the past few years, the water tables have been dropping significantly in most states at the rate of more than 30 cm/year, which raises serious concerns about the future of food security. It has reached a point where the government looks into the possibility of shifting paddy cultivation to wetter states. On the same issue, the McKinsey Report (2009) mentions that water demand in India will grow by more than two-folds by 2030 (from 740 billion m^3 to almost 1.5 trillion m^3, 2010 baseline data), principally driven by population growth and the domestic need for agriculture. As per the World Health Organization (WHO, 2013), with respect to water demand and supply there are about 173 million people in India (urban and rural) who do not have an improved source of drinking water and more than 136 million people with poor sanitation facilities.

At some point, in the distant future, this water scarcity and increasing demand for water might lead to mass migration of people and relocation of major water dependent industries to other wetter states.

Climate change impacts such as increased glacial meltdowns and erratic monsoons in the Himalayan region are creating a huge problem for predicting future water securities and risk assessments. More glacial melt will cause increased summer flow in the rivers for a few decades followed by drought years as the glacier disappears. Research conducted on the historical trends and climate variability in the Brahmaputra river basin indicates that climate warming would impact the hydrology within the entire river basin. The author also mentions that a large part of the variations in monsoon precipitation along the river basin is related to the temperature gradient between the Tibetan Plateau and the agricultural floodplains of India and Bangladesh. Low air temperature on the Tibetan Plateau will mean weaker monsoon on the floodplains and *vice versa* (Immerzeel, 2008).

With no proportional increase in water availability and an ever increasing demand, a water crisis is imminent in rural and urban sectors, creating regional/inter-state tensions, impacting local sanitation and health for millions of people.

Diminishing Water Resources

It is a fact that without enough water and fuel, any nation could be brought down on its knees. Early human civilisations have thrived along major river basins because of easier access to this bountiful blue gold. It is in fact tied to food, culture, energy and economy. But in recent times, according to Chellaney (2011), "water has gone from being an economic issue to becoming a security issue."

Climate Warming: Melting Himalayan Glaciers

The impacts of climate warming on Himalayan water resources could be significant as it will lead to an increase in the glacial meltdown, increase in evapotranspiration and changes in regional precipitation patterns. Glacial retreat alone could impact the water supply for many Himalayan rivers.

From the mid-1970s until late 2000, the average air temperature rose by 1°C in the Himalayan region, that is almost twice as fast as the global average warming of 0.6°C reported by the Intergovernmental Panel on Climate Change (IPCC), this trend being most pronounced at high altitude sites (Thomas and Rai, 2005). IPCC (2007) also states that the current trend of melting glaciers suggests that the Ganges, Indus, Brahmaputra and other rivers across the northern Indian plains could most likely become seasonal rivers in the near future. The glaciers in the Himalayan mountains have retreated by almost 67 per cent in the past few decades (IPCC, 2001), and it was also observed that the Gangotri glacier in the Indian Himalaya is retreating at the rate of 30 m per year (United Nations [UNESCO], 2007).

Even China's National Climate Change Program report (2007) has estimated that the area of glaciers in western China (the Tibetan Plateau) will decrease by 27 per cent by 2050. The same concerns are also reflected in many scholarly articles, warning that such meltdowns will result in massive flooding followed by severe droughts.

Researchers from the International Centre for Integrated Mountain Development (ICIMOD) have mentioned that the Himalayan glaciers in eastern Nepal near the Dudh Koshi region are retreating at rates ranging from 10 to 60 m per year, and many glaciers smaller than 0.2 km^2 have already disappeared (Bajracharya *et al.*, 2008).

No trace of radioactive substances or distinctive signatures of nuclear testing of the early 1950s and 1960s were found by researchers in the ice core of the Tibetan glaciers, suggesting that ice layers or the accumulated snow since 1950s have sublimated or melted (Nature, 2013). These findings have also raised questions about the fate of the water reservoir and billions of people depending on it.

Other research studies have indicated that the black soot depositions on these glaciers are also responsible for accelerating the rate of meltdown due to reduced surface reflection and more heat accumulation. According to a United Nation Environment Programme (UNEP, 2008) report, glaciers in India such as the Siachen, Gangotri and Chhota Shigiri are also retreating and their retreat has accelerated in the past three-and-a-half decades due to the solar heating of the atmosphere from the Atmospheric Brown

Cloud and decreased reflection from the snow and ice layers due to the deposition of black carbon. Similar deposition of black carbons was also observed by a team of scientists who recently visited the Himalayan glaciers (Roger and Neil, 2013).

These findings are also supported by an earlier research conducted by Sharma (2012), who mentions that the glaciers in the Indian Himalaya are losing 1 metre of ice every year compared to 0.42 m from previous records and the main contributor towards this melting is black carbon, emanating from forest fires and burning of agricultural waste. The loss in the mass of glaciers in the Indian Himalaya has significantly gone up from 1998 onwards.

Glacier melting leads to the formation of glacial lakes. The banks of such lakes are made of moraines (accumulated sediments deposited by the glacier) that may collapse when the lakes fill up, leading to sudden and violent flooding in the downstream valleys. Any flood of this sort (referred to as GLOF, or glacial lake outburst flood) can have disastrous consequences for the population and biodiversity of the entire region downstream of the lakes. The formation of glacial lakes on the higher reaches of the mountain continues to pose a serious threat to downstream communities of Himalayan states.

Climate Change/Warming Impacts

In a recent study on flashflood risk and management in the Himalaya, it has been mentioned that flashfloods and landslides are triggered by the intense seasonal precipitation in the central and eastern Himalaya during the summer monsoon (June-September) and in the western Himalaya during winter (ICIMOD, 2013).

The devastation and destruction caused by a series of cloud burst events that occurred in India (Ladakh, 2010) and in Pakistan (2011) and the recent Kedarnath disaster (June 2013) in the Indian state of Uttarakhand are testimony to how vulnerable these Himalayan states are to nature's fury.

An earlier study by ICIMOD (2013) recorded that there were more than 1,600 glacial lakes in Nepal, of which about half a dozen were considered very dangerous. In the Bhote Koshi/Sun Koshi basin alone, there were 139 glacial lakes that were identified as potentially dangerous. The 1981 GLOF event that swept away about 40 houses, two highway bridges and others cost Nepal a loss of US$ 750,000. Recent research forecasted that the number, area and ice reserves of glaciers in this basin are declining leading to an increase in the number of glacial lakes. The study even warns communities in Nepal of more GLOFs in the near future with double the magnitude experienced in 1981. In the past, 24 GLOF events have been reported, out of which 10 occurred in the Tibetan catchments of rivers.

In 2002, Greenpeace reported that the pro-glacial Imja Lake in Nepal (not existing before 1960) continues to grow as the glacier front retreats nearly 10 metres per year (Greenpeace Briefing, 2002). Other researchers from ICIMOD have also reported that this glacial lake is growing by just under 50 metres per year and is in danger of bursting its banks. They have even warned that more than 7,500 human lives will be affected by it, including tourist hiking routes at the Everest Base Camp (*The Telegraph*, 2011). BBC (2011) also ran a similar story in its environment section about the dangers of a glacial lake overlooking an ethnic community of Halji village residing in Nepal's western province.

In the Himalayan regions of India, a new glacial lake was reported at the snout of South Lhonak glacier in Sikkim. A study further revealed that this lake was bound only by loose soil and debris and could cause havoc downstream if it ruptured (Digital Media Corporation, 2013). On 16 and 17 June (2013), the Indian state of Uttarakhand witnessed one of the most horrific furies of nature in terms of cloud burst and flash flooding in the Kedarnath valley. Human casualties were in the thousands and economic loss was estimated to be around US$ 2 billion. According to LANDSAT images and the geomorphologic set-up, Kedarnath town is situated in the outwash plane of Chorabari and its companion glaciers. The Chorabari lake (3,960 m a.s.l.) located within 2 km further up from Kedarnath town is a glacial lake which is fed by seasonal monsoon with no natural outflow. The first flashflood event occurred due to the intense rainfall in the area and the second event of flashflood that devastated the whole of Kedarnath town occurred due to the overflow and collapse of this glacial lake (Dobhal *et al.*, 2013).

Weakening of the Indian Monsoon

As early as 1884, English meteorologist Henry F. Blanford, who worked in India, had an inspired idea that the snow in Tibet and the Indian monsoon were causally connected. He also suggested in his writings that the less it snows in winter (in Tibet), the earlier the snowmelt, and the earlier the monsoon. More recent research on the Indian monsoon has also indicated that the increased snow cover on the Tibetan Plateau will lead to a subsequent reduction in precipitation in Southeast Asia. Researchers relate the intensity of the Indian monsoon to the energy balance and the land-ocean thermal contrast between the Tibetan Plateau and the Bay of Bengal (Immerzeel and Bierkensb, 2009).

The seasonal monsoon wind shift and weather associated with the heating and cooling of the Tibetan Plateau is believed to be the strongest such monsoon on earth. This monsoon recharges most of these mighty rivers and allows them to flow further down to many downstream countries. The Tibetan Plateau's seasonal heating during summer and spring plays a principal role in determining the large-scale air circulation in summer. Heating over the Tibetan Plateau tends to generate a surface cyclonic circulation and upper-atmosphere anti-cyclonic circulation which results in the appearance of a large air motion in the eastern side of the plateau. During summer, the Tibetan Plateau acts as an elevated heat source driving the Asian monsoon. The differential heating between the land and the sea intensifies the pressure gradient between the south Asian landmass and the Indian Ocean leading to the flow of air and moisture from the sea.

In the July issue of *Nature Climate Change*, Tandong and colleagues (2012) reported on the changing status of Tibetan Plateau's glaciers over the past three decades. The authors attribute the varying glacier statuses to changing precipitation levels from the weakening Indian monsoon (decreasing precipitation) and strengthening of westerlies (westerly winds) to increasing precipitation in the eastern Pamir ranges. They also mention that from 1979 to 2010, precipitation decreased in the Himalaya and this period saw the most dramatic glacier shrinkage in the southeastern part of the Tibetan Plateau where glacier length decreased on an average by 48 m^2 per year (Tandong *et al.*, 2012).

Water Availability and Management in China

It would be unfair on my part to discuss the water availability in the Himalayan regions and other riparian states without briefly discussing the water demand in China and its damming activities and policies.

According to survey data analysed by the Joint Monitoring Program for Water and Sanitation of WHO and UNICEF, about 200 million Chinese (2% of rural and 13% of urban population) still do not have access to an improved drinking water source and about 400 million do not have access to improved sanitation. Progress in rural areas appears to lag behind what has been achieved in urban areas (WHO, 2013).

In some regions of China, water demand outpaces supply, mainly in the lowland industrial and agricultural provinces. Close to 16 provinces in China suffer from less than adequate water resources per capita compared to average world standards. This could trigger a huge demand to exploit the abundant water reserve in western Tibet since these water stressed regions in China are the major contributors to gross regional product, where major secondary industries are located (HSBC, 2011). And the ever expanding Chinese middle class and changes in their food consumption, mainly in beef, (National Geographic, 2009) could blindly force policymakers to take drastic action in the water abundant regions in Tibet without a second thought. It remains to be seen whether the riparian states can collectively do something to reach a multilateral consensus on these trans-boundary rivers.

The current water scarcity threatens the ability of China's farmers to irrigate their crops, impacting food security as well as social stability, especially in northern China. Water shortage costs the country an estimated 40-60 billion RMB ($6.3-9.5 billion) in lost economic output per year. Continued scarcity and uncertainty will affect the willingness of foreign and domestic companies to invest in China, further lowering the production of existing facilities, and ultimately affecting the job market (Hu, 2012).

In certain parts of China, more public funds are spent on bottled water than on metered water due to the low quality of water, and poor people have no alternative but to consume inferior quality water (World Bank, 2009). This indicates a weak water supply system, low sewerage pricing and a bleak future for water sustainability.

Chinese authorities have so far failed to combat the main reason behind inefficient water usage—the substantial under-pricing of water. The main reason for this failure lies in the ever-present sense of insecurity amongst the Communist party about farmers and factory owners protesting against the proper pricing of water (Forbes, 2011).

The current situation necessitates a change in the Chinese government's approach towards the development of water infrastructure. China needs to step away from a protectionist stance and move towards a more global perspective, which involves understanding that increasing foreign involvement will be a necessary part of strengthening China's national water security (Hu, 2012).

On a larger scale, Ma Jun writes that "Environmental protection policies are subordinate to the broader economic picture. Environmental impact assessments can be breached if they are a barrier to investment. Once a crackdown has ended, polluting industries can pick up where they left off—as long as it will benefit GDP (gross domestic product) growth. Faced with the choice between economic growth and protecting water resources, local governments favour the economy" (Chinadialogue, 2009).

Damming Tibetan and Himalayan Rivers

> More than 60% of the world's 227 largest rivers have been fragmented by infrastructures such as dams and diversions. Rivers are turned on and off instead of flowing by natural rhythms. Many rivers are thus but shadows of their former selves and the blue lines on the map are often tokens of faded glories (UNESCO-IHP, 2012).

Rivers originating in the Himalayan ranges and other regions in Tibet drain approximately 6 million sq km or more. The snow peaks and glaciers enable these regions to be the source of major rivers that flow into Asia, approximately sustaining 1.3 billion people.

One can easily observe the Chinese dam building frenzy from its past records. As per the World Commission on Dams, China had only 22 large dams in 1949 and today there are more than 87,000 dams in China (International Rivers, 2013). China even plans to dam the rivers that still remain free flowing, such as the Arun (Arun flows from Tibet as Bhumchu to Nepal and India) and the Subansiri (Subansiri river is a tributary of Brahmaputra river flowing from Tibet to the Indian states of Assam and Arunachal Pradesh) before flowing into India (The Jakarta Globe, 2011).

According to the South China Morning Post (2013), on 23 January 2013, the Chinese state council released an energy-sector blue print for 2011-2015 in which it has decided to construct at least 54 hydro-power stations with a total capacity of 120 GW on the upper reaches of Yangtse, Mekong and Salween. This construction clearly disregards geological risks, global biodiversity, resettlement and impacts on downstream communities (International Rivers, 2013a). The plan also includes the re-opening of damming projects on Salween river that were previously shelved due to environmental concerns (South China Morning Post, 2013).

According to International Rivers (2013a; 2013b), many of these damming projects have forced over 23 million people to leave their homes and land, many of whom are still suffering the impacts of displacement and dislocation. Yet, despite serious impacts of dam construction in China, the Chinese government has ambitious plans to expand hydro-power generation. Not only are these rivers subjected to hydro-power projects, but these free-flowing rivers and their potential for hydro-power source attracts major extractive industries from distant mainland due to availability of cheap power and water resources. The strong policy backing from Beijing towards the mining sector, designates it as one of the 'Four Pillar' industries in central Tibet. The fate of these trans-boundary rivers and rivulets has already been decided and measured in terms of economic benefits, rather than ecological values. Western rivers such as Yarlung Tsangpo (Brahmaputra) and its major tributaries in Tibet (Kyichu, Nyangchu, Tongchu, Nyang Trib Chu and Drakchu, Wolga Chu, Chllong Chu, Yiwong Chu and Parlung Chu) are now being increasingly interrupted by medium-sized dams. Such activities paint a bleak picture as they will definitely impede the downstream flow of water and alluvial sediment to the floodplains of India and Bangladesh. Two new additional dams (Bayu and Daigu) are also being planned along the mainstream of Yarlung Tsangpo along with the construction of a 510 megawatt (MW) project at Rdzam/Zangmu (Figure 12.3).

The official narration from China towards these damming is, as usual, the same except for a small change in the date. "The Chinese side always takes a responsible attitude towards the exploitation of cross-border rivers and every new project will be planned and reasoned in a scientific way—before being started" was the response by Hong Lei of the Foreign Ministry during a daily press briefing (Xinhua, 2013).

China is (indeed) the central (poker) player in many of the controversies surrounding shared water resources in Asia with more damming plans for its upstream reserves that will have dramatic impacts on the lower riparian countries (Economy, 2012).

On this side of the political border, the hydro-power potential for the remaining Himalayan countries also remains very attractive for power companies. Pomeranz (2011) estimated that for Pakistan, India, Bhutan and Nepal, the hydro-power potential could be a jaw dropping 192,000 megawatts with almost half of it on the Indian side.

According to Pandit and Grumbine (2012), the hydro-power potential within the Indian Himalayan rivers (Brahmaputra, Ganges and Indus) is enormous (50,000 MW) and the Government of India (GoI) is keen to invest in these water resources. They also mention that this region could have one of the highest dam density in the world if all the dams were to be constructed as planned (Figure 12.3), resulting in huge loss and extinction of terrestrial species and changes in land cover. A separate article published by *Hindustan*

Times-Darjeeling discusses the grand master plan as envisioned by the central government of India in identifying the north-eastern region as 'India's future powerhouse' by building about 160 or more dams. It also quoted a statement from a former West Bengal State Planning Board member that the earthquake that struck Sikkim on September 2011 could have been induced or accelerated by the multiple dams on Teesta river (Hindustan Times, 2011).

A UNESCO-IHP report mentioned that both water and culture are strongly interrelated and their perfect blending is crucial for the flourishing of human culture (UNESCO, 2007). But, by looking at the current pace of damming activities and their various impacts, it appears that we have moved too far for a complete U-turn to a point close to 'A', but still, timely enough to admit our past errors in understanding the true value of these resources to sustain our ancestral culture and traditions.

A Sitting Time Bomb: Himalayan Dams

The geological nature of the Tibetan Plateau and the Himalayan belt is such that the whole region in its entirety is still rising higher and is often jolted with strong and weak earthquakes. The dams constructed on the seismic-prone zones and near active faultlines can be a perfect recipe for future disasters. In most cases, the locals were poorly informed or not consulted during this maddening spree of damming and traversing of the natural rhythm of rivers in the name of developments (Figure 12.4).

In China, dam safety has always been treated as a sensitive subject. Now, incidents at a number of dams and reservoirs have cast doubt on the quality of these projects, but they are rarely reported to the general public (Zongshu and Nianzu, 2011). In 2012, in a study conducted by 'Probe International,' Jackson (2012) mentioned that more than 99.7 per cent of the large dams in western China (in Tibet) were located in zones of moderate to very high seismic hazard (as defined by the UN Global Seismic Hazards Assessment Program).

Figure 12.4 explains the seismic-prone areas within the Himalayan belt and warns us about the imminent threat posed by those 200 or more dams that are built or are under construction throughout the Himalayan regions.

Development Cost: Social Impacts and Threats to Biodiversity

On the high alpine pastures of Tibet, damming activities and climate warming have not only caused various landscape changes, but also resulted in the final eviction of nomads from their ancestral pastures. Unlike the hydro-power projects planned in the Indian Himalayan states and in other parts of the Himalayan regions, those that are currently operational and under construction in Tibet have and are still attracting many extractive industries and migrant workers from mainland China. As such they not only indulge in land grabbing and polluting the local water sources but also marginalise local/ethnic Tibetans. No clear information is available as to how the local residents are really benefiting from these so-called development initiatives. In most cases, the local residents are uninformed about the consequences and excluded from any decision-making processes. Not only are there no local consultations and public hearing regarding these dam constructions, there is no media reporting and blogging on these constructions.

Current Chinese policies of settling the nomads as 'ecological migrants' in low land permanent settlements and restoring the grassland ecosystem are justified on account of the so-called 'overgrazing of pastures' and 'upbringing of the backward nomadic culture'. According to field reports and policies, these programmes (Breivik, 2007) aimed to protect and restore the grasslands have affected the social lifestyles of the displaced herders and pastoralist who have for millennia safeguarded these rangelands and water resources (Isom, 2009). Some programmes have even gone as far to simulate the effect of grazing by clipping plots of grasslands (in Tibet) and to indicate the positive effects of grazing (Klein *et al.*, 2007) and the effect of grazing herds on pulling back the carbon dioxide from atmosphere (Lovell and Ward, 2009). Researchers mentioned that abandoning and depopulating these grasslands will lead to the domination of the invasive species, diminution of biodiversity and could cause more harm to the grasslands (Foggin, 2008). The grasslands of Tibet, when grazed moderately and intermittently could actually maintain a higher biodiversity and healthier pastures (Breivik, 2007).

According to Foggin (2011):

> Ecological Migration (EM) was a policy that remains an untested social experiment at an enormous scale and is threatening not only local pastoralists' livelihood and community structure, but also regional stability as quota driven resettlements are married with high levels of unemployment and loss of hope.

This programme could prove devastating and if continued in the future, have long-term (generational) social, cultural and possibly environmental consequences.

Similar concerns related to loss of biodiversity, cultural values and environmental destruction were also raised around damming projects in different parts of Sikkim, Uttarakhand and Arunachal Pradesh in India. The Himalayan state of Arunachal Pradesh is home to about 1.5 million people comprising 20 or more tribal communities. More than 150 dams are being proposed on the major river basins that are home to many tribal communities and which are rich in biodiversity (Overdorf, 2012).

An ecological modelling conducted on the consequences of damming on Brahmaputra, Ganges and Indus within the Indian Himalayan region projected that these dams (in future) will responsible for the extinction of 22 flowering plants and 7 vertebrate animals by 2025. About 54,117 ha of forests will be submerged and 114,361 ha will be damaged by dam-related activities. It was also estimated that nearly 90 per cent of Indian Himalayan valleys will be affected by dam building and 27 per cent of these dams will also affect dense forests (Pandit and Grumbine, 2012).

Even today, those people living downstream of the first big dam (Ranganadi Hydroelectric project, 450 MW) are facing social challenges and migrating to other parts of Arunachal Pradesh due to continuous threats posed by these floodgates. According to Overdorf: "It was the huge upfront payments made by the dam builders that allow the governments to gloss over the other impacts caused by these dams" (Overdorf, 2012). Other researchers have mentioned the extent to which these dam builders are pushing forward with their pet projects as clean energy sources to seek carbon credits and in the process undermining the plight of the indigenous communities (Yumnam, 2013). In the uplands of Sikkim and Arunachal Pradesh, minority indigenous communities such as the Lepchas and Idu Mishmis have expressed concern about the impacts of multiple mega projects in their homelands (Vagholikar and Das, 2010). As such, these projects require extensive tunneling in a geologically, ecologically and culturally sensitive area (Ghosh, 2011). Others also mention the utter disregard and callousness towards local communities and the natural environment in the way in which these projects are being implemented.

Conclusion and Recommendations

The Tibetan Plateau and the Himalaya are the land bridge connecting South Asia with East Asia. The very survival of almost 1.3 billion people depends on the water resources originating from them. The impacts on landscape and natural resources due to climate warming and human intervention will be enormous and irreversible.

Rivers originating from Tibet and the Himalayan regions are one of nature's best gifts to all life forms. They currently face various natural and manmade blows that could seriously affect regional harmony, social integrity and local cultures. These river waters should be well respected and treated as a medium or a natural platform to develop and promote peace and harmony within the region. They could play a pivotal role in safeguarding ancestral cultures and indigenous knowledge for understanding mother earth.

Hence, policymakers must actively engage with scientists, local communities and experts on the problems facing the Himalaya and its people prior to initiating any developmental projects. Human interventions coupled with climate warming have transformed these natural ecosystems and affected native biodiversity and the communities who have thrived on these rugged terrains for generations.

Downstream users of river waters originating from Tibet should establish a regional forum to create policies on trans-boundary issues that effectively safeguard access and quality of water from the source region. Special priority for such a regional and international forum should be the long-term planning to address reduction in current flows due to accelerating glacier melt, industrial demand and damming.

References

Atisha, T.P (1990). "The Tibetan Approach to Ecology", Paper presented at the *Ecological Conference on Tibet.* San Francisco.

Bajracharya, S.R., P.K. Mool and B.R. Shrestha (2008). *Global Climate Change and Melting of Himalayan Glaciers.* Nepal: ICIMOD. *http://geoportal.icimod.org/Publication/Files/cf894b1a-d2df-46ca-9e7a-e0577d24ea4f.pdf*

BBC News Report (2011). "Himalaya Village Caught Between Culture and Nature", by Navin Singh Khadia. 24 August. *http://www.bbc.co.uk/news/science-environment-14620091.*

Blanford Henry F (1884). "On the Connection of the Himalaya Snowfall with Dry Winds and Seasons of Drought in India", *Proceedings of the Royal Society of London* 37: 3-22.

Breivik, Irene (2007). *The Political Ecology of Grassland Conservation in Qinghai Province, Chine: Discouse, Polocies and the Herders.* MA thesis. Noragric: Norwegian University of Life Sciences , Department of International Environment and Development Studies.

Chellaney Brahma (2011). *Water: Asia's New Battleground.* HarperCollins Publishers India.

Chinadialogue (2009). "Defending Water Security", 19 March. *http://www.chinadialogue.cn/article/show/single/en/2847*

Choephel, Tsering and Tsephel (2003). *Environment Conditions in Ngari Prefecture of Tibet.* DIIR Publication. Tibetan version.

Digital Media Corporation (2013). "Huge Glacial Lake Atop Himalayas Poses Danger in Sikkim", *http://www.dnaindia.com/scitech/report_huge-glacial-lake-atop-himalayas-poses-danger-in-sikkim_1798401-all*

Dobhal, D.P., Anil K. Gupta, Manish Mehta and D.D. Khandelwal (2013). "Kedarnath Disaster: Facts and Plausible Causes", *Current Science* 105(2): 171-74, 25 July. *http://www.currentscience.ac.in/volumes/105/02/0171.pdf*

Economic Times (2012). "Rice Production Should Shift to Eastern Parts of the Country, Feel Scientists", *Economic Times. http://articles.economictimes.indiatimes.com/2012-10-09/news/34343185_1_alternative-crops-eastern-states-food-grain*

Economy, Elizabeth (2012). "China's Global Quest for Resources and Implications for the United States", *Testimony Before the U.S.-China Economic and Security Review Commission.* 26 January. *http://www.uscc.gov/sites/default/files/1.26.12economy_testimony.pdf*

Environment and Development Desk (1992). *Tibet: Environment and Development Issues (1992): Wildlife Conservation Decree Issued by Tagdra Rinpoche the Regent of Tibet in 1944).* Dharamshala: DIIR, CTA.

————. (2000). *Tibet 2000, Environment and Development Issue.* Dharamsala: DIIR-Publication, CTA.

————. (2012). "Tibet: Environment and Development", *EDD-Blog, http://tibet-edd.blogspot.in/2012/02/geological-evolution-and-seismicity-of.html*

Foggin, J. Marc (2008). "Depopulating the Tibetan Grasslands, National Policies and Perspectives for the Future of Tibetan Herders in Qinghai Province", *China, Mountain Research and Development* 28(1): 26–31, Feb. doi:10.1659/mrd.0972

———. (2011). "Rethinking 'Ecological Migration' and the Value of Cultural Continuity: A Response to Wang, Song, and Hu". AMBIO 40:100–101, doi 10.1007/s13280-010-0105-5, Royal Swedish Academy of Sciences 2010. *http://www.researchgate.net/publication/226138803_Response_to_Rethinking_Ecological_Migration_and_the_Value_of_Cultural_Continuity*

Forbes (2011). "China's Strict New Water Policy", *http://www.forbes.com/sites/gordonchang/2011/04/03/chinas-strict-new-water-policy/*

French, Rebecca Redwood (1995). *The Golden Yoke: The Legal Cosmology of Buddhist Tibet.* Ithaca, New York: Snow Lion Publications.

Ghosh, Subir (2011). "Going Underground: Indian Dam Projects Threaten Teesta River", *http://asiancorrespondent.com/64398/india-theres-more-to-teesta-than-just-water-sharing/*

Greenpeace Briefing (2002). *http://www.greenpeace.org/international/PageFiles/24845/glacier_media.pdf*

Harrabin, Roger and Neil Paton (2013). "Travelling to a Himalayan Glacier", *http://www.bbc.co.uk/news/science-environment-24208687*

Hindustan Times (2011). "Sikkim Quake May Have Been Induced by Dams Across Teesta", *Hindustan Times,* Darjeeling, 21 September. *http://www.hindustantimes.com/India-news/WestBengal/Sikkim-quake-may-have-been-induced-by-dams-across-Teesta/Article1-748547.aspx*

HSBC Research (2011). "China's Rising Climate Risk", *http://www.research.hsbc.com/midas/Res/RDV?ao=20&key=Fxjcu6AJgD&n=309614.PDF*

Hu, Yusha (2012). "Foreign Investment in China's Water Infrastructure, A New Strategy for National Security", *http://www.chinasecurity.us/index.php?option=com_content&view=article&id=308&Itemid=8*

Huber, Toni (2004). *Territorial Control by "Sealing": A Religio-Political Practice in Tibet.* ZAS 33.

ICIMOD (2013). *Case Studies on Flash Flood Risk Management in the Himalayas in Support of Specific Flash Flood Policies.*

ICIMOD and USAID (2013). "Case Studies on Flash Flood Risk Management in the Himalayas", *http://lib.icimod.org/record/27767/files/Case-study-on%20%20FFRM.pdf*

Immerzeel, Walter (2008). "Historical Trends and Future Predictions of Climate Variability in the Brahmaputra Basin", *Int. J. Climatol.* 28: 243–54. doi: 10.1002/joc.1528.

Immerzeel, Walter and M.F.P. Bierkensb (2009). "Seasonal Prediction of Monsoon Rainfall in Three Asian River Basins: The Importance of Snow Cover on the Tibetan Plateau", *Int. J. Climatol.* doi: 10.1002/joc.2033.

International Rivers (2013a). "China Moves to Dam the Nu, Ignoring Seismic, Ecological and Social Risks", *http://www.internationalrivers.org/resources/china-moves-to-dam-the-nu-ignoring-seismic-ecological-and-social-risks-7807*

———. (2013b). "China". *http://www.internationalrivers.org/programs/china*

IPCC (2007). "Chapter 10: Asia, Section 10.6.2 The Himalayan Glaciers", *Climate Change 2007: Working Group II: Impacts, Adaptation and Vulnerability. http://www.ipcc.ch/publications_and_data/ar4/wg2/en/ch10s10-6-2.html*

———. (2001). "Chapter 11: Australia and New Zealand, Section 11.2.1.2 Human Systems: Sensitivity/Vulnerability to Climate and Weather", *Working Group II: Impacts, Adaptation and Vulnerability. http://www.ipcc.ch/publications_and_data/ar4/wg2/en/ch11s11-2-2.html*

Isom, John (2009). "Tibet's Nomadic Pastoralists: Tradition, Transformation and Prospects", *http://www.iwgia.org/publications/search-pubs?publication_id=402*

Jackson, John (2012). *A Probe International Study, Earthquake Hazards and Large Dams in Western China.*

JakartaGlobe (2011). "China Holds the Key to Asia's 'Blue Gold'", 15 December. *http://www.thejakartaglobe.com/opinion/china-holds-the-key-to-asias-blue-gold/484739*

Klein Julia A., Harte John and Zhao Xin-Quan (2007). "Experimental Warming, Not Grazing, Decreases Rangeland Quality on the Tibetan Plateau", *Ecological Applications* 17(2).

Lovell, Tony and Bruce Ward (2009). "Regenerating Grasslands", *http://www.guardian.co.uk/environment/2009/jul/13/manchester-report-grasslands*

Lu, Zongshu and Shen Nianzu (2011). "Dams Gone Wrong: Is Danger Lurking in China's Dams?", 24 August. *http://journal.probeinternational.org/2011/08/24/dams-gone-wrong-is-danger-lurking-in-china%E2%80%99s-dams/*

Mckinsey Report (2009). *Charting our Water Future. http://www.mckinsey.com/App_Media/Reports/Water/Charting_Our_Water_Future_Exec%20Summary_001.pdf*

National Climate Change Program, China (2007). *http://www.china.org.cn/english/environment/213624.htm*

National Geographic (2009). "Booming Middle-Class Diet May Stress Asia's Water Needs", *Thirsty Beef. http://news.nationalgeographic.co.in/news/2009/08/090827-asian-water-crisis/*

National Research Council (2012). *Himalayan Glaciers: Climate Change, Water Resources, and Water Security.* Washington, DC: The National Academies Press. *http://www.nap.edu/catalog.php?record_id=13449*

Nature (2013). "Jane Qiu, Tibetan Glaciers are Shrinking at Their Summits", *Nature News.* 17 September. *http://www.nature.com/news/tibetan-glaciers-are-shrinking-at-their-summits-1.13767* (accessed October 2013).

NBC News Science (2013). "Surprising Ally Protecting Snow Leopards: Buddhist Monks", *http://www.nbcnews.com/science/surprising-ally-protecting-snow-leopards-buddhist-monks-8C11088007*

Norbu, Jamyang (2009). "High Sanctuary, Wildlfe and Nature Conservancy in Old Tibet", 6 December. *http://www.jamyangnorbu.com/blog/2009/12/06/high-sanctuary/*

Overdorf, Jason (2012). "Damnation, The True Cost of India's Energy Demand", Part 1-4. *http://www.globalpost.com/dispatch/news/regions/asia-pacific/india/120315/dam-nation-arunachal-pradesh-hydropower-electricity-part-1?page=0,1*

Pandit Maharaj, K. and Grumbine R. Edward (2012). "Potential Effects of Ongoing and Proposed Hydropower Development on Terrestrial Biological Diversity in the Indian Himalaya", *Conservation Biology* 26(6): 1061–71. Society for Conservation Biology. Doi: 10.1111/j.1523-1739.2012.01918.x

Pomeranz Kenneth (2011) The Asia-Pacific Journal: Japan Focus, 'The Great Himalayan Watershed: Water Shortages, Mega-Projects and Environmental Politics in China, India, and Southeast Asia, http://japanfocus.org/-kenneth-pomeranz/3195 (accessed October 2013).

Sharma, Dinesh C. (2012). "Himalayan Scare from Melting Ice", *http://www.dailymail.co.uk/indiahome/article-2133382/Himalayan-scare-melting-ice.html*

South China Morning Post (2013). "Ban Lifted on Controversial Nu River Dam Projects", January. *http://www.scmp.com/news/china/article/1135463/ban-lifted-controversial-nu-river-dam-projects*

Styron, R., M. Taylor and K. Okoronkwo (2010). *"Database of Active Structures from the Indo-Asian Collision", Eos Trans. AGU, 91(20).*0-1. doi: 10.1029/2010EO200001.

Tandong Yao, Lonnie Thompson,Wei Yang,Wusheng Yu, Yang Gao, Xuejun Guo, Xiaoxin Yang, Keqin Duan, Huabiao Zhao, Baiqing Xu, Jiancheng Pu, Anxin Lu, Yang Xiang, Dambaru B. Kattel and Daniel Joswiak (2012). *Different Glacier Status with atmospheric Circulations in Tibetan Plateau and Surroundings*. Published online: 15 July 2012.Doi: 10.1038/nclimate1580.

The Telegraph (2011). "Nelson Dean, Everest Glacier 'Turning into a Lake' Due to Global Warming", *http://www.telegraph.co.uk/earth/environment/8538974/Everest-glacier-turning-into-a-lake-due-to-global-warming.html*

Thomas, J. and S. Rai (2005). "Executive Summary", *An Overview of Glaciers, Glacier Retreat, and Subsequent Impacts in Nepal, India and China*. WWF, Nepal Program. *http://www.panda.org/downloads/climate_change/glacierssummary.pdf*

UNEP (2008). "Atmospheric Brown Cloude", *Regional Assessment Report With Focus on Asia. http://www.unep.org/pdf/ABCSummaryFinal.pdf*

UNESCO and World Heritage Centre (2007). "Case Studies on Climate Change and World Heritage", CLT/WHC/07/30. *http://www.unesco.org/new/en/media-services/single-view/news/now_available_online_water_cultural_diversity_and_global_environmental_change_emerging_trends_sustainable_futures/*

UNESCO-IHP (2012). "Water, Cultural Diversity, and Global Environmental Change, Emerging Trends and Sustainable Futures", *http://www.unesco.org/new/en/media-services/singleview/news/now_available_online_water_cultural_diversity_and_global_environmental_change_emerging_trends_sustainable_futures/*

Vagholikar, Neeraj and Partha J. Das (2010). "Damming Northeast India", *http://chimalaya.files.wordpress.com/2010/12/damming-northeast-india-final.pdf*

World Bank (2009). *Addressing China's Water Scarcity*. JianXie, Andres Liebenthal, Jeremy J. Warford, John A. Dixon, Manchuan, Wang, ShijiGao, Shuilin Wang, Yong Jiang and Zhong Ma. pp.89.

World Health Organization (2013). "Progress on Sanitation and Drinking Water", *www.who.int/iris/bitstream/10665/81245/1/9789241505390_eng.pdf*

World Health Organization and UNICEF (2013). "Progress on Sanitation and Drinking-Water, 2013: Update". *www.who.int/iris/bitstream/10665/81245/1/9789241505390_eng.pdf*

Xinhua (2013). "China Justifies Yarlung Zangbo River Exploitation", Updated on 30-01-2013, *http://usa.chinadaily.com.cn/china/2013-01/30/content_16188880.htm*

Yumnam, Jiten (2013). "Mega Dams and CDM Fraud in Sikkim", *http://carbonmarketwatch.org/mega-dams-and-cdm-fraud-in-sikkim/*

Zhi, Lu (2010). "Biodiversity is Life", *Beijing Review* 26, July. *http://www.bjreview.com.cn/ quotes/txt/2010-07/01/content_282315.htm*

Figure 12.1

Active Structures of the Tibetan Plateau (Based on Styron et al., 2010)

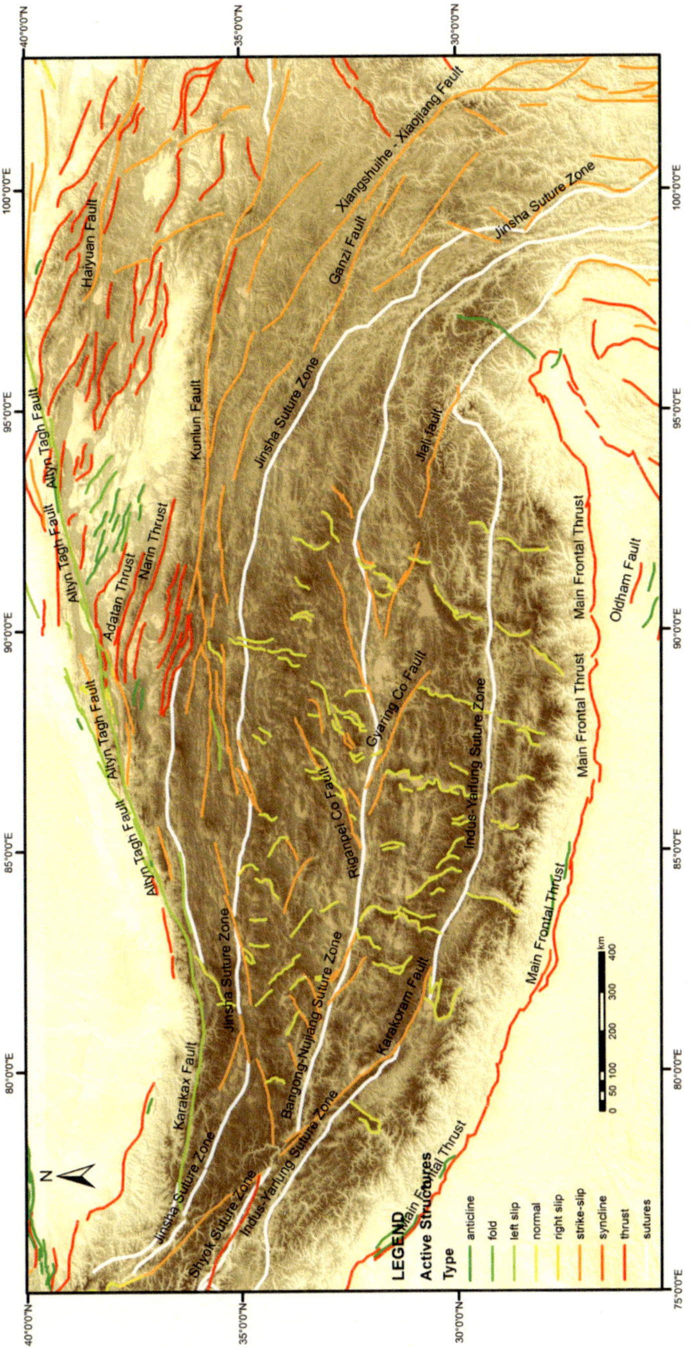

Source: EDD/DIIR (2013) CTA.

Figure 12.2

Drainage Basin of Major Rivers Originating from Tibet

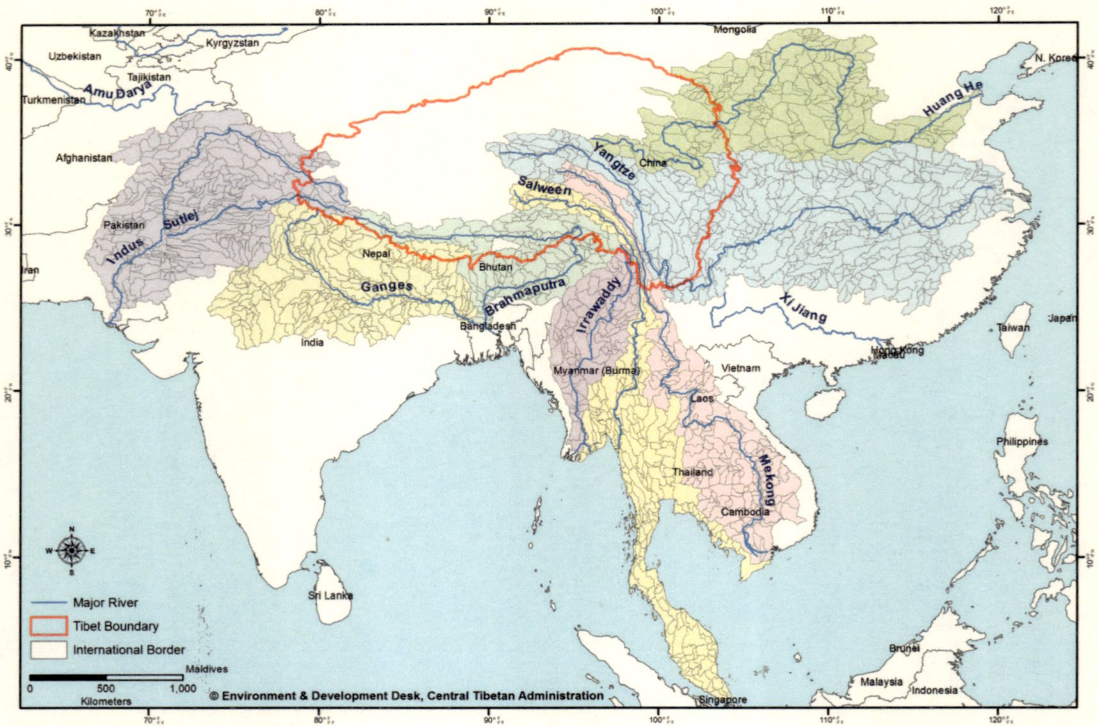

Source: EDD/DIIR (2012) CTA.

Figure 12.3

Distribution of Dams Under Various Planning Stages on the Rivers Flowing from Tibet and on the Indian Himalayan Regions

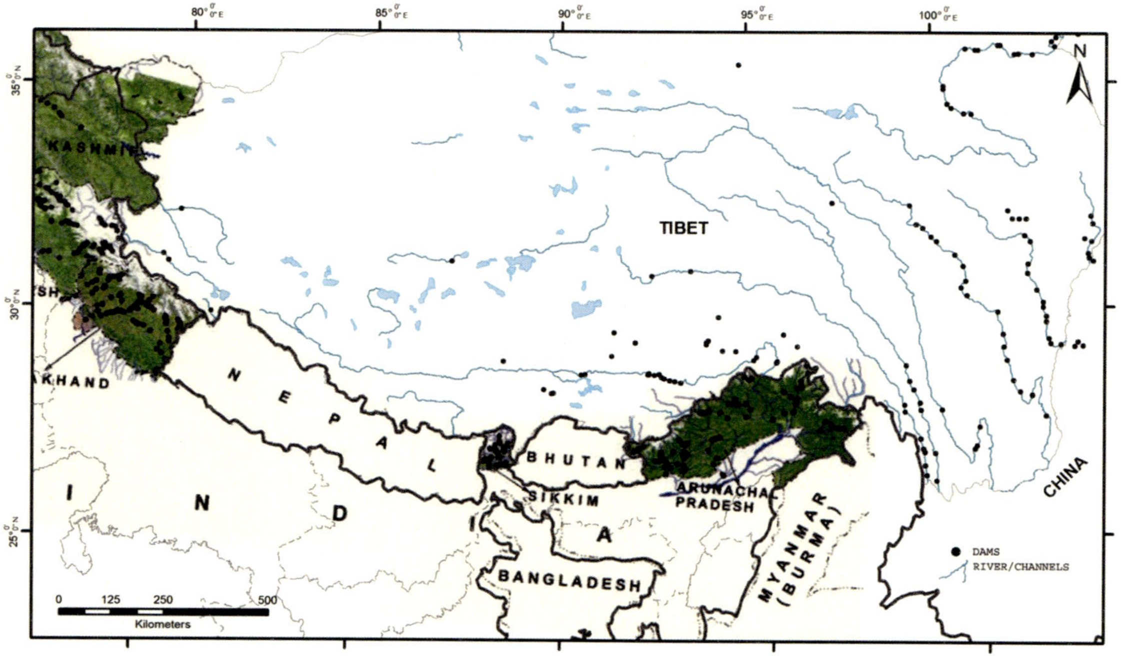

Source: Adapted from Zoomer and Tashi (2013) and Pandit and Grumbine (2012).

Figure 12.4

Seismic Events (magnitude ≥ 5) that Occurred Between 1973 and 2013 and Active Structures within the Himalayan Regions

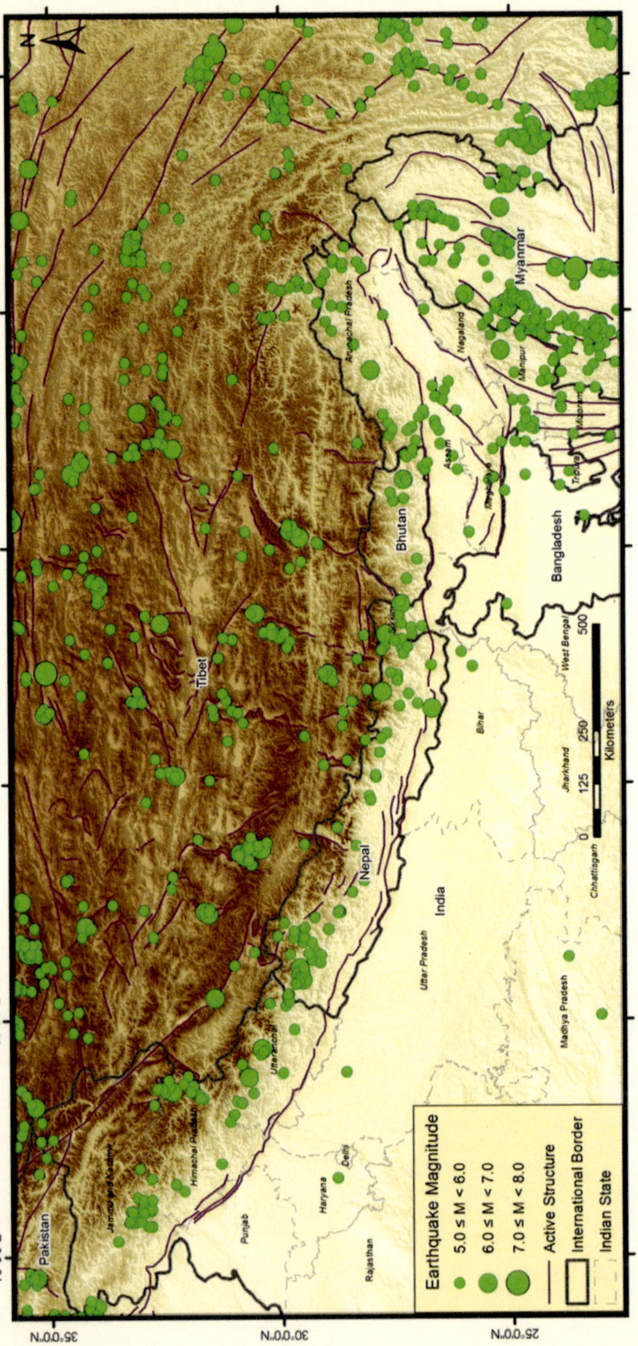

Source: EDD/DIIR (2013).

13

ANANTA SWARUP BIJENDRA DE GURUNG

Tibet and Security Implications for China

A Brief Appraisal

Introduction

Tibet saw its documented foreign intervention with the successful penetration of Colonel Younghusband in 1904. It has been on one occasion the arena of the great game between imperial Britain and czarist Russia. Tibet has always been one of the most vibrant and significant centres for Buddhist pilgrims in the world. Lamaist Buddhism reigns supreme in the land. Until recently, the subsequent incarnations of the Dalai Lama (the true embodiment of God himself according to the Tibetans) formed the apex body and supervised spiritual and political needs resulting in a hazy divide between the holy and the worldly. Bordered by the Himalayan belt in the south, it remained mysterious and little known to the world till the first half of the 20th century.

During the British Raj in India, the European power was well aware of the fact that it could not afford to have a foreign influence in the region that could prove detrimental to its interests. This policy in relation to Tibet was later pursued by independent India but it could not hold on to it for too long. Contested over decades, Tibet has now been officially recognised as a part of China. Thus, the sovereignty of the geographical space remains altered. It is an ignominy that international society could not interfere to secure Tibet's sovereignty. In the contemporary era, it forms a geostrategic, political and economic buffer between two nuclear powers in South Asia, viz., China and India.

Tibet is better known in international echelons as the 'Roof of the World'. But many a times, it is also acknowledged as the

Water Tower of Asia because of the huge reserves of fresh water in the form of glaciers and natural lakes. These reserves naturally flow into and feed some of the main rivers in China, India and Southeast Asia. China is the fastest growing economy and its urge to sustain the growth has left huge energy demands. This has led to unprecedented consumption and exhaustion of natural resources in interior China, which are diminishing at a fast rate. To tackle this problem it has located huge pockets of natural reserves such as coal, gold, oil shale gas and important base metals (for example, copper, iron ore, aluminium, chromium, lead and zinc) within the Tibetan Plateau, which could prove vital in sustaining its heavy industries and the inflating economic growth. Infrastructural build up such as the Qinghai-Tibet railway, China National Highway 219 (G219) and China National Highway 109, to mention a few, could easily use these resources. Thus, Tibet has serious security implications for China.

Intervention in Tibet by China has several aspects which can be clubbed together to form a single motive. First, historically, China has justified its intrusion in the name of liberation and humanitarian cause, securing a readymade answer for the international audience so that Tibet can in turn be used as a buffer state. Secondly, and most importantly, the intervention had long-term economic implications for China as Tibet now promises to be an avenue through which uninterrupted flow of energy demands could be met. Extracting minerals *via* Tibet may prove to be the most viable option for China to safeguard and realise its long-term national interests. It could alter the power and international position of China, especially when there are avenues of economic prospects to be explored in Tibet. This exploitative mindset can be described as a remnant of the colonial and imperial legacy once employed by the European powers to exploit their colonies in Africa and Asia. China's growing assertiveness and rapacious behaviour in the international forum puts a serious question to the decolonisation process which marked an end to colonial policies once pursued by many powerful western nation-states. Without refuting the role of real politics, the paper argues that China's contemporary rationale for securing Tibet emanates not only from the prism of a conventional security dilemma but also from non-traditional security concerns (maintaining its energy security and national growth rate). It also makes an attempt to understand how these contribute to China and India's relationship.

Land of Opportunities (Tibet) and Resource Seeking (China)

The interactions between Tibet and China became regular in the 7th, 8th and 9th centuries when Tibet was at the pinnacle of its power (Rockhill, 1910). The relationship before and during this period between the two was the opposite of what it is in the contemporary era. It was not China that had leverage in influencing the relationship between the two, but it was Tibet that was supreme over China in their bilateral relationship. But when there was a decline Tibet's power, China began to be an independent entity, free of Tibetan dominance. The power vacuum created with the fall of monarchy from second-half of the 8th century in Tibet was slowly filled by a select few religious leaders who became temporal and religious heads of the land.

While it was the Chinese imperial Manchu army which conquered Tibet for the first time somewhere in 1909 (Bradsher, 1969), it was the Shimla conference (1914) between British India and China, which bestowed China exclusive rights over the foreign affairs and suzerainty of Tibet (Alexandrowicz, 1953). It also established the McMahon line as the international border between British India and China (Anand, 2009), which the latter did not accept as legitimate. Later during the 1950s, the Red army claimed absolute sovereignty over the region. Gradually, China's policy over Tibet began to grow assertive. Consequently, the power relationship that we see in Sino-Tibet is the legacy of China's gradual growth in supremacy in international affairs. Such an approach has reduced the status of Tibetans to second class citizens.

China has a history of peasant repression by imperial rulers and has also seen many uprisings against them. Later, under the peasant revolutionary forces, overthrow the aristocratic system and established a type of socialism under Mao Tse-Tung. After a successful revolution, China now saw the need to liberate its immediate neighbour, Tibet, from a perceived oppressive system. It is true that political power, administrative departments and large part of the pastured land in Tibet were owned by the nobility, composed of high aristocrats and rent free Lamaseries (Riggs, 1950). But whether there really existed an exploitative system that was detrimental to the interests of the general Tibetans, lacks supportive evidence. Nonetheless, China exploited this fact to its advantage and made it the focal point through which it validated its liberating stance for the people of Tibet. This line of thought formed the basis for China's intervention along with its creed to free Tibet from the feudal aristocratic system, which according to it had ushered poverty and hunger for the general masses. In the immediate year that followed, China successfully signed a treaty of 'Agreement of the Central People's Government and the Local Government of Tibet for peaceful Liberation of Tibet' (1951) that affirmed that Tibet had long been a part of China (Bradsher, 1969). China through its long history of an oppressive monarchial system had realised that a strong socialist nation could be an answer to development that is free of oppressive domestic systems at home and from foreign domination. It wanted to superimpose this logic to further its claim over Tibet, in addition to the historical justification laid by it. But the plan backfired as Tibet saw such a move as aggressive and fatal to its sovereignty. The monks who had practised installed religious sovereign, over centuries, did not see the need for a socialist regime and a revolution. They were content with the simple life of a monk with daily prayers and worships. The displeasure later conglomerated into a fierce Lhasa uprising of 1959, which was crushed with an iron hand by Chinese authorities.

The intervention had manifold policy implications. First, China wanted to project itself as the vanguard of good life and human rights, which could be achieved only through socialism. It firmly believed in the credo that the condition of the oppressed would improve in a class-less society cultivated through a successful revolution against the oppressor. But what China failed to realise was that Tibet did not have an antagonistic outlook against the ruling elite. The general masses did not feel cheated and oppressed by the monastery. The incarnation of the Dalai Lama was seen with the holiest of attitude and reverence. He was the embodiment of God himself who had come to earth and deferred his own *nirvana* for the benefit of the whole human race. The Tibetans as such had no intention to go against their God. Second, China was well aware that a foreign influence in the region could be detrimental to its national interests to exert its own influence in the region. It wanted to secure Tibet to secure itself in the long run. Third, if we look closely towards the logic of China's incursion, the invasion was purely for economic motifs, simply to secure its strategic economic national interest. Tibet was made a scapegoat for the wider political and economic interests sought by the Chinese political elite. And it is this third implication that has the most important contemporary relevance.

China has the fastest growing economy, therefore it needs huge and uncut power supply and minerals. This the Chinese are procuring through dams, mines, deforestation, etc., from its peripheral region. Tibet was once looted of its valuables from its monasteries by the invading imperial British who wanted to open Tibet to use it as a back door to enter the vast potential market of China (Mehra, 2005; Anand, 2009). In the contemporary era, it is China that wants to open Tibet to procure and exploit the natural resources in the region for its own development. A disturbing relationship with a colonial fervour is thus developing between the two, where the powerful core (China) seeks to exploit the resource rich but weak periphery (Tibet).

The Red army was consistent in giving shape to this policy from the very beginning. By 1976 strategic requirements had been completed where it had carved out 91 highways totaling 15,800 km, which linked Lhasa with interior China (Norbu, 1979). The reasons for such policies then was to wipe out the British, Soviet and American influence from the region and exert its own influence, whereas in the contemporary era the logic of such expansionism and infrastructural build-up is basically for resource extraction. On a positive note, by 1965, there were 1,682 primary schools, 7 middle schools, 15 hospitals and 149 clinics, and 60 small and middle-sized industrial plants established by China in Tibet (Bradsher, 1969). No doubt that a modern education system, health and sanitation facilities have been established in Tibet, but the oppressive structure and imposing rule that the Chinese employ against the Tibetans still continues. The Dalai Lama remains the primary symbol of the nation of Tibet (Kolas, 1996) and for the people, despite it being illegal as far as the Chinese code of conduct and rules are concerned.

Tibet and Security Implications for China: A Brief Appraisal

There are two significant reasons for China's repressive as well as assertive policies. The first is predominantly geostrategic and the second is the contemporary manifestation of the former, which is a combination of geostrategy as well as economy. They are nonetheless related to one another and form a single conglomerate whole.

Conventional Security

China was aware of the geostrategic significance of Tibet. It wanted to curtail the influence of other European and Eurasian powers such as imperial Britain and czarist Russia in the region from the very beginning. Creating a buffer in Tibet would create a situation of balance in the region devoid of foreign intervention. We find traces of such logic as early as 1788 when China chose to close Tibet to all external influences (Riggs, 1950). Even Jiang Zhiyu, one of the two officials left in Lhasa by Gen. Huang Musong after the 1934 Chinese Mission to Tibet, felt the need to procure Tibet at the earliest even if it meant using brute force to bring the region under Chinese control (Lin, 2002).

In addition, China was suspicious of American intentions *vis-à-vis* Tibet, because by 1949 it knew a group of American secret agents under Lowell Thomas had already studied the country in terms of military, strategic and economic prospects (Patterson, 1960; Riggs, 1950). With historic attempts by imperial Britain and czarist Russia to woo Tibet on their side and now America showing an active interest in the region, China could not afford to leave its peripheral neighbour unsecured. If Tibet fell under foreign forces it would leave China vulnerable to their attacks. Thus, securing Tibet was more like securing itself for the Red army which culminated in the final invasion of Tibet in the 1950s. To further check foreign influence in the region, the first air field in central Tibet was built during 1955-

1956 and by 1963, 12 airfields near the frontier of Nepal, Sikkim and Bhutan were complete (Norbu, 1979).

Discontent Khambas of eastern Tibet did launch a rebellion as early as 1954 and 1957, but by then it was too late for the people of Tibet (Bradsher, 1969). The climax of the mutiny was witnessed with the death of the Lhasa uprising in 1959, which resulted in the escape of His Holiness the 14th Dalai Lama into India *via* the North-East Frontier Agency (NEFA). After the Great Games and with the fall of czarist Russia and the British empire, a secure Tibet acted as a safe buffer between mainland China and post-colonial India. While the immediate concern of the Chinese occupation of Tibet in the 1950s was to check the influence of India in the Himalaya, China's long-term vision was more intricate and well mapped. Extraction and exploitation of resources were soon to follow.

We should know that during this period an extended landmass was also an important source of national power, which China sought to acquire. What is interesting here is that China was able to reveal that the conventional understanding of national power in the form of a extended landmass could hold true. Further, balance of power was maintained in the region through infrastructural development such as roads and railways. Szechuan-Tibet Highway (South Military Road), Chinghai-Tibet Highway (Northern Military Road), Drodam Highway (extreme west) and the Yunnan-Tibet Highway (starts from south) are some of the important highways that connect Tibet with interior China (Norbu, 1979). Among the latest actions in the region are the massive militarisation of Tibet, where an estimated 300,000 to 500,000 troops are stationed (Mota, 2007). All this infrastructural build-up within Tibet was not only aimed at developing and effectively dealing with domestic challenges in the region, but also to check and play a balancing act against foreign interventions and their influence in its extended backyard.

Non-conventional Security

The term non-conventional security is of recent origin and can be a serious threat as the enemy is within rather than outside. With the demise of military warfare, innovation of WMDs (weapons of mass destruction) and the evolution of interdependency at the global level, traditional security has lost some of its face value. In the contemporary era, actors in the international arena concentrate more on combating safety concerns emanating from non-conventional security threats. Economic development, energy security, food security deficit and climate change are some predicaments that every developing and developed nation-state faces. In the traditional era, development deficit was met directly by conquest and exploitation of natural resources of the subjugated. The scramble for Africa is one such account in the history of world affairs. The weapon of choice then was colonialism and imperialism, but such concepts have been put to an end with the final colonial state being liberated during the late 1960s. Or has it not? The question is still debatable. The following section tries to explain the linkages between non-conventional security threats and peripheral resource exploitation to meet these safety concerns.

Tibet is geostrategic ally placed and rich in natural resources but this very resource became the foundation for its exploitation. Scholars like Gabriel Lafitte have labelled such dilemmas 'resource curse' where the plunder of a region is solely due to the presence of its own natural resources. Thus the core rationale driving such exploitation, it could be argued, is the mirror image of colonialism. Some of the major manifestations can be summed up as:

Water Security

Water security is one of the most challenging security concerns faced by nation-states today. Tibet is the stockroom of fresh water reserves in Asia and therefore is known as the Third Pole because of its freshwater reserves in the form of glaciers and lakes. Thirty per cent of the fresh water supply of China is met from the rivers flowing from Tibet (Tibet: Environment and Development, 2011). A crisis will hatch when these valuable resources are to be shared between two or more nation-states. Consequently, sharing transnational river(s) has become a contentious affair in inter-state relations. For example, the recent Teesta water sharing dispute between India and Bangladesh. Teesta runs an entire length of 393 km and provides livelihood for its residents along the entire length. The same scenario can be replayed in the context of the relationship between India and China. Besides, China is a non-signatory to the 1997 UN Convention on the Law of Non-navigational Uses of International Watercourses which gives it an upper hand in defending its water policies. While damming of rivers inside Tibet is China's policy leap towards energy security, these rivers in turn form an essential life line for the economy of the whole of India's north, north-east (hydroelectricity and agriculture depend heavily on water supply from Tibet) and West Bengal.

Tibet ensures 70 per cent of summer flow in the Ganges in the west to 33.6 per cent of water in the east in the form of Brahmaputra (Central Tibetan Administration: Restoring Freedom and For Tibetans, 2009). The region between the Indus Valley in the west and Yellow River Valley in the east sustain approximately 47 per cent of the world's population (Department of Information and International Relations, 2000). But the Himalayan and Tibetan glaciers have been shrinking at an alarming rate, threatening the livelihood of over a billion people dependent on the major river systems of Asia (Chanda, 2009). Global warming and unaccountable human activities are the main causes behind it (Department of Information and International Relations, 2011). Due to this, there is already reduced flow in many of the rivers originating in Tibet (Norbu, 2012), for example, Drichu is confronting a pollution crisis, Gyalmo Ngyulchu again is threatened by dam construction and Zachu threatened by overfishing (Tibet: Environment and Development, 2012). In the short run, the glacier melt may increase water availability, but eventually when the base flow from glaciers ceases, it will have a drastic impact on river hydrology (Department of Information and International Relations, 2009). And so far, China has dammed every minor river and its tributaries in Tibet and has unveiled plans to construct even more dams which are clearly stipulated in its 12th Five Year Plan (2011-2015) (Central Tibetan Administration: Restoring Freedom and For Tibetans, 2013). According to this plan, China has a vision to build at least 54 hydro-power stations with a total capacity of 120 GW on the upper reaches of Yangtse, Mekong and Salween (Norbu, 2013). Further, a 510 MW dam of Dzam (Ch: Zangmu) on Yarlung Tasngpo (Brahmaputra) in Tibet has been commissioned in 2010 (Tibet: Environment and Development, 2012a).

China had only 22 dams in 1949 and this has increased to 22,000 dams in 2000 (Norbu, 2013). As for India, driven by population growth and the domestic needs of agriculture, its water demand will double by 2030 reaching 1.5 trillion cubic metres (Tibet: Environment and Development, 2012b). China's effort to dam the course of water then, is a serious concern for the lower riparian areas of India, Bangladesh and Southeast Asia. As a result, blocking Yarlung Tsangpo will spell disaster for the lower regions. It could withhold the river's fertile sediments from reaching the floodplains of Assam in north-east India and Bangladesh (The Guardian, 2010) hence affecting the soil quality and agricultural yield of the region. In addition, dams and reservoirs are responsible for almost a quarter of all human-caused methane emission (Tibet: Environment and Development, 2012c), increasing global warming.

India has a similar vision of tapping hydro-power potential of its north-eastern states (all the eight sisters of north-east India). But the paradox is that these rivers are directly fed by glacier run-off which has most of its origins in the Tibetan Plateau. If the rivers are dammed right at their source, how will India realise its energy security? Besides, glacier run-off has decreased drastically due to China's effort to use these rivers for commercial purposes (Department of Information and International Relations [DIIR], 2009).

Water is very important for irrigating the plains of India too. Irrigation is widespread in both the Indus (15 MHA) and Ganga/Brahmaputra basin (29 MHA) and in the Indus basin, water consumption is for cotton production; in Brahmaputra basin, water use is dominated by rice production; and in Ganga basin-irrigated water is used primarily for wheat production.[1] The use of water in the agricultural sector has increased over the past few decades and will continue to increase further (Norbu, 2013). But the decrease in the water run-off due to the dam building spree has hampered food

1. National Academy of Science, 2012, *http://www.nasonline.org/*

security in the region. For example, 70-80 per cent of Sengye Khabab (Indus river) water is fed by Tibetan glaciers and the decrease in the flow puts a question mark on its irrigation potential which is about 36 million acres.[2]

River waters are used by heavy industries located in the mineral-rich industrial but water deficit complexes of northern China. Industries use up to 23 per cent of the total water available in China. Of this about 80 per cent is used to operate and cool China's 10,000 coal burning generating units at 550 power plants (Schneider, 2010), for example, the giant Baotou Iron and Steel Company plant located in Inner Mongolia, which produces roughly 10 million metric tonnes of steel annually. Mining industries also demand a huge amount of water to tap in pools of oil and shale gas reserves deep inside the earth. The existing hydro-fracking technology requires that each horizontally drilled well receives 19,000-26,000 cubic metres (5-7 million gallons) of water mixed with chemicals and sand to crack the rock to release the valuable gas (Schneider, 2012).

Other than increased use of river water for generation of electricity and irrigation, river water contamination is on the rise in Tibet. Zinc and nickel contamination in the Gyalmo Ngulchu (Salween river) and high concentration of Nickel were identified in a tributary of the Drichu (Yangtse).[3] Lead poisoning of the water supply due to pollution from the Ganhetan Industrial District in Rushar (Ch: Huangzhong) county in Qinghai province was reported in 2006 (DIIR, 2011). Similarly, presence of heavy metal in the surface water in Gyama town has also been reported (Dhundup, 2013). This is a matter of grave concern, as these contaminated rivers unsuitable for consumption and irrigation finally pour down to India and many states in south and Southeast Asia.

Minerals and Petrochemical Deposits

Tibet is blessed with great reserves of coal, gold, copper, tin, lead, iron ore, corundum, oil and shale gas. It could be the largest mineral resource in the country with a potential value of more than $125

2. Ibid
3. Ibid.

billion (Interfax-China, 2006). The presence of such minerals was speculated by Mr J.C. White, the British Political Officer stationed in Sikkim, in his report dated as early as 1902 (Freshfield, 1904). The Chinese simply capitalised on this opportunity. Oil shale exploration is going on in TAR (Tibet Autonomous Region) and China is currently looking forward to exploiting these deposits when oil prices get high enough to make it worthwhile (Tibet: Environment and Development, 2011a). China was extracting essential natural resources from the Tibetan Plateau and border areas from the first half of the 20th century (Lin, 2002). Security for China is not only securing its international border but the source of rivers which flow into China to meet its energy crunch. Thus for China, acquiring Tibet became synonymous with securing its international border and energy.

China's economic structure relies on heavy industries and is energy intensive (Tang and Croix, 1993). China is the fastest growing economy in Asia and the world. Its economy is propelled by coal, which still is the major contributor to its energy sector. It is the world's largest coal producer and consumer (Schneider, 2010). China's energy demand is rising so fast that, without a breakthrough in supply or efficiency, coal will still fuel 70 per cent of the nation's energy portfolio in the next decade. But the coal sector is also the nation's second-largest industrial consumer of water, so a finite water supply will likely limit the coal industry's growth (Circle of Blue, 2013). China mines and processes more than 3 billion metric tonnes of coal annually to fuel its expanding economy.

China's actions toward reassuring its dominance over its territories have been growing lately, and Tibet has been experiencing the most interventions (Mota, 2007). Latest estimates show that Tibet may hold 40 per cent of China's mineral resources including petroleum, coal, gold, uranium and copper (Chokyi, 2012; Mota, 2007). According to surveys conducted by the Geographical Survey of China since 1999, more than 600 new sites have been discovered in Qinghai-Tibet of which the Nyixung reserve alone contains 300-500 million tonnes of high-grade iron ore.[4] Damming and mining in

4. See for example, "Huge Mineral Resources Found on Qinghai-Tibet Plateau", Xinhua (2007), *http://www.chinadaily.com.cn/bizchina/2007-02/13/content833286.html*

the region is at full swing where any protest against the projects is met with serious repressive measures. For example, Chen Tao was falsely accused and executed by Chinese authorities for his alleged participation in protests against dams (Beitarie, 2011). The benefits derived from such projects have little benefit for the Tibetans. The resources no doubt are exploited within Tibet but their remuneration is taken and invested to develop mainland China.

There were 94 different kinds of minerals discovered in 1,719 sites within Tibet, including 39 containing impressive reserves within which 12 reserves would be the most important for the industrialisation process of China.[5] They contained chromites (used in tanning industries), corundum (used to manufacture aluminium), copper (used in electrometallurgy and some disinfectants), lithium (used in dry cells and nuclear reactors), iron ore, with hundreds of the sites containing gold layers.[6]

Most of the proven reserves of oil are located in the north-eastern provinces, chiefly the Songlian and Bohai basins, which produce 90 per cent of China's crude oil but have reached their mature stage (Tang and Croix, 1993). This has made China look for an alternative in its peripheral areas to reduce its energy dependency on other oil producing states. The exploration and discovery of fossil fuel (oil shale reserves which could be transformed into oil) in Tibet was an opportunity for an industrialised nation like China to fuel its economy.[7] The oil-bearing fields of Amdo produce more than 1 million tonnes of crude oil per annum for energy deficient China (Tibetan Plateau, 2011). This is just a part of the menacing story of China's full-scale exploitation of Tibet (Tibet: Environment and Development, 2011b). In north-east Qinghai (Amdo), Tsaidam Basin, Thangthang and Lunpoli Basin within TAR, a number of coal mines and petroleum deposits are in operation with little respect to the natives and the ecosystem. In 1994, Tibet produced 115,000 tonnes

5. "The Mineral Resources of Tibet", *http://www.lhassa.org/en/geography-of-tibet/mineral-resources-of-Tibet.php*

6. Ibid.

7. See for example, "Huge Mineral Resources Found on Qinghai-Tibet Plateau", Xinhua, 2007 *http://www.chinadaily.com.cn/bizchina/2007-02/13/content833286.html*

of chromite, 23,000 tonnes of borax, 27,000 tonnes of lead and zinc and 5,800 tonnes of coal (Tibetan Plateau, 2012) .

China is more prone to oil price swings than other industrialised or industrialising nations (Downs, 2004). Therefore if it could find potential sources other than international energy markets, then it could be more immune to these shocks. Although China has its venture in the South China Sea to procure oil, these reserves are highly contested and at times politically controversial. The most cost-effective approach for procuring petroleum and natural shale gas would, in this context, be from the reserves of the Tibetan Plateau. Therefore, the rational stand would be to tap resources at hand. For this purpose, China has exploited Tibet's coal reserves and other minerals and ore-rich mines to sustain its current pace of development (Kambara, 1974).

Gold is another essential precious metal, deposits of which are located in Tibet. Tsaidam belt (Tanjianshan gold mine) and Songpan-Ganze Mobile belt in Qinghai, are associated with gold deposits which have been exploited by China since the 1950s.[8] Gouli and Guloulongwa near Panchen Shingde are also being explored for gold (Tibetan Plateau, 2011). Trucks, backhoes and thousands of men claw these mines and are busy extracting the resource-rich bounty of the region (Schneider, 2011). Aluminum Corp of China or Chinalco, Western Mining Co., Zijin Mining Group Co. Ltd., Leyshon Resources (developing gold mine in Heilongjiang), Central China Goldfiled (CCG), Continental Minerals Corporation and Eldorado Gold Corp of Vancouver, Canada, are some of the developers which have established themselves in different capabilities in the region to extract the potential resources (Times of India, 2010).[9]

Although there has been immense examination of the Tibetan Plateau, nearly 2.6 million km^2 of the region remains unexplored (Asia News, 2007). The only fear emanating from such venture is that these developments and exploitations will benefit only the ethnic

8. "The Mineral Resources of Tibet", *http://www.lhassa.org/en/geography-of-tibet/mineral-resources-of-Tibet.php*

9. Also see, "Tibet Railway Opens the Gates Formining", MAC: Mines and Communities, China Update, 29 July 2006, *http://www.minesandcommunities.org/article.php?a=819*

Han Chinese which is a worrisome concern for Tibetans (Asia News, 2007). What China gains from such policies is clear from the view of Ivanova (2013), who states that China took only 30 years to reach the developmental level of the western countries that took them more than a century. And Tibet has contributed immensely towards this feat.

Deforestation, Erosion and Floods

Deforestation is a major concern in Tibet. Forest covers are exploited in various scales but mostly under very poor environmental norms and regulations (Chokyi, 2012). Unchecked deforestation as a result has led to large-scale soil erosion, siltation and landslides in the region of high deforestation (Daniel, 2008; Schneider and Pope, 2008). By China's own estimate, 80 per cent forest reserve inside Tibet have been destroyed (Central Tibetan Administration: Restoring Freedom and For Tibetans, 2013). The Yangtze flood of 1998 and frequent floods in Bangladesh have been associated by scientists with deforestation in Tibet (Central Tibetan Administration: Restoring Freedom and For Tibetans, 2013). The rapid scale of deforestation has increased the possibility of frequent floods in the lower riparian region. But there may come a time, when the water flow across the lower belt of the Himalaya is drastically reduced because forests and grasslands play a vital role in sustaining the hydrological cycle.

According to a report by the International Centre for Integrated Mountain Development (ICIMOD), there are 8,790 glacial lakes within a selected area of Hindu Kush Himalaya of which more than 200 are identified as potentially dangerous (Tibet: Environment and Development, 2012d). Severe floods have been reported in the Sutlej and Sinag rivers that flow from Tibet through Himachal Pradesh and Arunachal Pradesh in the Indian territory giving rise to landslides and infrastructural damage (Blaikie and Muldavin, 2004). It even increases the chances of glacial lake outburst flood (GLOF) events as is evident from the history of the region. On 10 June 2000, a dam broke in Yidwong Tsangpo (tributary of Yarlung Tsangpo) which caused severe flash floods within and outside the immediate region (Department of Information and International Relations (DIIR),

2009). This flash floods in five downstream districts of Arunachal Pradesh in eastern India left 50,000 people homeless and damaged more than 20 big bridges along with other infrastructure. Further, in 9 of these 15 GLOF events from 1930 to 2002, the debris entered Nepal, India and Bhutan causing serious loss of life and property (DIIR, 2009). GLOFs around these regions are transnational in character which lead to social, economic and infrastructural damage not only inside Tibet but also in India, Nepal and Bhutan.

WMDs and Militarisation

Increased militarisation at the borders is bound to raise inter-state tensions, especially when the area houses WMDs. There have been increasing reports of deployment of WMDs in the Tibetan Plateau. Dumping of radioactive (nuclear) waste, which has a life span of over thousands of years in the border areas is another cause of concern. These highly toxic pollutants may prove catastrophic especially if they find an outlet in the form of river systems which are transnational in nature. This increases the chances of nuclear seepage and possibility of cancer if not properly disposed off. This could prove dangerous for adjacent states, particularly if the dumping site is quite close to international borders.

Furthermore, nearly half a million heavily armed Chinese soldiers and stockpiles of China's most advanced military and nuclear weapon systems are stationed in the Tibetan Plateau (DIIR, 2000). There are increasing reports of Tibet being used as a dumping area (including for ballistic missiles) due to its geostrategic location given its remoteness and proximity to other nation-states. Xinhua (The Chinese official news agency) has reported that there is a "20 square meter dump for radioactive pollutants" in Haibei Tibetan Autonomous Prefecture near the shore of Lake Kokonor, the largest lake in the Tibetan Plateau (Central Tibetan Administration: Restoring Freedom and for Tibetans, 2013). The dumping site is dangerously close to rivers and water systems, which increases possibilities of downstream radioactive material run-off pollution.

The first nuclear weapon was brought into Tibet as early as 1971 and stationed in the Tsaidam (Ch: Qaidam) Basin, north of

Amdo. There are confirmed reports of installation of Dongfeng Intercontinental Ballistic Missiles with a range of 7,000 km in Large Tsaidam, Small Tsaidam and Terlingkha (Ch: Delingha) (Central Tibetan Administration: Restoring Freedom and For Tibetans, 2013). China has conducted numerous documented nuclear tests at Loponor in Xinjing province, northwest of Tibet (Central Tibetan Administration: Restoring Freedom and For Tibetans, 2013). Altogether it is estimated that there are 17 secret radar stations, 14 military airfields, eight missile bases (in Nyingtri Kongpo, Lhasa, Drotsang, Siling, Terlingkha, Small Tsaidam, Large Tsaidam and Nagchuka), at least eight intercontinental ballistic missiles (ICBMs), 70 medium-range missiles and 20 intermediate range missiles in the whole of Tibet (DIIR, 2000). As per Vincent Matten of the International Campaign for Tibet (29 February 2012), there were at least 4 nuclear missile launch sites located in Qinghai Province alone (Meenakshi, 2012). The Chengdu Railway Bureau has 14 military officers holding critical posts in key departments at all major stations and the Military Transportation Department of the People's Liberation Army (PLA) General Logistics Department has equipped over 1000 railway stations with military transportation facilities, which enhances the PLA strategic projection capability (Meenakshi, 2012).

In a region which already has three nuclear capable nations side by side, chances of border frictions increase, as everyone would like to get an upper hand in the larger politics of the geographical space. This may make the region prone to sporadic border skirmishes which are evident in the history of all the three neighbouring states of Pakistan, India and China. It is to be noted that there has been a drastic increase in the deployment of foot soldiers too. For example, up to 1947, 75 Indian policemen were enough to guard the Indo-Tibetan border, which has now increased to deployment of seven to eight divisions in the Himalaya. While, up to 1911, 250-300 Chinese soldiers were present in Lhasa this member had increased to 150,000 soldiers (Norbu, 2000).

Increased militarisation and armament can be an irritant in fostering stronger ties. In addition, it requires infrastructural build-up in the form of military outposts, roads and railways. The same cycle of deforestation for military bases, missile launch sites (though secretive), connectivity in the form of all weather roads and railways, permafrost-ecological-environmental degradation and CO_2 and CH_4 release is repeated. Such an arrangement increases the chances of developing mutual distrust and suspicion between India and China, which will prove detrimental to their interests.

Grassland, Meadows and Wetlands

Tibet's rangeland covers approximately 70 per cent of the total area of Tibet and its highlands hold 51 per cent of the total natural wetlands (Central Tibetan Administration: Restoring Freedom and For Tibetans, 2013). The alpine grasslands at high altitudes occupy over 60 per cent of the total rangeland in Tibet (Tibet: Environment and Development, 2012e). These rangelands (meadows during the growing season) and wetlands and alpine grasslands in Tibet absorb CO_2 at 1840-3050 mg/m^2 per day to 7,400 million tonnes in the upper reaches of the region (Central Tibetan Administration: Restoring Freedom and For Tibetans, 2013). The wetlands of Lhalu on the northwest edge of Lhasa alone, with a total area of 6.2 sq km could absorb 78,800 tonnes of CO_2 and produce 57,330 tonnes of oxygen annually (Tibet: Environment and Development, 2012f). They act as a natural storage for greenhouse gases (GHGs) mainly CO_2 and CH_4. But they are disappearing due to China's strict pastoral policy which restricts the movement of native herders, the Drogpas, and their yaks which actually contribute to the growth of grasslands (Norbu, 2012). These restrictions upset the natural cycle of growth of carbon sinks (grassland, meadows and wetlands), drastically reducing their capacity to absorb and purify GHGs from the atmosphere (DIIR, 2009). Household Contract Responsibility System or the Grassland Law (1985) and the Four-way Program are some examples which discourage seasonal movement and encourage permanent settlements.

The wetlands not only trap carbon-rich sediments but act as a sponge, absorbing water during the summer when the water is in access and releasing it when the run-off is short in the winters (Central Tibetan Administration: Restoring Freedom and for

Tibetans, 2013). They also produce substantial amount of oxygen-rich clean air essential for all living organisms on earth. But the wetlands on the plateau have shrunk more than 10 per cent overall in the past 4 years, with wetlands of the Drichu (Yangtze)'s origin alone contracting at an alarming 29 per cent (DIIR, 2009). Thus the water regulation capacity of all the wetlands has also declined (Tibet: Environment and Development, (2012g).

In the late 1950s and in the following few decades, the PLA, in order to maximise agricultural production (winter crop) from the alpine grasslands ploughed 20 million ha of grassland in Tibet and Inner Mongolia, and claimed it as 'newly claimed virgin croplands' but later failed to reap any harvest which now stands severely degraded (Norbu, 2011). They even introduced hybrid seeds and artificial chemical fertilisers in the traditional fragile organic Tibetan ecosystem to increase the final output. China has spent billions of dollars to build a system of canals to tap water from the Himalayan snowmelt and glaciers and transports it hundreds of miles north and east to the country's farm and industrial regions (Schneider and Pope, 2008). Securing water is essential because the HYVs (high yielding varieties) of seeds are water intensive and require huge doses of chemical fertilisers. Population pressure also played a role in exerting pressure over agricultural yield. Food security has enormous connotations for growing mouths as well as livestock farming in China. Further, a growing economy cannot afford to have a hungry labour pool. A huge population that is unhealthy and impoverished is a liability, not an asset. Therefore feeding the Chinese population at the cost of marginalising others has been the prime policy employed in the region to secure its national growth.

Accelerated degradation of the grasslands is attributed to permafrost dilapidation, mining, road construction, conversion of grasslands into cropland, gold mining, etc. (Department of Information and International Relations [DIIR], 2011). Meanwhile, anthropogenic activities play an important role as amplifiers and accelerators in the wetland degradation process (Tibet: Environment and Development, (2012h). China is a signatory to the Ramsar Convention, 1971 (Convention on Wetlands of International

Importance), (Tibet: Environment and Development, (2012h) but it does not follow the protocols of the international convention.

This has serious consequences for the lower riparian areas because it regulates the flow of water, which could easily flood and dry the whole of north and north-east India during the summer and winter season respectively. The northern plains of India, mainly Uttar Pradesh (UP) that is one of the essential cereal producers of India and whereas north-east India that has economic prospects in terms of hydrology and can provide an outlet to the whole of Southeast Asia, could be at the mercy of China's water. This could prompt a resource war between the two nuclear capable nations of South Asia, which might not be in the best interest of both the countries.

Migration

China is the most populous country in the world. On the other hand, Tibet has vast land reserves which could benefit China in lessening the population explosion pressure. Tibet is already under the official policy of birth control as in mainland China. China has also encouraged thousands of Han Chinese to migrate to Lhasa, making them ethnically and politically powerful and rendering the Tibetans powerless in the capital (Daniel, 2013). These days, more than 65 per cent of Lhasa's population is Chinese immigrant, and with the current expansion of the railway network, this trend is expected to increase further (Chokyi, 2012). This is why even His Holiness the 14th Dalai Lama has labelled the construction of railways the "2nd invasion of Tibet" (Mota, 2007).

As a result, Tibetans are in a minority with massive immigration of the Chinese Han population in their own land. By 1999, Beijing had already moved 60,000 immigrants of Chinese origin into Tibet (Daniel, 2013). Such immigrations could ease the population pressure within resource thinning China, but is bound to cause serious ethnic tensions in Tibet and movement across international borders.

Roads and Railways

The final piece of the puzzle that completes resource extraction, population and mineral appropriation in Tibet is the huge infrastructural build-up that links Tibet with interior China. It was originally designed by Dr Sun Yatsen, but put to action during the 2nd Five Year Plan (1958-1962) in the era of Chairman Mao Zedong (DIIR, 2009a). The Gormo-Lhasa railway, Qinghai-Tibet railway, China National Highway 219 (G219) and China National Highway 109 are a few of the huge web of roads and railways that open up Tibet. These roads and railways are used not only by tourists and local commuters, but also for the transportation of heavy machinery used in mining industries and bringing home the final output that is used in China to sustain its energy-hungry industries.

The opening of the Gormo-Lhasa railway has allowed China to extract Tibet's resources more efficiently and at a faster rate (DIIR, 2009a). It has extended railroads to Shigatse, Tibet, which will allow greater access to remote, yet mineral-rich deposits of the region (The New York Times, 2007). As with other policies and plans, the wider implication of building roads and rail networks then and now is to check foreign influence on the one hand and maintain China's colonial grip and access to the most energy-rich district (Tibet) on the other.

Environmental Degradation and Climate Change Inside Tibet and its Repercussion for India

Tibet is 2 per cent of the land surface of our planet (DIIR, 2009). It is the highest and the largest plateau on earth, occupying an area of more than 2.5 million sq km with an average elevation exceeding 4,000 metres (DIIR, 2000a). India shares the 2,000 mile long Himalayan frontier with Tibet (Lal, 2008). The plateau has contributed basic necessities to sustain life in and around the Asian subcontinent (Tibet: Environment and Development (2012h). It has always defined India's security interest not only in conventional but also in the non-conventional sense. It is to be borne in mind that trouble in Tibet means trouble downstream and downwind from Tibet, across Asia (Central Tibetan Administration: Restoring Freedom and For Tibetans, 2009). While there was a strict environmental protection law called 'ri-rlung-tsatsig' (Mountain Valley Edicts) which prohibited felling, hunting and mining in Tibet

(Tibet: Environment and Development (2012i), such edicts are not given importance by Beijing.

One of the most important phenomenon which connects the whole of Himalaya is that cimate change in the Tibetan Plateau does not occur in isolation (Central Tibetan Administration: Restoring Freedom and For Tibetans, 2011) and environmental degradation inside Tibet is causing some of the most dramatic changes in regional and global climatic patterns (DIIR, 2000). In addition, various anthropogenic factors in the Tibetan Plateau are accelerating these changes. Rampant use of fossil fuels and degradation of the environment release GHGs inside Tibet, which have immediate repercussions for India's water, food and energy security. The Chinese governments policy to bring changes in land use (conversion of grassland into cropland to maximise agriculture production), developmental projects and mining activities are some of the immediate causes of environmental degradation (Tibet: Environment and Development, 2012j). Diversion of rivers is yet another challenge and concern, which poses a serious environmental threat to the whole of Asia (Central Tibetan Administration: Restoring Freedom and For Tibetans, 2008).

Tibet, due to its geostrategic location and geological formation, is the principle watershed for Asia (Central Tibetan Administration: Restoring Freedom and for Tibetans, 2003). It is the source of most of Asia's rivers like Yarlung Tsangpo (Brahmaputra), Drichu (Yangtze), Zachu (Huan He or Yellow river), Sengye Khabab (Indus), Gyalmo Ngulchu (Salween), Meakong (Zachu), Phung Chu/Bhumchu (Arun), Macha Khabab (Karnali/Gaghara) and Langchen Khabab (Sutlej), which sustain the lives of more than half of the Asian populations in India, China, Bhutan, Bangladesh, Nepal, Pakistan, Thailand, Myanmar, Laos, Cambodia and Vietnam (Central Tibetan Administration: Restoring Freedom and For Tibetans, 2003a). More than 15,000 lakes are found in Tibet of which the most prominent are Mansarovar (Mapham Yumtso), Namtso, Yamdrok Yumtso and the largest, Kokonor Lake (Tso Ngonpo) (Central Tibetan Administration: Restoring Freedom and For Tibetans, 2013). But rivers like Drichu (Yangtze), Gyalmo Ngulchu (Salween), Meakong

(Zachu) and Sengye Khabab (Indus), are enlisted and considered endangered by the World Wide Fund (WWF) (Central Tibetan Administration: Restoring Freedom and For Tibetans, 2013). This poses an immediate threat to water security downstream states like India, which are heavily dependent on these rivers.

Climate change and human-induced environmental degradation threaten natural resources all over the world (Tsultrim, 2007). And ecological damage mainly in the upper riparian area can have a devastating impact in the lower regions. Gyalwang Karmapa Ogyen Trinley Dorje, during a recent conference on Environment Protection for Khoryug (2012) emphasised the importance of Tibet's environment and appealed for its conservation for the benefit of the whole of Asia (Central Tibetan Administration: Restoring Freedom and For Tibetans, 2012).

Tibet's plateau contains more than 46,000 glaciers covering an area of 105,000 km^2 and glacier-fed rivers originating from the Tibetan Plateau make up the largest river run-off from any single location in the world, feeding approximately 1.3 million people living in more than 5.6 million km^2 (Central Tibetan Administration: Restoring Freedom and for Tibetans, 2013). Besides, it holds the Hindu Kush ice sheet which is considered the largest ice mass outside the two poles. But Tibet's glaciers are retreating at an alarming rate because of black shoot deposits[10] and GHG emissions (Central Tibetan Administration: Restoring Freedom and for Tibetans, 2009a). According to the Chinese Academy of Science, glaciers on the Tibetan Plateau are melting at a rate of 7 per cent annually (Tibet: Environment and Development, 2012k), and ecological degradation challenges the very existence of these water sources. Owing to these facts, there will be adverse effects on the stability and reliability of hydro-power, which is the key energy source for many developing countries and may lead to regional conflicts (Tsultrim, 2007).

Tibet has a fragile ecology which can easily get disturbed, yet and it is so vital that it can play an important role in checking carbon

10. Black soot deposits are usually by-products emitted by diesel engines, coal-fired power plants and outdoor cooking stoves which can increase the ability to retain radiation of the sun and increase the surface temperature of the earth, accelerating glacier meltdown.

diffusion in the atmosphere. But the irresponsible exploitation of natural resources continues in Tibet. With massive grasslands, Tibet is a vast carbon sink, soaking anthropogenic gases such as CO_2 (Tsultrim, 2007). These grasslands are fast disappearing because of unaccounted mining, logging, damming, expansion of urban areas, population transfer and construction of roads and railways, resulting in global warming. But Beijing justifies its actions in the name of development policy for its underdeveloped periphery.

A recent study showed that one-third of China's pollution comes from the production of its exports (Chanda, 2009). The forest cover, permafrost, grasslands and wetlands of Tibet could play a role in stabilising this atmospheric maladjustment by removing atmospheric carbon, but the whole region is itself in environmental retreat. Consequently, even the Tibetan Plateau is not free from ozone depletion (Tsultrim, 2007). These hitherto slow-motion changes have been accelerating along with fossil fuel generated economic growth (Chanda, 2009).

Conclusion

Tibet is considered a blessing in disguise and is very important for China to maintain its national image and fast growing international economic persona. It has long-term conventional and non-conventional security implications for China. It is now next only to the US in terms of economy. Beijing's urge to develop has incited the government to employ harsh policies to extract resources without seriously reflecting on the human rights, culture and environmental degradation of Tibet. One serious question that the crisis in Tibet raises is whether the world has witnessed the end of colonialism/ imperialism in its varied manifestations.

The reasons for annexation of Tibet by China were strategic and political at one point in history, but they are no longer only confined to its traditional realm of balance of power. Chinese presence in Tibet has transmogrified into a need-based issue because of the cushioning it can guarantee against non-conventional security concerns, for example, the destabilising effect that may arise from energy and food security in the country. Thus, control over Tibet can provide national and international security in terms of demographic and strategic space on the one hand and natural resources on the other. China hypothetically freed Tibet from the shackles of exploitation to extend its control and utilise its natural resources. It also brings home the point that Tibet is an integral part of China and no other actors in the international arena can interfere in its internal matters.

Ultimately China has two agendas in Tibet: procuring essential fresh water, minerals (gold, coal, fossil fuels and essential ores) for its energy deficient industries and at the same time portraying to the world that Tibet is an integral part of China and thus it has the sole right to exploit what is rightfully its. A closer look at the Chinese policy towards Tibet reveals a more implicit design with a colonial fervour to maintain its record of economic growth, military capability and industrialisation. But Tibet holds importance not only for China, but for India as well, both geostrategic ally and environmentally. Disturbing the ecology of Tibet could spell disaster for China in general and for India in particular. Therefore the manner in which India chooses to raise its concerns over these issues *vis-à-vis* China will steer their bilateral relations to a large extent.

References

Alexandrowicz, C.H. (1953). "India and the Tibetan Tragedy", *Foreign Affairs* 31(3): 495-500. Council of Foreign Relations. *http://www.jstor.org/stable/20030982*

Anand, Dibyesh (2009a). "Strategic Hypocrisy: The British Imperial Scripting of Tibet's Geopolitical Identity", *The Journal of Asian Studies, http://www.jstor.org/stable/20619680*

————.(2009b). *Tibet: A Victim of Geopolitics*. New Delhi: Routledge.

Asia News (2007). "Train to Lhasa to Take Out Tibet's Mineral Riches", *www.asianews.it/news-en/Train-to-Lhasa-to-take-out-Tibet's-mineral-riches-8577.html*

Beitarie, Rachel (2011). "Surge of New Dams in Southwest China Produces Power and Public Ire", *www.circleofblue.org.*

Blaikie, Piers M. and Joshua S.S. Muldavin (2004). "Upstream, Downstream, China, India: The Politics of Environment in the Himalayan Region", *Annals of the Association of American Geographers* 94(3): 520-48. Taylor and Francis Ltd. *http://www.jstor.org/stable/3693928*

Bradsher, Henry S. (1969). "Tibet Struggles to Survive', *Foreign Affairs* 47(4): 759-762. Council of Foreign Relations. *http://www.jstor.org/stable/20039413*

Central Tibetan Administration (2003), (2008), (2009), (2011), (2012), (2013). Various publications.

Chanda, Nayan (2009). *Climate Change: Talks of Borders Just Fogs the Issue. Central Tibetan Administration: Restoring Freedom and For Tibetans. http://tibet.net/2009/05/26/climate-change-talk-of-borders-just-fogs-the-issue/*

Chokyi (2012). "China Rushes to Build a New Generation of Mega-Dams", *Annual Newletter*, 14 September. Dharamsala: Environment and Development Desk, Department of Information and International Relations (DIIR). Central Tibetan Administration

Circle of Blue (2013). *China's Provincial Energy Production (1997-2010)*. 31 January. *http://www.circleof blue.org/waternews/2013/world/infographic-china-energy-production-data/*

Daniel, K. (2008). "What Unethical Action Done on Tibet by the Chinese Government Cause the Tibetan Protest?", *http://jspivey.wikispaces.com/Final+Project+Daniel+K*

DIIR (2000), (2009), (2011). Various publications.

Dhundup, Tshering (2013). "Scarring the Land, Scraping the Wounds", *Tibet Burning: A Symposium on the Crisis in Tibetan Politics and Culture, http://www.india-seminar.com/semsearch.html*

Downs, Erica S. (2004). "The Chinese Energy Security Debate", *The China Quarterly* 177: 21-41. Cambridge University Press on behalf of the School of Oriental and African Studies. *http://www.jstor.org/stable/20192303*

Freshfield, Douglas W. (1904). "Tibet. I. Notes from Tibet", *The Geographical Journal* 23(3): 361-66, Whiley on behalf of the Royal Geographical Society. *http://www.jstor.org/stable/1774992*

Interfax-China (2006). "Tibet Railway Opens the Gates for Mining", 28 July. *http://www.resourceinvestor.com/2006/07/27/tibet-railway-opens-gates-mining*

Jaffe, Aaron and Keith Schneider (2011). "A Dry and Anxious North Awaits China's Giant, Unproven Water Transport Scheme", *Circle of Blue*, 1 March. *http://www.circleofblue.org*

Kambara, Tatsu (1974). "The Petroleum Industry in China", *The China Quarterly* 60: 699-719. Cambridge University Press on behalf of the School of Oriental and African Studies. *http://www.jstor.org/stable/652373*

Kolas, Ashid (1996). "Tibetan Nationalism: The Politics of Religion", *Journal of Peace Research* 33(1): 51-66. Sage Publication Ltd. *http://www.jstor.org/stable/425133*

Lal, Dinesh (2008). *Indo-Tibet-China Conflict*. Delhi: Kalpaz Publications.

Lawrence, Walter (1904). "The British Mission to Tibet", *The North American Review*,178(571): 869-81. University of Northern Iowa. *http://www.jstor.org/stable/25150992*

Lin, Hsiao-Ting (2002). "The 1934 Chinese Mission to Tibet: A Re-Examination", *Journal of the Royal Asiatic Society* 12(3). Cambridge University Press on behalf of the Royal Asiatic Society of Great Britain and Ireland, *http://www.jstor.org/stable/25188291*

Meenakshi, S. Swathi, (2012). "One Railroad Serves all (Purposes): Geopolitical Analysis of the Qinghai-Tibet Railroad", *tibet-edd.blogspot.in, http://tibet-edd.blogspot.in/2012/06/one-rail road-servesallpurposes.html?pfstyle=wp*

Mehra, Parshotam (2005). "In the Eyes of Its Beholder: The Younghusband Expedition (1903-04) and Contemporary Media", *Modern Asian Studies* 39(3): 725-39. Cambridge University Press. *http://www.jstor.org/stable/3876591*

Mota, Alan (2007). "Tibet Mineral Deposits Worth Billions: Discovery Could Have Major Negative Impacts for Region, World", *OhmyNews, http://www.tew.org/archived/min.worth.billion.html*

Nadya, Ivanova (2013). "Toxic Water: Across Much of China, Huge Harvests Irrigated with Industrial and Agricultural Runoff", *http://www.circleofblue.org*

Norbu, Dawa (1979). "Strategic Development in Tibet: Implications for its Neighbors", *Asian Survey* 19(3): 245-59. University of California Press. *http://www.jstor.org/stable/2643692*

———. (2012). *A Culture Endangered: Depopulating the Grassland Plateau.* Dharamsala: Environment and Development Desk, Department of Information and International Relations (DIIR). Central Tibetan Administration.

———. (2013). *Tibet: The Third Pole and the Himalayas.* Dharamsala: Environment and Development Desk, Department of Information and International Relations (DIIR). Central Tibetan Administration.

Patterson, George N. (1960). *Tibet in Revolt*. London: Faber and Faber.

Phillips, Tom (2012). "China Defends 3bn Tibet Theme Park", in *Green Tibet* (ed. Chokyi). Annual Newsletter. Dharamsala: Environment and Development Desk, Department of Information and International Relations (DIIR). Central Tibetan Administration.

Praag, Michael C. Van Walt Van (1987). *The Status of Tibet: History, Rights and Prospects in International Law.* London: Wisdom Publication.

Riggs, Fred W. (1950). "Tibet in Extremis", *Far Eastern Survey* 19(21): 224-30. Institute of Pacific Relations. *http://www.jstor.org/stable/3023858*

Schneider, Keith (2010). "China's Climate Emissions Are Global Issue, But Water Scarcity Is Greater Domestic Priority", *Circle of Blue*, 7 October. *http://www.circleofblue.org*

———. (2011). "China: Confronting Water Scarcity and Energy Demand in the World's Largest Country", *Circle of Blue*, 15 February. *http://www.circleofblue.org*

———. (2012). "Food Supply, Fracking, and Water Scarcity Challenge China's Juggernaut Economy", *Circle of Blue*, 17 October. *http://www.circleofblue.org*

Schneider, Keith and C. T. Pope (2008). "China, Tibet, and the Strategic Power of Water", *Circle of Blue, http://www.circleofblue.org/waternews/2008/world/china-tibet-and-the-strategic-power-of -water/*

Tang, Chuanlong and Sumer J. La Croix (1993). "Energy Consumption and Economic Activity in China", *The Energy Journal* 14(4): 21-36. International Association for Energy Economics. *http://www.jstor.org/stable/41322525*

The Guardian (2010). "Chinese Engineers Propose World's Biggest Hydro-electric Project in Tibet", *http://ww.theguardian.com/environment/2010/may/24/chinese-hydroengineers-propose-tibet-dam*

Tibet: Environment and Development (2000), (2011), (2012). Various publications.

Tibetan Plateau (2012). "Best Data on Tibet's Minerals and Petroleum Deposits", *http://tibetanplateau.blogspot.in/2012/07/best-data-on-tibets-mineral-and.html*

The New York Times (2007). "Valuable Mineral Deposits Found Along Tibet Railroad Route", *www.nytimes.com/2007/01/25/your-money/25iht-mine.4338449.html?_r=2&*

The Times of India (2010). "Now, China finds $100bn Mineral Deposits in Tibet", 6 December, *http://articles.timesofindia.indiatimes.com/2010-12-06/china/28247188_1_mineral-reserves-mineral-resources-rich-deposits*

Tsultrim, Tenzin (2007). C*orporate Responses to Climate Change and the Role of Tibet. Central Tibetan Administration: Restoring Freedom and For Tibetans. http://tibet.net/2007/06/22/corporate-response-to-climate-change-and-the-role-of-tibet/*

Reports:

Accused of Ruining Tibet, 26 April 2000, *http://news.bbc.co.uk/2/hi/asia-pacific/726412.stm*

"China to Develop Mineral Bases in Tibet", 7 February 2011, *http://www.financialexpress.com/news/china-to-develop-mineral-bases-in-tibet/747063*

"China and Britain Ready to Exploit Tibet's Natural Resources", 27 July 2008, *telegraph.co.uk, http://www.phayul.com/news/article.aspx?id=22092&t=1.*

"China Discovers Huge Minerals Resources in Tibet", 14 February 2007, *http://articles.economictimes.indiatimes.com/2007-02-14/news/28471246_1_mineral-reserves-tibetan-plateau-china-geological-survey*

"China's Provincial Energy Production 1997-2010", 31 January 2013, *http://www.circleofblue.org*

"China's Provincial Grain Production 1997-2010", 12 December 2012, http://www.circleofblue.org

"The Mineral Resources of Tibet", *http://www.lhassa.org/en/geography-of-tibet/mineral-resources-of-Tibet.php*

"Glacial Meltdown and Glacial Lake Outburst Floods", 2012, *tibet-edd.blogspot.in, http://tibetedd.blogspot.in/2012/03/glacial-meltdown-and-glacial-lake.html*

"Huge Mineral Resources Found on Qinghai-Tibet Plateau", 12 February 2007, *Xinhua, http://www.chinadaily.com.cn/bizchina/2007-02/13/content_833286.htm*

"Origins of Tibet and Beginnings of its History", *http://www.lhassa.org/en/history-of-tibet*

"Resource Extraction and Deforestation in Tibet", 2 May 2012, *http://tibet-edd.blogspot.in/2012/05/resource-extraction-and-deforestation.html#more*

Tibet: A Human Development and Environmental Report, 2009. Dharmasala: Environment and Development Desk, Department of Information and International Relations (DIIR) and Central Tibetan Administration.

"Tibetans Forcibly Removed to Make Way for Mining Development", 18 January 2013, *http://tibet-edd.blogspot.in/2013/01/tibetans-forcibly-removed-to-make-way.html#more*

"Transforming Yamdrok Yumtso: Development for Whom and At What Cost?", 19 June 2012, *http://tibet-edd.blogspot.in/search/label/HYDROLOGY*

Index